Abnormal Behavior

PSYCHOLOGY INFORMATION GUIDE SERIES

Series Editors: Sydney Schultz, M.L.S., Consultant, Library and Publications Services, and Duane Schultz, Adjunct Professor of Psychology, American University, Washington, D.C.

Also in this series:

B.F. SKINNER AND BEHAVIORISM—*Edited by Carol Filipczak**

COMMUNICATION—*Edited by A. George Gitter and Robert Grunin*

CRIMINAL JUSTICE AND BEHAVIOR—*Edited by Harold J. Vetter**

FREUD AND PSYCHOANALYSIS—*Edited by Reuben Fine**

GROUP BEHAVIOR—*Edited by Gloria Behar Gottsegen*

HISTORY OF PSYCHOLOGY—*Edited by Wayne Viney, Michael Wertheimer, and Marilyn Lou Wertheimer*

HUMANISTIC PSYCHOLOGY—*Edited by Gloria Behar Gottsegen and Abby J. Gottsegen**

HUMAN MOTIVATION—*Edited by Charles N. Cofer**

PSYCHOLOGY AND INDUSTRY—*Edited by Sydney Schultz and Duane Schultz**

PSYCHOLOGY IN HEALTH AND REHABILITATION—*Edited by Durand F. Jacobs and Jack G. Wiggins, Jr.**

PSYCHOLOGY OF WOMEN—*Edited by Helen R. Kearney**

*in preparation

The above series is part of the
GALE INFORMATION GUIDE LIBRARY

The Library consists of a number of separate series of guides covering major areas in the social sciences, humanities, and current affairs.

General Editor: Paul Wasserman, Professor and former Dean, School of Library and Information Services, University of Maryland

Managing Editor: Denise Allard Adzigian, Gale Research Company

Abnormal Behavior

A GUIDE TO INFORMATION SOURCES

Volume 5 in the Psychology Information Guide Series

Henry Leland

Professor of Psychology
The Ohio State University
Nisonger Center for Developmental Disabilities
Columbus

Marilyn W. Deutsch

Lecturer in Psychology
The Ohio State University
Nisonger Center for Developmental Disabilities
Columbus

Gale Research Company
Book Tower, Detroit, Michigan 48226

Library of Congress Cataloging in Publication Data

Leland, Henry.
    Abnormal behavior.

    (Psychology information guide series ; v. 5) (Gale
information guide library)
      Includes indexes.
      1. Psychology, Pathological—Information Service.
I. Deutsch, Marilyn W., joint author. II. Title.
III. Series.
RC454.L39   157.'07   80-65
ISBN 0-8103-1416-9

VITAE

Henry Leland, Ph.D., is currently a professor of psychology at The Ohio State University and is director of psychological services at the Nisonger Center for Developmental Disabilities. He has worked in the areas of mental retardation, emotional disturbance, brain damage, and other abnormal behaviors for twenty-six years. He received his doctor's degree from the Sorbonne, Paris, France in 1952.

Professor Leland has been very active in clinical, research, service, and training activities; has published numerous research reports in a variety of clinical and scientific journals; has authored two books (with Daniel E. Smith) as well as a variety of other instructional and assessment works; and is one of the developers of the Adaptive Behavior Scales. He is active in professional organizations and is presently a member of the American Psychological Association Council of Representatives.

Marilyn Weisberg Deutsch, Ph.D., is currently a lecturer of psychology at The Ohio State University and is on the psychology staff at the Nisonger Center for Developmental Disabilities. Her major areas of interest include assessment, diagnosis, and therapeutic interventions with emotionally disturbed, mentally retarded individuals. Dr. Deutsch has written several articles on these topics, and has presented her research findings and instructional materials at professional meetings, including The American Association on Mental Deficiency.

Prior to her present position, Dr. Deutsch worked at a children's psychiatric treatment center in Ohio, and a facility for mentally retarded individuals in Pennsylvania. She received her doctoral and master's degrees from The Ohio State University, and her B.A. from Temple University.

CONTENTS

Contents

Contents

ACKNOWLEDGMENTS

The editors wish to thank The Ohio State University, Nisonger Center for Developmental Disabilities, Dr. Michael J. Guralnick, Director, who generously allowed time and provided space and facilities for the completion of this work.

Recognizing that the real work is always done by the backup staff of secretaries, graduate research assistants, and other helpers, we want to give a great and heartfelt thank you to Ron Bridges, Carol Cohen, Jenny Curry, Henri Deutsch, Teni Garrett, Sherrie Ireland, Carrie-Ellen Jacobs, Annick Parker, and Mary Shaeffer.

INTRODUCTION

The study of abnormal behavior is ancient, and throughout history there have been various descriptions of people whom we would today describe under some of the categories of disturbed behaviors or personality disorders. These reports cover the biological and the social and behavioral sciences as well as professions ranging from medicine, psychology, education, and social work through sociology, anthropology, genetics, and communication. This reference guide covers a period of approximately ten years and includes materials that are generally available in the United States in a form that is readily usable by both professionals and laypersons.

The volume has been organized somewhat along the lines offered by THE DI-AGNOSTIC AND STATISTICAL MANUAL OF MENTAL DISORDERS (DSM II) of the American Psychiatric Association (see item 29). This has been done for the convenience of the reader, with the expectation that standard and commonly used terms become the most convenient reference points from which to start searching for information. We recognize that the American Psychiatric Association is currently revising its manual, and it is certainly in keeping with the growth of both the science and profession that there should be constant and regular revisions as information and knowledge develop. However, accessibility is also a major concern, and, until the new system becomes as familiar as the old one, it was deemed helpful to use the more popular or familiar base.

In an effort to make this guide as current as possible, the major portion of the references have been drawn from journals and periodicals; a listing of the most important of these, with their mailing addresses, is found in the appendix. Also, because of the bulkiness of the material, a major effort has gone into giving as complete a listing in the various areas as feasible, but with brief annotations. In some instances the title of the work seemed sufficiently explanatory. In other instances a summary of content areas, a short statement of explanation, or a general comment is provided. Works deemed to be of major importance are marked with an asterisk. This judgment is based primarily on the completeness of the exposition rather than being an editorial judgment to support one or another school of thought.

Chapter 1

INTRODUCTION TO RESOURCES AND MATERIALS IN ABNORMAL BEHAVIOR AND PERSONALITY ABERRATIONS

This chapter is designed to acquaint the reader with the available resources in the field and includes a listing of (1) the annual reviews and series, (2) the handbooks and encyclopedias covering the areas under discussion in the rest of the guide, (3) resource books and annotated bibliographies, and (4) a group of references to persons and volumes considered classic in the field. This latter group includes those who have made major introductory contributions as well as those who continue to have a strong impact on the field. In this chapter no effort has been made to designate references with an asterisk, because it is considered that all of the items listed are of major importance.

ANNUAL REVIEWS AND SERIES

Because it would be inefficient to attempt to review each volume in this area, we are including the name of the series, the publisher, the date of the first volume, and additional information that we feel would be useful to potential readers. It is not always possible to cite the editor in charge of specific volumes, but, where the series has had a continuing editor or editors, that information is provided.

1   ANNUAL OF PSYCHOANALYSIS. Edited by the Chicago Institute for Psychoanalysis. New York: (Quadrangle/New York Times Books, 1973.) International Universities Press, 1973-- .

This annual includes essays on the diverse topics related to psychoanalytic thought.

2   ANNUAL PROGRESS IN CHILD PSYCHIATRY AND CHILD DEVELOPMENT. Edited by Stella Chess and Alexander Thomas. New York: Brunner/Mazel, 1968-- .

This annual progress series is targeted toward professionals working with normal and disturbed children. It tries to keep abreast of the current status of research and treatment in the area.

3   ANNUAL REVIEW OF BEHAVIOR THERAPY: THEORY AND PRACTICE. Edited by Cyril M. Franks and G. Terrence Wilson. New York: Brunner/Mazel, 1973-- .

These volumes cover a wide range of topics involving both children and adults in the growing area of behavior therapy.

4   ANNUAL REVIEW OF PSYCHOLOGY. Palo Alto, Calif.: Annual Reviews, 1950-- .

Each year's volume has representative reviews of current research areas of psychology. Over time the series contains material on all major areas of psychology.

5   ANNUAL REVIEW OF THE SCHIZOPHRENIC SYNDROME. Edited by Robert Cancro. New York: Brunner/Mazel, 1971-- .

This series covers the latest and "most important" work on the various aspects of the schizophrenic syndrome.

6   LIFE HISTORY RESEARCH IN PSYCHOPATHOLOGY. Minneapolis: University of Minnesota Press, 1970-- . Annual.

The volumes contain studies dealing with life history variables associated with psychopathology. These include high-risk behaviors in children. Provides empirical data to support the concept that important determinants of current disturbances in adulthood are found in childhood experiences and developmental events.

7   MENTAL RETARDATION AND DEVELOPMENTAL DISABILITIES: AN ANNUAL REVIEW. Edited by Joseph Wortis. New York: Brunner/ Mazel, 1969-- .

The series covers the research, programs, and conceptual development in the field of mental retardation and developmental disabilities.

8   PROGRESS IN CLINICAL PSYCHOLOGY. Edited by Lawrence E. Abt and Bernard S. Riess. New York: Grune and Stratton, 1952-- . Annual.

This series addresses itself to the evaluation and understanding of areas that form the background and content of work in clinical psychology, including psychodiagnosis and psychotherapy.

9   PROGRESS IN NEUROLOGY AND PSYCHIATRY: AN ANNUAL REVIEW. Edited by Ernest A. Spiegel. New York: Grune and Stratton, 1946-- .

These reviews are dedicated to current progress in treatment and related research.

10 PROGRESS IN PSYCHIATRIC DRUG TREATMENT. New York: Brunner/Mazel, 1975-- . Annual.

These articles and review papers were prepared especially for these volumes. They deal with the effects of psychiatric drugs on psychiatric patients.

11 THE PSYCHIATRIC CLINICS OF NORTH AMERICA. Philadelphia: W.B. Saunders Co., 1978-- . 3/year.

These reports are to keep practitioners abreast of ongoing clinical experiences.

12 PSYCHOANALYSIS AND CONTEMPORARY SCIENCE: AN ANNUAL OF INTEGRATIVE AND INTERDISCIPLINARY STUDIES. New York: International Universities Press, 1972-- .

This series presents essays that touch not only on psychoanalytic topics but on other relevant areas as well.

13 THE PSYCHOANALYTIC STUDY OF THE CHILD. New York: International Universities Press, 1945-- . Annual.

This comprehensive series of readings presents annually approximately twenty contributions in the field of child development, psychoanalytic theory, and related areas.

14 PSYCHOTHERAPY AND BEHAVIOR CHANGE. Chicago: Aldine, 1972-- . Annual.

These annuals contain articles on psychotherapy and behavior change from the preceding year that review ongoing research and theory and general approaches, both broad and eclectic.

15 RESEARCH ADVANCES IN ALCOHOL AND DRUG PROBLEMS. New York: Wiley Bio-Medical Health Publications, 1974-- . Annual.

This series reviews current research and treatment procedures in alcohol and drug dependence.

15A STRESS AND ANXIETY. Edited by Charles D. Spielberger and Irwin G. Sarason. Washington, D.C.: Hemisphere, 1975-- .

This series covers research and theoretical discussions in the areas of anxiety and stress and the development of procedures for measuring effects of stress and anxiety on behavior, environmental impacts, and clinical manifestations.

16 THE YEARBOOK OF NEUROLOGY, PSYCHIATRY AND NEUROSURGERY. Edited by Roland P. Mackey, Sam B. Wortis, and Oscar Sugar. Chicago: Yearbook Medical Publishers, 1907-- .

This is one of the oldest of the annual series, valuable for its current material as well as for the long-range overview.

HANDBOOKS AND ENCYCLOPEDIAS

17 Arieti, Silvano, ed. AMERICAN HANDBOOK OF PSYCHIATRY. 2d ed. 6 vols. New York: Basic Books, 1974-75. 6,105 p.

Comprehensive handbook covering adult, child, and adolescent psychiatry, with individual references to both usual and rare types of psychological and psychiatric disorders.

18 Batten, Loring, ed. PSYCHOLOGY ENCYCLOPEDIA 73/74. Guilford, Conn.: Dushkin Publishing Group, 1973. 311 p.

Single-volume encyclopedia designed to meet the needs of nonprofessional readers for help with terms needing clarification. More then one thousand articles arranged alphabetically with cross references.

19 Ellis, Norman R., ed. INTERNATIONAL REVIEW OF RESEARCH IN MENTAL RETARDATION. 9 vols. New York: Academic Press, 1966-76. 2,700 p.

Includes articles on the major research in mental retardation in such areas as learning, memory, and cognition.

20 Feinstein, Sherman C., and Giovacchini, Peter, eds. ADOLESCENT PSYCHIATRY. 4 vols. New York: Basic Books, Jason Aronson, 1971-75. 1,815 p.

21 Goldenson, Robert M.; Dunham, Jerome R.; and Dunham, Charles S., eds. DISABILITY AND REHABILITATION HANDBOOK. New York: McGraw-Hill, 1978. 846 p.

Illustrated guide to physically and mentally disabling conditions and their treatment.

22 Howells, John G. MODERN PERSPECTIVES IN PSYCHIATRY. 7 vols. New York: Brunner/Mazel, 1978. 4,871 p.

Attempts to cover all aspects of psychiatry.

23 Leigh, Denis; Pare, C.M.B.; and Marks, John, eds. A CONCISE ENCYCLOPEDIA OF PSYCHIATRY. Baltimore: University Park Press, 1977. 416 p. Illus.

A nonspecialized guide to profession-specific terms and jargon, defining and clarifying the vocabulary of psychiatry in easy-to-understand terms.

24 Mussen, Paul H., ed. CARMICHAEL'S MANUAL OF CHILD PSY-
CHOLOGY. 3d ed. 2 vols. New York: John Wiley and Sons,
1970. 2,391 p.

A text that provides a comprehensive reference to every established and influential theory of child psychology.

24A Noshpitz, Joseph D., ed. THE BASIC HANDBOOK OF CHILD PSY-
CHIATRY. 4 vols. New York: Basic Books, 1979. 3,090 p.

This book covers the field of child psychiatry through the first
twenty years of child development. It is an encyclopedic
reference and includes current research on children of varied
backgrounds, life-styles, religious patterns, and economic
groups in America; account of the theory and practice of
evaluating children; examination of disturbances in development, therapeutic interventions, and an overview of major
approaches to prevention of childhood psychiatric disorders.

25 Wolman, Benjamin B., ed. CLINICAL DIAGNOSIS OF MENTAL
DISORDERS: A HANDBOOK. New York: Plenum Publishing Corp.,
1978. 910 p.

26 _____. THE INTERNATIONAL ENCYCLOPEDIA OF PSYCHIATRY,
PSYCHOLOGY, PSYCHOANALYSIS, AND NEUROLOGY. 12 vols.
New York: Van Nostrand Reinhold, 1977.

Contains over two thousand articles written by more than one
thousand five hundred scholars.

27 Wolman, Benjamin B.; Egan, James; and Ross, Alan O., eds. THE
HANDBOOK OF TREATMENT OF MENTAL DISORDERS IN CHILD-
HOOD AND ADOLESCENCE. Englewood Cliffs, N.J.: Prentice-
Hall, 1978. 496 p.

28 Wright, Logan; Schaefer, Arlene B.; and Solomons, Gerald, eds.
ENCYCLOPEDIA OF PEDIATRIC PSYCHOLOGY. Baltimore: University Park Press, 1978. 600 p.

RESOURCE BOOKS AND ANNOTATED BIBLIOGRAPHIES

29 American Psychiatric Association. THE DIAGNOSTIC AND STATIS-
TICAL MANUAL OF MENTAL DISORDERS. 2d ed. Washington,
D.C.: 1968. 134 p.

The currently used diagnostic and statistical manual (DSM II)
soon to be replaced by the third edition.

30 _____. A PSYCHIATRIC GLOSSARY: THE MEANING OF TERMS FREQUENTLY USED IN PSYCHIATRY. 4th rev. ed. New York: Basic Books, 1975. 155 p.

A reference guide prepared by the subcommittee of the committee on public information.

31 Berlin, Irving N., ed. BIBLIOGRAPHY OF CHILD PSYCHIATRY AND CHILD MENTAL HEALTH. 2d ed. New York: Human Sciences Press, 1976. 508 p.

32 English, Horace B., and English, Ava Champney. A COMPREHENSIVE DICTIONARY OF PSYCHOLOGICAL AND PSYCHOANALYTICAL TERMS: A GUIDE TO USAGE. New York: Longmans, Green and Co., 1958. 508 p.

33 Frank, George. PSYCHIATRIC DIAGNOSIS: A REVIEW OF RESEARCH. Oxford, Engl.: Pergamon Press, 1975. 140 p.

A highly condensed annotated bibliography on diagnosis, psychotic reactions, and the neuroses.

34 Glick, Ira D., and Haley, Jay. FAMILY THERAPY AND RESEARCH: AN ANNOTATED BIBLIOGRAPHY OF ARTICLES AND BOOKS PUBLISHED, 1950-1970. New York: Grune and Stratton, 1971. 280 p.

35 Grossman, Herbert J., ed. A MANUAL ON TERMINOLOGY AND CLASSIFICATION IN MENTAL RETARDATION. Special Publications Series, no. 2. Washington, D.C.: American Association on Mental Deficiency, 1977. 204 p.

Currently used diagnostic classification manual in the area of mental retardation, including both behavioral and etiological listings.

36 Group for the Advancement of Psychiatry. PSYCHOPATHOLOGICAL DISORDERS IN CHILDHOOD: THEORETICAL CONSIDERATIONS AND A PROPOSED CLASSIFICATION. GAP Report no. 62. Washington, D.C.: American Psychiatric Association, 1966. 565 p.

37 Hinsie, Leland E., and Campbell, Robert Jean. PSYCHIATRIC DICTIONARY. 3d ed. New York: Oxford University Press, 1960. 788 p.

38 Hobbs, Nicholas, ed. ISSUES IN THE CLASSIFICATION OF CHILDREN. Vols. 1 and 2. San Francisco: Jossey-Bass Publishers, 1975. 965 p.

Sourcebooks presenting systematic and comprehensive summaries of current thinking about the classification of exceptional children and the consequences of such categorization and labeling.

39 Honigfeld, Gilbert, and Howard, Alfreda. PSYCHIATRIC DRUGS: A DESK REFERENCE. New York: Academic Press, 1978. 264 p.

40 Kalisch, Beatrice J. CHILD ABUSE AND NEGLECT. Westport, Conn.: Greenwood Press, 1978. 535 p.

An annotated bibliography.

41 Mental Health Materials Center. A SELECTIVE GUIDE TO MATERIALS FOR MENTAL HEALTH AND FAMILY LIFE EDUCATION. 3d ed. Detroit: Gale Research Co., 1976. 947 p.

Contains complete information on more than seven hundred materials chosen from an initial pool of 30,000.

42 Rutter, Michael; Shaffer, David; and Shepherd, Michael. A MULTI-AXIAL CLASSIFICATION OF CHILD PSYCHIATRIC DISORDERS: AN EVALUATION OF A PROPOSAL. Geneva: World Health Organization, 1975. 85 p.

43 Tymchuk, Alexander J. THE MENTAL RETARDATION DICTIONARY. Los Angeles: Western Psychological Services, 1973. 112 p.

44 Whittaker, James K., and Trieschman, Albert E., eds. CHILDREN AWAY FROM HOME: A SOURCE BOOK OF RESIDENTIAL TREATMENT. Chicago: Aldine-Atherton, 1972. 438 p.

Thirty-five selected readings on current issues related to the therapeutic milieu approach when dealing with emotionally disturbed children in a residential treatment facility. Addresses the changing status of institutions.

45 Wisconsin, University of. A BIBLIOGRAPHY OF MATERIALS FOR HANDICAPPED AND SPECIAL EDUCATION. Edited by Roger H. Lambert. 2d ed. Madison: Center for Studies in Vocational Technical Education, 1975. 81 p.

A bibliography of 1,621 references to materials related to the vocational and technical education of handicapped persons.

46 Wright, George N., and Jacks, James C. ANNOTATED BIBLIOGRAPHY ON EPILEPSY: SOCIAL, PSYCHOLOGICAL AND BEHAVIORAL LITERATURE FROM 1955 THROUGH 1965. Washington, D.C.: Epilepsy Foundation, 1966. 28 p.

47 Young, D.R., ed. THE DIRECTORY FOR EXCEPTIONAL CHILDREN.
6th ed. Boston: Porter Sargent, 1969. 1,150 p.

Provides extensive information on services for the mentally retarded.

"CLASSIC" TEXTS

It is almost impossible to compile a list of "classic" texts without leaving out
some favored authors or works. In this instance we have tried to choose the
people whose works have made a major impact in psychiatry and the psychology of emotional or mental disorders. In some cases the age of the reference
has made it a classic, or the fame of the author has been the important factor, and in some instances the nature of the work itself has been the deciding
point. Comments are offered only when the content of the text is not clearly
implied by the title.

48 Adler, Alfred. THE SCIENCE OF LIVING. New York: Greenberg,
1929. 266 p.

49 Allport, Gordon. BECOMING: BASIC CONSIDERATIONS FOR A
PSYCHOLOGY OF PERSONALITY. New Haven, Conn.: Yale University Press, 1955. 106 p.

50 Ansbacher, Heinz, and Ansbacher, Rowena. THE INDIVIDUAL PSY-
CHOLOGY OF ALFRED ADLER. New York: Basic Books, 1956.
503 p.

51 Bettelheim, Bruno. THE EMPTY FORTRESS. New York: Free Press,
1967. 484 p.

Presents classic theory, research, and case histories in the
area of childhood autism.

52 Binet, Alfred, and Simon, Thomas. THE DEVELOPMENT OF INTEL-
LIGENCE IN CHILDREN. Vineland, N.J.: Wilkins, Williams, and
Co., 1916. Reprint. New York: Arno Press, 1978. 336 p.

53 Durkheim, Emile. THE ELEMENTARY FORMS OF RELIGIOUS LIFE.
New York: Macmillan, 1915. 456 p.

Pioneering work in the field of sociology.

54 Ebbinghaus, Hermann. PSYCHOLOGY: AN ELEMENTARY TEXT
BOOK. Boston: D.C. Health, 1908. Reprint. New York: Arno
Press, 1978. 215 p.

55 Freud, Anna. INTRODUCTION TO THE TECHNIC OF CHILD ANAL-
    YSIS. New York: Nervous and Mental Disease Publishing Co., 1928.
    59 p.

56 Freud, Sigmund. THE STANDARD EDITION OF THE COMPLETE PSY-
    CHOLOGICAL WORKS OF SIGMUND FREUD. Translated by James
    Strachey, Anna Freud, Alix Strachey, and Alan Tyson. 24 vols.
    London: Hogarth Press, 1953.

57 Goddard, Henry H. THE KALLIKAK FAMILY: A STUDY IN THE
    HEREDITY OF FEEBLEMINDEDNESS. New York: Macmillan, 1912.
    Reprint. New York: Arno Press, 1978. 121 p.

58 Groos, Karl. THE PLAY OF MAN. New York: D. Appleton and
    Co., 1901. 424 p.

59 Haslam, John. SOUND MIND: OR CONTRIBUTION TO THE NAT-
    URAL HISTORY AND PHYSIOLOGY OF THE HUMAN INTELLECT.
    London: Longman, Horst, Rees, Orme and Brown, 1819. 209 p.

60 Jung, Carl G. PSYCHOLOGY OF THE UNCONSCIOUS: A STUDY
    OF THE TRANSFORMATIONS AND SYMBOLISM OF THE LIBIDO.
    New York: Moffet Yard and Co., 1916. 632 p.

61 Kanner, Leo. CHILDHOOD PSYCHOSES: INITIAL STUDIES AND
    NEW INSIGHTS. Washington, D.C.: V.H. Winston and Sons, 1973.
    283 p.

62 _____. "Infantile Autism and the Schizophrenics." BEHAVIORAL
    SCIENCE 10, no. 4 (1965): 412-20.

63 Klein, Melanie. THE PSYCHOANALYSIS OF CHILDREN. 1932. Rev.
    ed. New York: Delacorte Press/Seymour Lawrence, 1975. 326 p.

64 Kraepelin, Emil. LECTURES ON CLINICAL PSYCHIATRY. 1904.
    Rev. ed. New York: Hafner Publishing Co., 1968. 308 p.

65 LeBon, Gustave. THE CROWD: A STUDY OF THE POPULAR MIND.
    London: T. Fischer Unwin, 1896. 239 p.

    First major text addressing mob behavior.

66 Lewin, Kurt. A DYNAMIC THEORY OF PERSONALITY. New York:
    McGraw-Hill, 1936. 286 p.

67   McDougall, William. THE GROUP MIND: A SKETCH OF THE PRIN-
CIPLES OF COLLECTIVE PSYCHOLOGY WITH SOME ATTEMPT TO
APPLY THEM TO THE INTERPRETATION OF NATIONAL LIFE AND
CHARACTER. New York: G.P. Putnam's Sons, 1920. Reprint.
New York: Arno Press, 1978. 481 p.

68   Menninger, Karl. THE HUMAN MIND. 3d ed. New York: Knopf,
1945. 517 p.

Menninger's observations on personality, abnormality, and
maladjustment.

69   Moreno, Jacob L. PSYCHODRAMA. 3 vols. Boston: Beacon House
Press, 1946, 1959, 1969. 428 p.

70   Prince, Morton. THE DISASSOCIATION OF A PERSONALITY: A
BIOGRAPHICAL STUDY IN ABNORMAL PSYCHOLOGY. Westport,
Conn.: Greenwood Press, 1969. 175 p.

71   Rogers, Carl. CLIENT-CENTERED THERAPY. Boston: Houghton Mifflin, 1951. 560 p.

72   Rothgeb, Carrie Lee, ed. ABSTRACTS OF THE STANDARD EDITION
OF THE COMPLETE PSYCHOLOGICAL WORKS OF SIGMUND FREUD.
New York: Jason Aronson, 1973. 315 p.

73   Seguin, Edward. IDIOCY AND ITS TREATMENT BY THE PHYSIO-
LOGICAL METHOD. 1866. Reprint. New York: Augustus M.
Kelley, 1971. 457 p.

74   Szasz, Thomas S. MYTH OF MENTAL ILLNESS. Rev. ed. New
York: Harper and Row, 1974. 297 p.

Book expresses dissatisfaction with the medical basis and conceptual framework of psychiatry's concept of mental illness.
Feels the concept of "mental illness" is in itself a myth.
Presents a systematic theory of personal conduct based on materials from psychiatry, psychoanalysis, and other disciplines
based on the notion that people do not recover from an "illness" but rather learn about themselves and life in general
and thus function better.

75   Tuke, Daniel H. ILLUSTRATIONS OF THE INFLUENCE OF THE
MIND UPON THE BODY IN HEALTH AND DISEASE. London: J.
and A. Churchill, 1872. 496 p.

76   Wechsler, David. THE RANGE OF HUMAN CAPACITIES. 2d ed.

Baltimore: Williams and Wilkins, 1952. 200 p.

77   Wolpe, Joseph.   PSYCHOTHERAPY BY RECIPROCAL INHIBITION.
     Stanford, Calif.:   Stanford University Press, 1958.   239 p.

     The original statement of Wolpe's theory and mode of treat-
     ment.

Chapter 2

GENERAL REFERENCE TEXTS AND OVERVIEWS IN ABNORMAL BEHAVIOR

This chapter presents a section of general references to the field of abnormal behavior, indicating some of the major textbooks in the area, some of the more philosophically or theoretically oriented texts, and works on some of the secondary but related issues such as ethics, legal questions, and similar areas. It seems appropriate to start these references with works that attempt to cover the historical perspective (though additional historical references are included when appropriate in the chapters on specific disorders, e.g., mental retardation). Key references in this chapter are marked with an asterisk and include the following numbers: 85, 91, 94, 99, 108, 121, 123, 140, 146, 180, 189, 215, 217, 239, 242, 243, 248, and 256.

HISTORICAL PERSPECTIVES

78 Alexander, Franz G., and Selesnick, Sheldon T. THE HISTORY OF PSYCHIATRY: AN EVALUATION OF PSYCHIATRIC THOUGHT AND PRACTICE FROM PREHISTORIC TIMES TO THE PRESENT. New York: Harper and Row, 1966. 471 p.

   Examination of 5,000 years of psychiatry covering all important historical periods and personages connected with the growth and development of Western psychiatry.

79 Allman, Lawrence R., and Jaffee, Dennis T., eds. READINGS IN ABNORMAL PSYCHOLOGY; CONTEMPORARY PERSPECTIVES. 1976–77 ed. New York: Harper and Row, 1976. 396 p.

   Series of reprinted pieces ranging from classics through popular articles designed for undergraduate courses.

80 Burvill, P.W. "Immigration and Mental Disease." AUSTRALIAN AND NEW ZEALAND JOURNAL OF PSYCHIATRY 7, no. 3 (1973): 155–62.

   Review of literature on immigration and mental illness, emphasizing the types of disorders, effects of time, the nature of the individual, and various other considerations. Sixty-seven references.

81 Dain, Norman. DISORDERED MINDS: THE FIRST CENTURY OF EASTERN STATE HOSPITAL IN WILLIAMSBURG, VA.: 1766-1866. Williamsburg, Va.: Colonial Williamsburg Foundation, 1976. 207 p.

82 Grob, Gerald N. MENTAL INSTITUTIONS IN AMERICA: SOCIAL POLICY TO 1875. New York: Free Press, 1973. 485 p.

History of social policy toward the mentally ill and the emergence of institutions to carry out these aims.

83 Hamilton, Max, ed. ABNORMAL PSYCHOLOGY. Baltimore: Penguin Books, 1967. 331 p.

Classic readings forming the base for the present field of abnormal psychology.

84 Hirsch, Charles. "From Mental Health to Social Action: Clinical Psychology in Historical Perspective." AMERICAN PSYCHOLOGIST 24, no. 10 (1969): 909-16.

Presents the shift from a clinical service framework to social action involvement of clinical psychology since World War II.

85 *Howells, John G., ed. WORLD HISTORY OF PSYCHIATRY. New York: Brunner/Mazel, 1973. 770 p.

The history of psychiatry for most geographical areas of the world. Discusses "scientific psychiatry" and how various cultures define and deal with abnormal behavior. Includes 130 illustrations from the psychiatric history of virtually every country.

86 Rosen, George. MADNESS IN SOCIETY: CHAPTERS IN THE HISTORICAL SOCIOLOGY OF MENTAL ILLNESS. Chicago: University of Chicago Press, 1968. 337 p.

"The place of the mentally ill . . . in society at different historical periods." Covers Greece, Rome, Biblical Palestine, Europe, and the United States.

87 Segal, Steven P., and Aviram, Uri. THE MENTALLY ILL IN COMMUNITY-BASED SHELTERED CARE. New York: Wiley-Interscience, 1978. 337 p.

In-depth historical review of sheltered care as a social policy. Study of 500 former mental patients in family care, boarding care, and halfway houses.

88   Sonado, Margaret M. "Sedatives and Hypnotics in Psychiatry." CA-
     NADIAN PSYCHIATRIC ASSOCIATION JOURNAL 14, no. 3 (1969):
     311-12.

     Describes the use of alcohol, hypnotics, and narcotics from
     ancient times to their current use in medicine and psychology.

89   Szasz, Thomas S. THE MANUFACTURE OF MADNESS. New York:
     Harper and Row, 1970. 383 p.

     Traces institutional psychiatry from its origins in Christian
     theology through its transition to present-day medical rhetoric.

90   _____, ed. THE AGE OF MADNESS: THE HISTORY OF THE IN-
     VOLUNTARY MENTAL HOSPITALIZATION PRESENTED IN SELECTED
     TEXTS. Garden City, N.Y.: Anchor, 1973. 372 p.

     An anthology spanning three centuries of work on involuntary
     hospitalization and treatment.

OVERVIEWS OF ABNORMAL BEHAVIOR
General

Although most complete descriptions of the various conditions described in this
volume are found under the headings for those conditions, there are a number
of textbooks that cover the field of abnormal psychology from a variety of
philosophical positions. The more encyclopedic approaches (professional
sourcebooks, classification manuals, etc.) are covered in the first chapter of
this guide. This section is dedicated to the textbooks themselves. Some may
consider it unfortunate that a topic of this sort has so many different schools,
but it nonetheless represents the current state of the art. Each of these
schools has a contribution to make, and, in the long run, the most important
information will probably be derived by studying the various positions presented. We may not touch here on every philosophical school, but we feel
that the major texts and most representative indications are all included.

Presented first are those texts that are general discussions of abnormal psychology and psychopathology, followed by a section listing texts that empha-
size the problems of children and adolescents.

91   *Arieti, Silvano. ON SCHIZOPHRENIA, PHOBIAS, DEPRESSION,
     PSYCHOTHERAPY AND THE FURTHER SHORES OF PSYCHIATRY:
     SELECTED PAPERS OF SILVANO ARIETI. New York: Brunner/Mazel,
     1977. 505 p.

     Thirty-one papers of importance for pediatricians and practi-
     tioners, with an introductory note by Arieti noting the signif-
     icance of the work and its impact on psychiatry.

92   _____, ed. THE WORLD BIENNIAL OF PSYCHIATRY AND PSY-CHOTHERAPY. Vol. 2. New York: Basic Books, 1973. 512 p.

To keep mental health professionals up to date on the work of their counterparts throughout the world.

93   Buss, Arnold H. PSYCHOPATHOLOGY. New York: John Wiley and Sons, 1966. 438 p.

A comprehensive review of abnormal psychology that attempts to separate accepted facts from theories. Presents an impartial description and evaluation of the theories.

94   *Coleman, James C. ABNORMAL PSYCHOLOGY IN MODERN LIFE. 5th ed. Glenview, Ill.: Scott, Foresman and Co., 1976. 816 p. Glossary.

Coleman's text has become the basic reference used for a comprehensive, eclectic introduction to abnormal psychology. Sections cover (1) perspectives on abnormal behavior, (2) the dynamics of adjustive behavior, (3) the patterns of abnormal behavior, and (4) modern methods of assessment, treatment and prevention.

95   Davis, D. Russell. AN INTRODUCTION TO PSYCHOPATHOLOGY. 3d ed. New York: Oxford University Press, 1973. 185 p.

Discusses and defines psychopathology as a science that seeks to explain disorders of behavior in terms of psychological processes. Eighteen pages of references.

96   Eysenck, H.J., ed. HANDBOOK OF ABNORMAL PSYCHOLOGY. 2d ed. San Diego, Calif.: Knapp, 1973. 906 p.

Formally marks the beginning of the experimental approach to abnormal psychology.

97   Farina, Amerigo. ABNORMAL PSYCHOLOGY. Englewood Cliffs, N.J.: Prentice-Hall, 1976. 207 p.

A simplified text for undergraduates and laypersons.

98   Garfield, Sol L. CLINICAL PSYCHOLOGY: THE STUDY OF PERSONALITY AND BEHAVIOR. Chicago: Aldine, 1974. 461 p.

A well-organized, simplified text suitable for undergraduates and laypersons.

99   *Garfield, Sol L., and Bergin, Allen E., eds. HANDBOOK OF PSYCHOTHERAPY AND BEHAVIOR CHANGE. 2d ed. New York: John Wiley and Sons, 1978. 928 p.

Source of empirical research on psychotherapy and behavior change. Covers marital and family therapy, cognitive-behavioral therapy, behavior therapy for children, crisis-oriented therapy, psychotherapy with the disadvantaged, the training of therapists, operant techniques in treatment, and related areas.

100 Hammer, Muriel; Salzinger, Kurt; and Sutton, Samuel, eds. PSY-CHOPATHOLOGY: CONTRIBUTIONS FROM THE SOCIAL, BEHAVIORAL, AND BIOLOGICAL SCIENCES. New York: Wiley-Interscience, 1973. 588 p.

Offers theoretical, methodological, and quantitative views appropriate for advanced graduate students and researchers.

101 Harnitz, Morton G. ABNORMAL PSYCHOLOGY. Englewood Cliffs, N.J.: Prentice-Hall, 1977. 608 p.

102 McMahon, Frank B. ABNORMAL BEHAVIOR: PSYCHOLOGY'S VIEW. Englewood Cliffs, N.J.: Prentice-Hall, 1976. 478 p.

General university-level textbook.

103 Maher, Brendan, ed. CONTEMPORARY ABNORMAL PSYCHOLOGY: SELECTED READINGS. Hardendsworth, Engl.: England Books, 1973. 442 p.

A series of readings concerning classification and diagnosis of abnormal behavior, psychosomatic disorders, schizophrenia, psychopathy, and neurotic disorders. Includes contemporary developments in treatment.

104 Martin, Barclay. ABNORMAL PSYCHOLOGY. Glenview, Ill.: Scott, Foresman and Co., 1973. 175 p.

Describes some of the more common forms of abnormal behavior and considers biological and psychological causes in treatment approaches.

105 Morris, Richard. PERSPECTIVES IN ABNORMAL BEHAVIOR. Pergamon General Psychology Series, vol. 37. New York: Pergamon Press, 1974. 554 p.

An interdisciplinary approach to the development and maintenance of abnormal behavior. Major content areas are identification, development, drug usage and alcohol, treatment, prevention, and the relationship of these areas to today's mental health problems.

106   Nathan, Peter E., and Harris, Sandra T. PSYCHOPATHOLOGY AND
      SOCIETY. New York: McGraw-Hill, 1976. 580 p.

      Discusses abnormal behavior through examples from present-
      day society. Details the relationships among psychobiology,
      genetics, personality, and psychopathology, and describes a
      variety of psychopathological conditions.

107   Neale, John M.; Davison, Gerald C.; and Price, Kenneth P., eds.
      CONTEMPORARY READINGS IN PSYCHOPATHOLOGY. New York:
      John Wiley and Sons, 1974. 337 p.

      Significant views on psychopathology written for undergraduate
      students or laypersons.

108   *Nicholi, Armand M., Jr., ed. THE HARVARD GUIDE TO MODERN
      PSYCHIATRY. Cambridge, Mass.: Harvard University Press, 1971.
      704 p.

      Synthesizes the biological, sociological, and psychological
      aspects of mental disorders by introducing viewpoints of emi-
      nent clinicians and scientists in the field of psychiatry.

109   Offer, Daniel, and Freedman, Daniel X., eds. MODERN PSYCHIA-
      TRY AND CLINICAL RESEARCH: ESSAYS IN HONOR OF ROY R.
      GRINKER, SR. New York: Basic Books, 1972. 320 p.

      Essays on clinical psychiatric syndromes, borderline states,
      anxieties, and the like, for students, professors, scientists,
      and practitioners.

110   Page, James D. PSYCHOPATHOLOGY: THE SCIENCE OF UNDER-
      STANDING DEVIANCE. 2d ed. Chicago: Aldine, 1975. 510 p.

      Takes an eclectic approach defining and delineating the field
      of psychopathology on the basis of impairment of voluntary
      control and behavior resulting in the suffering of a person,
      family, or society. Sees disordered behavior as the cumula-
      tive product of genetic factors, personal experiences, and
      environmental influences.

111   Price, Richard H. ABNORMAL BEHAVIOR: PERSPECTIVES IN CON-
      FLICT. New York: Holt, Rinehart and Winston, 1972. 216 p.

      Reviews six models of abnormal behavior--psychoanalytic, ill-
      ness, learning, moral, humanistic, and social--and uses these
      as perspectives for understanding abnormal behavior.

112   Rabkin, Leslie Y., and Carr, John E., eds. SOURCE BOOK IN
      ABNORMAL PSYCHOLOGY. Boston: Houghton Mifflin, 1967.
      519 p. Paper.

Original and important readings in abnormal psychology designed to complement standard texts.

113 Rakoff, Vivian M.; Stancer, Harvey C.; and Kedward, H.B., eds. PSYCHIATRIC DIAGNOSIS. New York: Brunner/Mazel, 1977. 240 p.

Designed to inform readers about current diagnostic practice. Discusses American Psychiatric Association diagnostic manuals including the proposed revision, DSM III (see item 29).

114 Reiss, Steven; Peterson, Robert A.; Eron, Leonard D.; and Reiss, M.M. ABNORMALITY: EXPERIMENTAL AND CLINICAL APPROACHES. New York: Macmillan, 1977. 662 p.

General text covering some of the more current research and clinical approaches.

115 Rimm, David C., and Somervill, John W. ABNORMAL PSYCHOLOGY. New York: Academic Press, 1977. 670 p.

Undergraduate text that confronts the basic questions concerning the nature of abnormal behavior, who defines it as abnormal, and how society views it. Presents overviews of diagnosis, treatment, and classification.

116 Sahakian, William S., ed. PSYCHOPATHOLOGY TODAY: EXPERIMENTATION, THEORY AND RESEARCH. Itasca, Ill.: Peacock, 1970. 730 p.

Reprints of articles (many abridged) having historic or contemporary importance in the field. Covers most of the broad areas of psychopathology.

117 Sarason, Irwin G. ABNORMAL PSYCHOLOGY: THE PROBLEM OF MALADAPTIVE BEHAVIOR. 2d ed. Englewood Cliffs, N.J.: Prentice-Hall, 1976. 678 p.

University-level text dealing with abnormal psychology from an adaptive and societal frame of reference.

118 Suinn, Richard M. FUNDAMENTALS OF BEHAVIOR PATHOLOGY. 2d ed. New York: John Wiley and Sons, 1975. 595 p.

Basic text dealing with biological, social, and psychological factors influencing abnormal development. Major portion of the work devoted to discussing dysfunctions as classified by the American Psychiatric Association classification manual (see item no. 29).

119   Thio, Alex.   DEVIANT BEHAVIOR.   Boston: Houghton Mifflin, 1978.
      416 p.

> Explores many theories of deviance and provides an overview
> of aspects of deviant behavior.   Contains case studies of
> value to professionals in the field.

120   Ullmann, Leonard P., and Krasner, Leonard.   A PSYCHOLOGICAL
      APPROACH TO ABNORMAL BEHAVIOR.   2d ed.   Englewood Cliffs,
      N.J.:   Prentice-Hall, 1975.   776 p.

> Textbook designed as an introduction to abnormal behavior.
> Represents a strong social learning viewpoint, which considers
> behaviors traditionally called abnormal as no different in their
> development and maintenance from other behaviors.   Traces
> the conceptual research and therapeutic implications of not
> labeling these behaviors as mental illness.

Children and Adolescents

121   *Achenbach, Thomas M.   DEVELOPMENTAL PSYCHOPATHOLOGY.
      New York: Ronald Press, 1974.   726 p.

> A comprehensive overview of the historical context, major
> theories, research, and treatment of childhood psychopathol-
> ogy, emphasizing the need to view it as separate and distinct
> from adult psychopathology.   Sixty-six pages of references.

122   Anthony, Elwyn James, ed.   EXPLORATIONS IN CHILD PSYCHIATRY.
      New York: Plenum Publishing Corp., 1975.   500 p.

> A presentation of contemporary research and important devel-
> opments in child psychiatry from clinical, experimental, nat-
> uralistic, and developmental approaches.

123   *Chess, Stella, and Hassibi, Mahin, eds.   PRINCIPLES AND PRAC-
      TICE OF CHILD PSYCHIATRY.   New York: Plenum Publishing Corp.,
      1978.   500 p.

> An objective assessment of theories and research findings as
> well as conceptualizations based on extensive clinical exper-
> ience in the field of child psychiatry.   Geared to profession-
> als who work with children.

124   Copel, Sidney L., ed.   BEHAVIOR PATHOLOGY OF CHILDHOOD
      AND ADOLESCENCE.   New York: Basic Books, 1974.   492 p.

> Psychoanalytically oriented book emphasizing individual dy-
> namics from a classical frame of reference.

125 Davids, Anthony. CHILDREN IN CONFLICT: A CASE BOOK. New
York: John Wiley and Sons, 1974. 227 p.

Collection of fifteen case histories on emotionally disturbed
children, with significant factors and treatment issues related
to each type of disorder. Includes psychosomatic, behavioral,
learning, neurotic, and psychotic types.

126 _____, ed. CHILD PERSONALITY AND PSYCHOPATHOLOGY.
New York: John Wiley and Sons, 1974. 239 p.

Readings on advances in child psychopathology.

127 _____. ISSUES IN ABNORMAL CHILD PSYCHOLOGY. Monterey,
Calif.: Brooks/Cole, 1973. 461 p.

A book of readings divided into general issues, childhood
psychopathology, therapeutic approaches, and ethical considerations in child psychology, primarily for beginning students
and laypersons.

128 Engel, Mary. PSYCHOPATHOLOGY IN CHILDHOOD: SOCIAL,
DIAGNOSTIC, AND THERAPEUTIC ASPECTS. New York: Harcourt
Brace Jovanovich, 1972. 183 p.

Book of supplemental readings in social, diagnostic, and therapeutic aspects of childhood psychopathology. A primer for
the uninitiated.

129 Faas, Larry A., ed. THE EMOTIONALLY DISTURBED CHILD: A
BOOK OF READINGS. Tempe: Arizona State University Press, 1975.
400 p.

Articles dealing with identification, understanding, and education of emotionally disturbed children in the schools. Includes a section on curricular and facility adaptations in the
creation of a therapeutic program for disturbed children in an
educational setting.

130 Freedman, Alfred M., and Kaplan, Harold I., eds. THE CHILD:
HIS PSYCHOLOGICAL AND CULTURAL DEVELOPMENT, Vol. II:
THE MAJOR PSYCHOLOGICAL DISORDERS AND THEIR TREATMENT.
New York: Atheneum, 1972. 417 p.

Discusses neuroses, anxiety, depression, phobic behavior, obsessive-compulsive behavior, mental retardation, and a variety
of other disorders as they relate to children.

131 Harrison, Saul I., and McDermott, John F., eds. CHILDHOOD PSY-
CHOPATHOLOGY: AN ANTHOLOGY OF BASIC READINGS. New
York: International Universities Press, 1972. 903 p.

Fifty-five papers ranging from the last century to the late 1960s representing an eclectic viewpoint of childhood psychopathology. For the student or professional. Forty-four pages of references.

132   Haslam, M.T. PSYCHIATRIC ILLNESS IN ADOLESCENTS: ITS PSY-CHOPATHOLOGY AND PROGNOSIS. London: Butterworths, 1975. 121 p.

Reviews the relevant literature concerning psychiatric disorders of adolescents, with special attention to possible causation. Discusses problems of deprivation, experience, and separation from parent figures.

133   Herbert, Martin. EMOTIONAL PROBLEMS OF DEVELOPMENT IN CHILDREN. New York: Academic Press, 1974. 362 p.

Uses developmental psychology as a framework for understanding abnormal and psychopathological behavior in children. Covers a broad range of topics, including exceptionality and psychopathology, and discusses the problems of the child's influence on the parents.

134   Kohen-Raz, Reuven. THE CHILD FROM 9 TO 13: PSYCHOLOGY AND PSYCHOPATHOLOGY. Chicago: Aldine-Atherton, 1972. 239 p.

Considers this age period as an independent and critical formative stage in human development. Discusses various aspects of child psychopathology and problems of special education, and develops an interdisciplinary interpretation of human development around this age period.

135   Lahey, Benjamin B., and Kazdin, Alan E., eds. ADVANCES IN CLINICAL CHILD PSYCHOLOGY. Vol. 1. New York: Plenum Publishing Corp., 1977. 414 p.

Clinical reviews in the field of clinical and developmental psychology, including child psychotherapy, behavioral assessment, disruption and hyperactivity in school, perinatal influences on behavior, and learning problems. References for specialists and researchers in this field.

136   McMillan, M.F., and Henao, S., eds. CHILD PSYCHIATRY: TREATMENT AND RESEARCH. New York: Brunner/Mazel, 1977. 336 p.

An interdisciplinary approach to the field of child psychiatry. Includes research in genetics, neurophysiology, neuropsychology, and comparative child development. Gives practical approaches to day-to-day treatment issues.

137 Neubauer, Peter B. "Disorders of Early Childhood." In CHILD AND ADOLESCENT PSYCHIATRY, SOCIO-CULTURAL AND COMMUNITY PSYCHIATRY, 2d ed., edited by Gerald Caplan, chapter 3. American Handbook of Psychiatry, vol. 2. New York: Basic Books, 1974.

Discusses problems in establishing diagnoses, developmental factors, individual variations in development, and a wide range of early childhood disorders from a developmental frame of reference.

138 Quay, Herbert C., and Werry, John S. PSYCHOPATHOLOGICAL DISORDERS OF CHILDHOOD. New York: John Wiley and Sons, 1972. 469 p.

Discusses a wide variety of childhood disorders from a behavioral-social learning theory point of view.

139 Rexford, Evedeen W., and VanAmerongen, Suzanne T. "Psychological Disorders of the Grade School Years." In CHILD AND ADOLESCENT PSYCHIATRY, SOCIO-CULTURAL AND COMMUNITY PSYCHIATRY, 2d ed., edited by Gerald Caplan, chapter 4. American Handbook of Psychiatry, vol. 2. New York: Basic Books, 1974.

Discusses various groupings of children's emotional disturbances, including physiologically based disturbances, developmental irregularities or failures, psychoneuroses of childhood, and personality disorders.

140 *Rie, Herbert E., ed. PERSPECTIVES IN CHILD PSYCHOPATHOLOGY. Chicago: Aldine, 1971. 423 p.

Examines the need for redefinition of the field in response to the impact of developments in such varied areas as ego psychology, ethology and human behavior, genetics, early individual differences, early cognitive stimulation, family approaches, application of principles of learning, sociocultural factors, and community mental health.

141 Ross, Alan O. PSYCHOLOGICAL DISORDERS OF CHILDREN. New York: McGraw-Hill, 1974. 360 p.

Behaviorally oriented presentation of psychological disorders of children and their treatment through behavior therapy.

142 Schoolar, J.C., ed. CURRENT ISSUES IN ADOLESCENT PSYCHIATRY. New York: Brunner/Mazel, 1973. 288 p.

Readings in areas of normal development in adolescence, social stress in adolescence, major pathologies in adolescence, and psychiatry and the law.

143 Schopler, Eric, and Reichler, Robert, eds. PSYCHOPATHOLOGY
     IN CHILD DEVELOPMENT. New York: Plenum Publishing Corp.,
     1976. 395 p.

     An encyclopedic view of the concerns of clinicians dealing
     with developmental disorders as well as some insight into the
     process of investigative work on development.

144 Shaw, Charles R. THE PSYCHIATRIC DISORDERS OF CHILDHOOD.
     New York: Appleton-Century-Crofts, 1966. 442 p.

     A general overview of childhood psychiatric disorders for stu-
     dents and professionals.

145 Taufer, Moses. ADOLESCENT DISTURBANCE AND BREAKDOWN.
     Hammondsworth, Engl.: Penguin Books, 1975. 96 p.

     Discusses the normal psychological development of adolescents
     and the causes and symptoms that characterize mental disturb-
     ance, illness, or vulnerability to breakdown.

146 *Wolman, Benjamin B., ed. MANUAL OF CHILD PSYCHOPATHOL-
     OGY. New York: McGraw-Hill, 1972. 1,369 p.

     Reference book for students and practitioners in the field of
     child and adolescent psychopathology. Comprehensive manual
     describing normal development, the etiology of mental dis-
     orders in childhood and adolescence, organic mental disorders,
     major neuroses and psychoses, diagnostic procedures, and
     treatment methods. An eclectic and thorough compilation of
     materials.

147 Workman, Sidney L. "Psychiatric Disorders of Adolescents." In
     CHILD AND ADOLESCENT PSYCHIATRY, SOCIO-CULTURAL AND
     COMMUNITY PSYCHIATRY. 2d ed., edited by Gerald Caplan, chap-
     ter 14. American Handbook of Psychiatry, vol. 2. New York: Basic
     Books, 1974.

     Discusses early adolescence, mid-adolescence, and late ado-
     lescence in terms of age-linked concerns related to adolescent
     psychiatric disorders. Covers a wide range of adolescent prob-
     lems.

THEORIES AND GENERAL CONCEPTS

Over and above the abnormal psychology texts and the comprehensive texts
covering psychiatric and psychological references, there are a number of books
devoted specifically to the development of the theories and general concepts
on which the various schools are based. Also, there are books that attempt
to relate psychological phenomena to other types of social phenomena, on a

theoretical plane. The books in this section are for those interested in the theoretical bases or philosophical underpinnings of the various approaches to psychotherapy. Again, there is no attempt to touch on all theories or philosophical concepts but rather to include broad collections touching many theoretical positions and specific texts that introduce new concepts related to treatment concepts in other areas.

148   Allen, Vernon L., ed. PSYCHOLOGICAL FACTORS IN POVERTY. Chicago: Markham Publishing Co., 1970. 392 p.

A collection of papers addressing the state of the art as it relates to the adequacy of psychological theory and the sufficiency of the current data to cope with practical problems of poverty. Covers theoretical positions, socialization and learning, heredity and environment, behavior concomitance, intervention strategies, and problems and prospects.

149   Ames, Thomas-Robert H., and Levy, Philip H. "What is Mental Illness?" In MODIFICATION OF BEHAVIOR OF THE MENTALLY ILL: REHABILITATION APPROACHES, edited by R.E. Hardy and J.G. Cull, chapter 1. Springfield, Ill.: Charles C Thomas, 1974. 230 p.

Proposes a psychosocial view of mental illness and mental health, stressing the term "maladjustment" as superseding "mentally sick" or "abnormal." Describes normal adjusted behavior as that which contributes to the growth and fulfillment of the individual and the group.

150   Cole, Jonathan O.; Freedman, Alfred M.; and Friedhoff, Arnold J., eds. PSYCHOPATHOLOGY AND PSYCHOPHARMACOLOGY. Baltimore: Johns Hopkins University Press, 1973. 298 p.

Discusses models of schizophrenia that can be produced by certain drugs, therapeutic aspects of drugs as they relate to issues of differential diagnosis, and general issues as they relate to ongoing research. Primarily for advanced students and professionals.

151   Cullen, John H., ed. EXPERIMENTAL BEHAVIOR: A BASIS FOR THE STUDY OF MENTAL DISTURBANCE. New York: John Wiley and Sons, 1974. 440 p.

A collection of eleven papers on behavioral science perspectives of mental disturbance. Includes syndromes resulting from object deprivation, social isolation and communication defects, factors in family relationships that contribute to psychological problems, and an ethological view of madness. Also covers recent developments in behavioral engineering.

152   Delage, Jean. "Child Psychiatry." VIE MEDICALE AU CANADA

FRANCAIS 1, no. 6 (1972): 604-7.

Excellent theoretical discussion of child psychiatry and the "current state of the arts."

153 Dunlaw, H. Warren. "Society, Culture, and Mental Disorder." AR-CHIVES OF GENERAL PSYCHIATRY 33, no. 2 (1976): 147-56.

Examines theories and hypotheses that purport to explain the process by which selected sociocultural factors influence the personality and emerge as mental symptoms. Presents fifteen propositions to summarize the factual knowledge from sociopsychological, epidemiological, and cultural studies. Sixty references.

154 English, O. Spurgeon, and Pearson, Gerald H. EMOTIONAL PROBLEMS OF LIVING: AVOIDING THE NEUROTIC PATTERN. 3d ed. New York: W.W. Norton, 1963. 624 p.

Explains the major factors of emotional adjustment in infancy, childhood, adolescence, and adult life, and discusses methods of prevention and treatment.

155 Freedman, Daniel X., ed. BIOLOGY OF THE MAJOR PSYCHOSES: A COMPARATIVE ANALYSIS. New York: Raven Press, 1975. 384 p.

156 Freylhan, F.A. "Rationale and Indications for Biological Treatment of Psychiatric Disorders." COMPREHENSIVE PSYCHIATRY 6, no. 5 (1965): 283-90.

Attempts to establish what constitutes drug-treatable psychopathology and what requires psychological insight, resolution of conflicts, or changes in interpersonal relationships.

157 Giora, Zir. PSYCHOPATHOLOGY: A COGNITIVE VIEW. New York: Gardner, 1975. 182 p.

Attempts to integrate the fields of psychopathology and psychotherapy with the discipline of information processing. Emphasizes the role of cognition in the development of psychopathology.

158 Graziano, Anthony M., ed. BEHAVIOR THERAPY WITH CHILDREN. Chicago: Aldine, 1971. 458 p.

Readings on behavior therapy with children, ranging from case histories to experimental reports, and covering behavioral approaches to mental retardation, psychoses, and antisocial behavior. Presents a comparison between psychotherapy and behavior therapy. For advanced workers with an interest in behavior modification.

159 Grenell, R.G., and Gabay, S., eds. BIOLOGICAL FOUNDATIONS
OF PSYCHIATRY. 2 vols. New York: Raven Press, 1976. 613 p.,
477 p.

Examines normal and abnormal behavior on the basis of the
medical model, with the aim of enhancing therapeutic concepts and techniques and of clarifying the biological bases
of language and concepts developed on the psychiatric model.

160 Hansell, Norris. THE PERSON IN DISTRESS: ON THE BIOSOCIAL
DYNAMICS OF ADAPTATION. New York: Human Sciences Press,
1976. 248 p.

Applies clinical and research findings on adaptational behavior to the design of treatment strategies, especially for severely distressed individuals.

161 Horowitz, Mardi J. STATES OF MIND. New York: Plenum Publishing Corp., 1978. 225 p.

Analysis of change in psychotherapy, presenting a systematic
approach to understanding psychological problems and establishing a means for evaluating and restructuring therapeutic
strategies.

162 Kaplan, Burton H., ed. PSYCHIATRIC DISORDER AND THE URBAN
ENVIRONMENT: REPORT OF THE CORNELL SOCIAL SCIENCE
CENTER. New York: Behavioral Publications, 1971. 310 p.

163 Kornetsky, C. PHARMACOLOGY--DRUGS AFFECTING BEHAVIOR.
New York: John Wiley and Sons, 1976. 275 p.

Outlines the physiological and psychological effects of drugs
most often used in the treatment of mentally ill persons, ep-
ileptics, and hyperactive children. For clinical psychologists
and mental health professionals. Also useful for persons not
highly trained in medical sciences but with a limited background in physiology and chemistry.

164 McCall, Raymond J. THE VARIETIES OF ABNORMALITY: A PHE-
NOMENOLOGICAL ANALYSIS. Springfield, Ill.: Charles C.Thomas,
1975. 568 p.

Describes the characteristics of various psychopathologies and
offers a simple system for organizing these characteristics into
a taxonomy. Presents a phenomenological analysis of mental
abnormality based on the logical organization of the taxonomy
rather than on etiological issues.

165 Millon, Theodore, ed. THEORIES OF PSYCHOPATHOLOGY AND

PERSONALITY: ESSAYS AND CRITIQUES. 2d ed. Philadelphia: W.B. Saunders, 1973. 502 p.

Presents a series of readings on the biophysical, intrapsychic, phenomenological, behavioral, sociocultural, and integrative theories of personality and psychopathology.

166 Rosenhan, David L., and London, Perry, eds. THEORY AND RE-SEARCH IN ABNORMAL PSYCHOLOGY. 2d ed. New York: Holt, Rinehart and Winston, 1975. 464 p.

A reader containing popular and classic articles that reject the basic assumption of the disease model. Presents issues that transcend therapy approaches, but also describes the concepts on which they are based.

167 Sadow, Leo. "Ego Access in Psychopathology." ARCHIVES OF GEN-ERAL PSYCHIATRY 21, no. 1 (1969): 15-24.

Suggests a diagramatic schema to conceptualize the varieties of psychological illnesses that must be differentiated to pre-scribe the most potentially efficient treatment and the most reasonable goal. Twenty-six references.

168 Slater, E., and Cowle, V.A. THE GENETICS OF MENTAL DIS-ORDERS. New York: Oxford University Press, 1971. 413 p.

Provides an extensive view of the various models and methods of clinical genetics. Proposes a predisposition to certain anx-iety and vulnerable states, although genetic studies do not support unitary hypotheses in most cases, particularly the neu-roses in which environmental stress is important. A handbook for the clinician.

169 Tader, Malcolm. THE PSYCHOPHYSIOLOGY OF MENTAL ILLNESS. London: Routledge and Kegan Paul, 1975. 270 p.

Presents a comprehensive review of psychophysiological factors in anxiety, depression, schizophrenia, and other forms of mental disturbance. Forty-seven pages of references.

170 Wachtel, P.L. PSYCHOANALYSIS AND BEHAVIOR THERAPY. New York: Basic Books, 1977. 315 p.

Challenges the assumption that psychodynamic and behavioral approaches to psychotherapy and personality are irreconcil-able. Demonstrates how the two schools can provide impor-tant complementary perspectives on understanding and chang-ing troubling life patterns.

EPIDEMIOLOGY AND OTHER DISCUSSIONS OF CAUSATION

171   Bullard, Dexter M., Jr.; Glaser, Helen H.; Heagarty, Margaret C.; and Pizchik, Elizabeth C. "Failure to Thrive in the 'Neglected' Child." AMERICAN JOURNAL OF ORTHOPSYCHIATRY 37, no. 4 (1967): 680-90.

Discusses problems of children who fail to thrive without any obvious physical cause or other known etiology. Feels the term "neglect" is not appropriate to these children.

172   Dohrenwend, Bruce P. "Sociocultural and Social Psychological Factors in the Genesis of Mental Disorder." JOURNAL OF HEALTH AND SOCIAL BEHAVIOR 16, no. 4 (1975): 365-92.

Discusses the etiological implications of sociocultural and social-psychological factors in the occurrence and distribution of functional psychiatric disorders. Five pages of references.

173   Felner, Robert D.; Stolberg, Arnold; and Cowen, Emory T. "Crisis Events and School Mental Health Referrals of Young Children." JOURNAL OF CONSULTING AND CLINICAL PSYCHOLOGY 43, no. 3 (1975): 305-10.

174   Freeman, Thomas. "Childhood Psychopathology and Psychotic Phenomena in Adults." BRITISH JOURNAL OF PSYCHIATRY 124 (November 1974): 556-63.

Discusses similarities between aspects of childhood psychopathology and aspects of adult psychotic behaviors in the areas of delusions, fantasies, psychomotor phenomena, and disturbances of affect.

175   Hertzig, Margaret E., and Birch, Herbert G. "Neurologic Organization in Psychiatrically Disturbed Adolescents: A Comparative Consideration of Sex Differences." ARCHIVES OF GENERAL PSYCHIATRY 19 (June 1968): 528-30.

Indicates that both male and female disturbed adolescents have a frequency of occurrence of neurologic abnormality far in excess of the frequency found in psychiatrically unremarkable comparison groups. Describes four measurements of abnormality.

176   Levy, Leo, and Rowitz, Louis. THE ECOLOGY OF MENTAL DISORDER. New York: Behavioral Publications, 1973. 209 p.

A brief review of studies on the incidence and prevalence of mental disorder as a function of community characteristics.

177 Masterson, James F., Jr. "The Psychiatric Significance of Adolescent Turmoil." AMERICAN JOURNAL OF PSYCHIATRY 124, no. 11 (1962): 107-12.

   Suggests that the clinical effects of adolescent turmoil should be given less significance than previously thought as a basis for adolescent symptomatology. Place greater emphasis on psychiatric illness as the probable basis of the symptoms.

178 Melgas, Frederick T., and Bowlby, John. "Types of Hopelessness in Psychopathological Process." ARCHIVES OF GENERAL PSYCHIATRY 20, no. 6 (1969): 690-99.

   Describes the role of hopelessness as an underlying dynamic in psychopathological process, as exemplified by depressive conditions in sociopathic behavior.

179 Rutter, Michael; Tizard, Jack; Yule, W.; Graham, P.; and Whitmore, K. "Isle of Wight Studies, 1964-1974." PSYCHOLOGICAL MEDICINE 6, no. 2 (1976): 313-32.

   Reports a program of interrelated educational and psychiatric studies of school-aged children on the Isle of Wight as part of a series of epidemiological studies of educational, psychiatric, and physical disorders in nine eleven-year-old children, with follow-up studies in 1968 and 1969.

180 *Schwab, John J., and Schwab, Mary E. SOCIOCULTURAL ROOTS OF MENTAL ILLNESS. New York: Plenum Publishing Corp., 1978. 325 p.

   An epidemiologic survey of investigations in mental illness, covering the last two hundred years.

181 Whittaker, James K. "Crises of Childhood Disorders." SOCIAL WORK 21, no. 2 (1976): 91-96.

   Examines present status of the "family-etiology hypotheses" in view of recent research on autism and learning disabilities. Suggests that the etiology of these disorders may be neurological or perceptual rather than psychogenic, as previously thought.

GENERAL THERAPEUTIC APPROACHES

Adults

There is a group of authors who have specialized in the development of various theoretical approaches to the question of treatment and psychotherapy. Here again we have a large number of schools that overlap or approach the problem in a similar way while using a different vocabulary or label. Also, there are approaches that are clearly distinct and use unique or highly specialized techniques, such as psychopharmacology or hypnotism. We have attempted to encompass the major approaches by including those texts which serve a primary review function and those systems which seem to have a research base, a foundation in collected data, or a sufficient period of experience for an outside observer to feel that a degree of validity has been established.

The items are grouped as follows: generalized approaches to the treatment of adult problems of abnormal behavior, approaches to treatment and therapy with children, and approaches to family therapy.

182   Aguilera, Donna C., and Messick, Janice M. CRISIS INTERVENTION: THEORY AND METHODOLOGY. St. Louis: Mosby, 1974. 153 p.

A "cookbook" approach to crisis intervention, including a number of historical antecedents and case studies, and attempting to establish theoretical concepts and a mode of assessing specific problems. For professionals and nonprofessionals.

183.   Bannister, Donald, ed. ISSUES AND APPROACHES IN THE PSYCHOLOGICAL THERAPIES. New York: John Wiley and Sons, 1975. 286 p.

Confronts general issues on the nature of mental illness, the nature of cure, and the nature of the psychotherapeutic relationship between therapist and client.

184   Bauman, Gerald, and Grunes, R. PSYCHIATRIC REHABILITATION IN THE GHETTO. Lexington, Mass.: Lexington Books, 1974. 178 p.

Describes the mental health movement as it emerged in poverty community areas, and develops a valuable historical and political approach to community rehabilitation and treatment efforts. Emphasizes treatment as part of an education process, rather than the more strict psychotherapeutic approach.

185   Beck, Aaron T. COGNITIVE THERAPY AND THE EMOTIONAL DISORDERS. New York: International Universities Press, 1976. 356 p.

Traces the development of the cognitive approach to psychopathology and psychotherapy. Discusses the development of rational techniques, the importance of engaging the patient in the exploration of his or her inner world, and the necessity of obtaining a sharp delineation of specific thoughts. Ten pages of references.

186   Binder, Virginia; Binder, Arnold; and Rimland, Bernard, eds. MODERN THERAPIES. Englewood Cliffs, N.J.: Prentice-Hall, 1976. 230 p.

Describes the techniques and objectives of twelve modern
therapies from rational-emotive therapy, gestalt therapy, and
reality therapy to transcendental meditation and megavitamin
therapy. Emphasizes the achievement of long-term benefits
from short-term therapy.

187 Bockar, Joyce. PRIMER FOR THE NON-MEDICAL PSYCHOTHERA-
PIST. New York: Halsted, 1976. 131 p.

A guide to differentiating mentally ill from physically ill patients. Provides psychiatric diagnostic information as well as
indications for use and effects and side effects of all psychotropic drugs, both prescriptive and illicit (including alcohol).
Appendix of drugs used in psychotherapy and their effects.

188 Burton, Arthur, ed. WHAT MAKES BEHAVIOR CHANGE POSSIBLE?
New York: Brunner/Mazel, 1976. 352 p.

Presents sixteen research and clinical authorities discussing
behavior change from various psychotherapeutic view points.
Considers techniques and processes including psychoanalysis,
behavioral therapy, gestalt therapy, family therapy, cogni-
tive-rational therapy, the humanistic approach, and crisis intervention.

189 *Corsini, Raymond J., ed. CURRENT PSYCHOTHERAPIES. Itasca,
Ill.: Peacock, 1973. 502 p.

Reports by representatives of twelve major schools on their
systems of psychotherapy, following a specific outline: definition of the school, history of its development, current status, major theoretical concepts, comparison with other systems, concept of personality, description of the process and
management of psychotherapy, and a case study. Includes
the following schools: psychoanalysis, Adlerian therapy, an-
alytical psychotherapy, client-centered therapy, rational-emotive therapy, behavior therapy, gestalt therapy, reality ther-
apy, experiential therapy, transactional analysis, encounter
therapy, and eclectic therapies.

190 Enelow, Allen J. ELEMENTS OF PSYCHOTHERAPY. New York:
Oxford University Press, 1977. 160 p.

Compares major approaches to psychotherapy, illustrating with
case histories. Includes examples of interactions and samples
of patient-therapist dialogue.

191 Friessen, DeLoss D. "The Use of Behavior Modification Techniques
with the Mentally Ill." In MODIFICATION OF BEHAVIOR IN THE
MENTALLY ILL: REHABILITATION APPROACHES, edited by R.E.

Hardy and J.G. Cull, chapter 2. Springfield, Ill.: Charles C Thomas, 1974.

192   Heine, Ralph W. PSYCHOTHERAPY. Englewood Cliffs, N.J.: Prentice-Hall, 1971. 170 p.

    Basically eclectic in the investigative tradition. Discusses the concepts of the therapeutic process, problems of psycho-diagnostic testing, and problems of assessment. Text for undergraduates and laypersons.

193   Hurwitz, Thomas D. "Electroconvulsive Therapy: A Review." COMPREHENSIVE PSYCHIATRY 15, no. 4 (1974): 303-14.

    Reviews the research on electroconvulsive therapy (ECT), stressing studies of the convulsive stimulus and the convulsive and physiologic responses. Gives indications, contraindications, and potential complications. Fifty-four references.

194   Jurjevich, Ratibor-Ray M., ed. DIRECT PSYCHOTHERAPY: 28 AMERICAN ORIGINALS. Coral Gables: University of Miami Press, 1973. 513 p.

    Direct psychotherapy seen as nonpsychoanalytic psychotherapy. Presents articles by Berne, Kelly, Ellis, Glasser, and Mowrer.

195   Kaplan, Harold I., and Sadock, Benjamin J., eds. COMPREHENSIVE GROUP PSYCHOTHERAPY. Baltimore: Williams and Wilkins, 1971. 928 p.

    A comprehensive compendium incorporating classic and newer articles in group psychotherapy. Includes thirty collaborators, all experts in the field, presenting basic principles of group psychotherapy, specialized group therapy techniques, psychotherapy with groups in special categories, and training and research. For students and professionals involved in group therapy.

196   Kernberg, O.S.; Burstein, E.D.; Coyne, L.; Appelbaum, A.; Horwitz, L.; and Voth, H. PSYCHOTHERAPY AND PSYCHOANALYSIS: FINAL REPORT OF THE MENNINGER FOUNDATION'S PSYCHOTHERAPY RESEARCH PROJECT. Topeka, Kans.: Menninger Foundation, 1972. 275 p.

    Report of a project initiated in 1954, involving the analysis of characteristics of patients, delineation of treatment and appraisal of outcomes, and situational factors in psychotherapy and psychoanalysis.

197   Korchin, Seldon S. MODERN CLINICAL PSYCHOLOGY: PRINCIPLES OF INTERVENTION IN THE CLINIC AND COMMUNITY. New York: Basic Books, 1976. 672 p.

Presents modern clinical psychology in such breadth and depth that the book could be used as a graduate-level text.

198   Kroger, William S.   CLINICAL AND EXPERIMENTAL HYPNOSIS. 2d ed.   Philadelphia: J.B. Lippincott Co., 1977.   406 p.

Basic "how-to-do-it" text on hypnosis.

199   Kroger, William S., and Fezler, William D.   HYPNOSIS AND BE-HAVIOR MODIFICATION.   Philadelphia: J.B. Lippincott Co., 1976. 426 p.

Demonstrates how a number of leading behavior therapists have used hypnotic techniques to facilitate the therapeutic process.   Discusses both hypnosis and behavior modification viewpoints using a simple framework, with little effort to develop real theoretical depth.   Provides a focused review of relevant work using either hypnosis or behavior therapy for a wide variety of problems, and offers practical examples.

200   Leitenberg, Harold, ed.   HANDBOOK OF BEHAVIOR MODIFICA-TION AND BEHAVIOR THERAPY.   Englewood Cliffs, N.J.:   Prentice-Hall, 1976.   671 p.

Discussion by three experts on a wide range of questions relating to behavior modification and behavior therapy as they relate to work with adults, children, and youth.   Touches on most of the issues involved in this field.

201   Loew, C.; Clemens, A.; Grayson, Henry; and Loew, Gloria Heinman, eds.   THREE PSYCHOTHERAPIES: A CLINICAL COMPARISON.   New York: Brunner/Mazel, 1975.   268 p.

Contrasts techniques of behavior therapy, gestalt therapy, and psychoanalysis by having representatives of each therapy discuss the same three cases.

202   Malan, David H.   THE FRONTIER OF BRIEF PSYCHOTHERAPY.   New York: Plenum Publishing Corp., 1976.   388 p.

An attempt to converge research and clinical practice through the use of eighteen case studies.

203   Patterson, Cecil H., ed.   THEORIES OF COUNSELING AND PSY-CHOTHERAPY.   2d ed.   New York: Harper and Row, 1973.   554 p.

Presents fourteen theories of psychotherapy with a summary and evaluation of each.   Good overview of theories but with a heavy psychoanalytic bias.

204   Rabkin, Richard. STRATEGIC PSYCHOTHERAPY. New York: Basic
        Books, 1977. 257 p.

        Describes psychotherapies that flow from both psychodynamic
        and behavioral science theories. Attempts to isolate the
        problem, analyze the attempts to solve it, and offer methods
        that may work better. Gives good clinical examples and
        relevant research.

205   Rubin, Richard D.; Fensterheim, H.; Henderson, J.D.; and Ullman,
        L.P., eds. ADVANCES IN BEHAVIOR THERAPY: PROCEEDINGS
        OF THE 4TH CONFERENCE OF THE ASSOCIATION FOR ADVANCE-
        MENT OF BEHAVIOR THERAPY. New York: Academic Press, 1972.
        233 p.

        Describes theoretical formula development of tests, critical
        research evaluation, and related issues involving the use of
        behavioral therapy techniques.

206   Sloane, R. Bruce; Staples, Fred R.; Cristol, A.H.; Yorkston, N.J.;
        and Whipple, K. PSYCHOTHERAPY VERSUS BEHAVIOR THERAPY.
        Cambridge: Harvard University Press, 1975. 254 p.

        A report of a well-controlled study comparing psychoanalyti-
        cally oriented psychotherapy and behavior therapy, with ten
        patients in each treatment group.

207   Small, Leonard. THE BRIEFER PSYCHOTHERAPIES. New York: Brun-
        ner/Mazel, 1971. 262 p.

        A review of the literature in the general area of brief psy-
        chotherapy. Considers population characteristics, diagnosis,
        progress, studies of outcomes, and hazards in brief psycho-
        therapy.

208   Stein, Leonard I., and Test, Mary Ann, eds. ALTERNATIVES TO
        MENTAL HOSPITAL TREATMENT. New York: Plenum Publishing
        Corp., 1978. 336 p.

        Explores the rationale behind the need for alternatives to
        mental hospital treatment. Proposes that the community be
        the primary focus of care for the patient. Provides perspec-
        tives on planning and implementing community-based treatment
        models.

209   Stuart, Richard B. TRICK OR TREATMENT: HOW AND WHEN PSY-
        CHOTHERAPY FAILS. Champaign, Ill.: Research Press, 1970. 201 p.

        Comprehensive review of literature on therapy failure. Pre-
        sents strong indictment of the more traditional models of psy-
        chotherapy, arguing that a concentration on a description of

pathology to fit psychiatric nomenclature is the best method
to guarantee failure. A general anti-labeling text that supports behavior change through social learning and behavioral
approaches.

210 Suinn, Richard M., and Weigel, Richard G., eds. INNOVATIVE
MEDICAL-PSYCHIATRIC THERAPIES. Baltimore: University Park Press,
1976. 302 p.

Identifies and evaluates medical-psychiatric therapies of
proven value as well as cautionary issues. Presents reviews
of current research, and details techniques of therapy, side
effects, drugs, drastic therapies (ECT or psychosurgery), and
miscellaneous approaches. For professionals.

211 Usdin, Gene, ed. OVERVIEW OF PSYCHOTHERAPIES. New York:
Brunner/Mazel, 1974. 204 p.

212 Valenstein, Elliot S. BRAIN CONTROL: A CRITICAL EXAMINA-
TION OF BRAIN STIMULATION AND PSYCHOSURGERY. New York:
John Wiley and Sons, 1973. 407 p.

Broad survey of the subject, with a critical evaluation of the
control of human behavior by electronically stimulating or
surgically destroying parts of the brain. History of these
processes gives some of the more important controversies,
looking at the legal situation, the question of civil rights,
and suggestions for guaranteeing maximal consideration of
patients' rights and interests. Includes 490 references.

213 Weiner, Irving B., ed. CLINICAL METHODS IN PSYCHOLOGY.
New York: John Wiley and Sons, 1976. 678 p.

Experts discussing major assessment and intervention methods
currently used in clinical psychology. Includes assessment
interviews, projective techniques, measures of intelligence
and conceptual thinking, individual psychotherapy, group
and family therapy, behavior modification, and crisis intervention. Useful reference book for beginning and experienced clinicians.

214 Winter, Arthur, ed. THE SURGICAL CONTROL OF BEHAVIOR: A
SYMPOSIUM. Springfield, Ill.: Charles C Thomas, 1971. 90 p.

215 *Wolman, Benjamin B., ed. THE THERAPIST'S HANDBOOK: TREAT-
MENT METHODS OF MENTAL DISORDERS. New York: Reinhold,
1976. 539 p.

Important handbook reflecting the major schools of thought

and approaches to treating mental illness. Covers the inter-
relationship of research, training, and service. Covers topics
ranging from theory to specific treatment modalities and including psychosomatic disorders, schizophrenia, depression,
neurosis, antisocial behavior, drug addiction, and alcoholism.

216   Yalom, Irvin D. THE THEORY AND PRACTICE OF GROUP PSYCHO-
      THERAPY. New York: Basic Books, 1975. 529 p.

      Presents a well-rounded view of group therapy processes.
      Discusses the training of therapists and the exploration of the
      scientific basis of group psychotherapy. Presents clinical ex-
      amples and heavily-referenced review material. Outlines
      how group variations are influenced by the therapist, by the
      group composition, by the setting, and by specific types of
      problems.

Children and Adolescents

217   *Anthony, James K. "Child Therapy Techniques." In CHILD AND
      ADOLESCENT PSYCHIATRY, SOCIO-CULTURAL AND COMMUNITY
      PSYCHIATRY, 2d ed., edited by Gerald Caplan, chapter 9. Ameri-
      can Handbook of Psychiatry, vol. 2. New York: Basic Books, 1974.

      Discusses various child therapy techniques: development of
      child analysis, nondirective psychotherapy, child therapy and
      the delinquent, release therapy, conditioning therapy, and
      other areas. Describes the therapeutic environment, course
      of treatment, role of the therapist, and evaluation of the
      procedures. Offers a comprehensive outline of the area.

218   Axline, Virginia M. PLAY THERAPY. Boston: Houghton Mifflin,
      1947. Rev. ed. New York: Ballantine Books, 1969. 374 p. Paper.

      Basic text on nondirective play therapy.

219   Dupont, Henry, ed. EDUCATING EMOTIONALLY DISTURBED CHIL-
      DREN: READINGS. 2d ed. New York: Holt, Rinehart and Winston,
      1975. 500 p.

      Readings designed to provide a current overview of the edu-
      cation of emotionally disturbed children and to encourage dis-
      cussion of policy issues and their relationship to conceptual
      models and program development.

220   Fish, Barbara. "Drug Use in Psychiatric Disorders of Children."
      AMERICAN JOURNAL OF PSYCHIATRY 124, no. 8 (1968): 31-36.

221   Gittelman-Klein, Rachel. RECENT ADVANCES IN CHILD PSYCHO-
      PHARMACOLOGY. New York: Human Sciences Press, 1976. 272 p.

222   Kahan, Vladimir L. MENTAL ILLNESS IN CHILDHOOD. New York: Barnes and Noble, 1974. 219 p.

   Describes a six-year review of seventy-one severely disturbed children. Considers types of treatment, symptoms and behaviors of the children, and the therapeutic potential of total environmental management of severely disturbed children.

223   Laufer, Maurice W.; Laffey, John J.; and Davidson, Robert E. "Residential Treatment for Children and Its Derivatives." In CHILD AND ADOLESCENT PSYCHIATRY, SOCIO-CULTURAL AND COMMUNITY PSYCHIATRY, 2d ed., edited by Gerald Caplan, chapter 12. American Handbook of Psychiatry, vol. 2. New York: Basic Books, 1974.

   A broad description of residential institutions for children, including day hospitals, residential units, group homes, and other similar settings. Includes 120 references.

224   Leland, Henry, and Smith, Daniel E. PLAY THERAPY WITH MENTALLY SUBNORMAL CHILDREN. New York: Grune and Stratton, 1965. 256 p.

   Defines four systems of play therapy useful with mentally retarded developmentally disabled children.

225   Lovaas, O. Ivar, and Bucher, Bradley, D., eds. PERSPECTIVES IN BEHAVIOR MODIFICATION WITH DEVIANT CHILDREN. Englewood Cliffs, N.J.: Prentice-Hall, 1974. 562 p.

   Deals with fears and phobias, self-injurious behavior, and improvement of self-help and social skills. For advanced students.

226   Magrab, Phyllis R., ed. PSYCHOLOGICAL MANAGEMENT OF PEDIATRIC PROBLEMS, vol. 1. EARLY LIFE CONDITIONS AND CHRONIC DISEASES. Baltimore: University Park Press, 1978. 400 p.

   Discusses multiple pediatric medical problems from a psychological perspective, presenting a developmental approach to the management of acute and chronic medical conditions of children and adolescents.

227   _____. PSYCHOLOGICAL MANAGEMENT OF PEDIATRIC PROBLEMS, vol. 2. SENSORINEURAL CONDITIONS AND SOCIAL CONCERNS. Baltimore: University Park Press, 1978. 352 p.

228   Moustakas, Clark. CHILDREN IN PLAY THERAPY. New York: Jason Aronson, 1973. 218 p.

   Discusses some of the general principles and benefits of the nondirective play therapy approach.

229   Reisman, John M. PRINCIPLES OF PSYCHOTHERAPY WITH CHIL-
DREN. New York: Wiley-Interscience, 1973. 329 p.

        Reflects on orientation toward a Rogerian type of psychother-
apy, which the author calls "integrative psychotherapy."

230   Rosenthal, Alan J., and Levine, Saul V. "Brief Psychotherapy with
Children: Progress of Therapy." AMERICAN JOURNAL OF PSYCHI-
ATRY 128, no. 2 (1971): 141-46.

        Outlines the concept of brief psychotherapy with children and
describes the results of a study using brief psychotherapy procedures.

231   Schaefer, Charles, and Millman, Howard, eds. THERAPIES FOR CHIL-
DREN. San Francisco: Jossey-Bass, 1977. 684 p.

        Presents condensations of 134 articles by professionals, to pro-
vide an eclectic guide for child therapy.

232   Smilansky, Sara. THE EFFECTS OF SOCIODRAMATIC PLAY ON DIS-
ADVANTAGED PRE-SCHOOL CHILDREN. New York: John Wiley
and Sons, 1968. 164 p.

233   Weber, George H., and Haberlein, Bernard J. RESIDENTIAL TREAT-
MENT OF EMOTIONALLY DISTURBED CHILDREN. New York: Behavioral Press, 1972. 327 p.

        Twenty articles on residential treatment for students and work-
ers in the field.

234   Weiner, Jerry M., ed. PSYCHOPHARMACOLOGY IN CHILDHOOD
AND ADOLESCENCE. New York: Basic Books, 1977. 226 p.

        Describes a historical and theoretical perspective on the use
of drugs in the treatment of childhood and adolescent problems. Assesses the scientific basis and current clinical usage
of drugs, taking a conservative view on drug use with young
persons. Intended primarily for clinicians who treat children.

235   Werry, John S., and Wallersheim, Janet P. "Behavior Therapy with
Children: A Broad Overview." JOURNAL OF THE AMERICAN
ACADEMY OF CHILD PSYCHIATRY 6, no. 2 (1967): 346-70.

        Reviews behavior therapy as applied to the treatment of psy-
chopathology of childhood. Four pages of references.

Parents and Families

236   Arnold, L. Eugene, ed. HELPING PARENTS HELP THEIR CHILDREN.

New York: Brunner/Mazel, 1977. 420 p.

Practical volume for professionals on the issue of recognizing parents as an important element in child mental health work. Discusses various aspects of parental guidance and deals with parents' potential roles in the final outcome.

237   Cooper, Shirley. "Treatment of Parents." In CHILD AND ADOLES-CENT PSYCHIATRY, SOCIO-CULTURAL AND COMMUNITY PSYCHI-ATRY, 2d ed., edited by Gerald Caplan, chapter 10. American Handbook of Psychiatry, vol. 2. New York: Basic Books, 1974.

Discusses the changing roles of the family, direct work with parents, the importance of the exchange of information, the work with poor and/or minority families, and the broad as-pects of issues emerging in these areas. Twenty references.

238   Krewman, Delores E., and Joy, Virginia D. "Family Response to the Mental Illness of a Relative: A Review of Literature." SCHIZO-PHRENIA BULLETIN, no. 10 (1974): 34–57.

Reviews data on the role of the family in the mental illness of one of its members. Describes psychological and non-psy-chological views of illness, effects of distance and closeness of the relationship to the patient and typologies based on re-sponses of families. Eighty-eight references.

239   *Minuchin, Salvador. "Structural Family Therapy." In CHILD AND ADOLESCENT PSYCHIATRY, SOCIO-CULTURAL AND COMMUNITY PSYCHIATRY, 2d ed., edited by Gerald Caplan, chapter 11. Amer-ican Handbook of Psychiatry, vol. 2. New York: Basic Books, 1974.

Presents broad aspects of family therapy, including various techniques, therapeutic tactics, case examples, and issues re-lating to family therapy. Thirty-eight references.

240   Morrison, Gilbert C., ed. EMERGENCIES IN CHILD PSYCHIATRY: EMOTIONAL CRISES OF CHILDREN, YOUTH AND THEIR FAMILIES. Springfield, Ill.: Charles C Thomas, 1975. 482 p.

Presents detailed theoretical and empirical studies on urgent emotional problems of childhood and adolescence. Addresses the interrelationships of psychological risk and crises, all em-bedded in a family matrix.

241   Rohner, Ronald P. THEY LOVE ME, THEY LOVE ME NOT. New Haven, Conn.: HRAF Press, 1976. 300 p.

Describes a new "universalist" approach to behavioral science and its applicability to the crosscultural study of the effects of parental acceptance and rejection. Covers a variety of topics on relationships between children and their parents and personality disturbances resulting from problems in these relationships.

242 *Sager, Clifford J., and Kaplan, Helen F., eds. PROGRESS IN GROUP AND FAMILY THERAPY. New York: Brunner/Mazel, 1972. 935 p.

Combines work from the current literature and specially prepared original papers. Includes fifty-two papers in major areas on group therapy, family therapy, sex and marriage, and special populations.

243 *Satir, Virginia; Stachowiak, James; and Taschman, Harvey A. HELPING FAMILIES TO CHANGE. New York: Jason Aronson, 1976. 296 p.

Reviews ideas, techniques, and issues in the family field over the last twenty years. Presents a theoretical and practical framework for guiding and evaluating the process implicit in family counseling.

244 Schuham, Anthony I. "Power Relations in Emotionally Disturbed and Normal Family Triads." JOURNAL OF ABNORMAL PSYCHOLOGY 75, no. 1 (1970): 30–37.

Reports a study of fourteen normal and fourteen disturbed family triads, and presents a series of outcomes and process measures delineating their differential power structures and the manner in which they were formulated.

245 Spotnitz, Hyman. "Objected-Oriented Approaches to Severely Disturbed Adolescents." In THE ADOLESCENT IN GROUP AND FAMILY THERAPY, edited by Max Sugar, chapter 14. New York: Brunner/Mazel, 1975.

LEGAL AND ETHICAL ISSUES AND THE RIGHTS OF THE MENTALLY HANDICAPPED

These works deal with the legal and ethical considerations of institutionalization, patient rights, and the question of general and special rights for mentally handicapped persons. This is a major area involving individuals receiving help in the community, in institutions, or through other agencies.

246 Arieti, Silvano. "Psychiatric Controversy: Man's Ethical Dimension." AMERICAN JOURNAL OF PSYCHIATRY 132, no. 1 (1975): 39–42.

Discusses the relationship of moral values to the problems of

psychiatry. Suggests that psychiatrists should influence patients to exert their will, make conscious choices, and as-
sume a sense of responsibility for their own actions. Asserts
that psychiatric treatment must consider the ethical dimension.

247   Berlin, Irving N. "The Rights of the Retarded Child and His or Her
       Family." In his ADVOCACY FOR CHILD MENTAL HEALTH, chapter
       15. New York: Brunner/Mazel, 1975.

       Presents a complete history of the rights of retarded children,
       and notes recent advances in research and technology affect-
       ing the retarded. Twenty-seven references.

248   *Ennis, Bruce J., and Friedman, Paul R., eds. LEGAL RIGHTS OF
       THE MENTALLY HANDICAPPED. 3 vols. New York: Practicing
       Law Institute, Mental Health Law Project, 1974. 1,538 p.

       Reviews cases on patient rights and related questions for the
       mentally handicapped. Part of a national mental health law
       project overseeing cases in the various states.

249   Felicetti, Daniel A. "Mental Health, Retardation, and Government:
       An Overview." In his MENTAL HEALTH AND RETARDATION POLI-
       TICS: THE MIND LOBBIES IN CONGRESS, chapter 3. New York:
       Praeger, 1975.

       Gives a background on the development of federal policy on
       mental illness and mental retardation, starting with the pri-
       vate physician-patient-family relationship and moving through
       the heavy involvement of state, local, and federal agencies
       in the 1970s. Fifty-nine references.

250   Ginsberg, Leon H. "An Examination of the Civil Rights of Mentally
       Ill Children." CHILD WELFARE 211, no. 1 (1973): 14-25.

251   Golann, Stuart, and Fremouw, William J., eds. THE RIGHT TO
       TREATMENT FOR MENTAL PATIENTS. New York: Irvington, 1976.
       246 p.

       A collection of nine papers on the right to treatment. In-
       cludes such topics as the background of the Wyatt versus Stick-
       ney case, judicial action and social change, the use of liti-
       gation to achieve the right to habilitation, and perspectives
       on the right-to-treatment issue.

252   Goldstein, Joseph; Freud, Anna; and Solnit, A.J. BEYOND THE
       BEST INTEREST OF THE CHILD. New York: Free Press, 1973.
       170 p.

       Examines parent-child placement statutes and procedures as

they relate to psychoanalytic theory. Suggests that current practices may result in permanent emotional damage. Discusses developing place of practices that involve "the least detrimental psychological alternative."

253 Halleck, Seymour I. "Legal and Ethical Aspects of Behavior." AMERICAN JOURNAL OF PSYCHIATRY 131, no. 4 (1974): 381-85.

Highlights a new climate of concern over the power of psychiatrists to shape behavior, a question made more critical by the increasing effectiveness of psychiatric treatment, including drugs and behavior therapy techniques. Stresses the need for truly informed consent, appropriate safeguards (including the use of an oversight agency), and a new system of internal regulation for psychiatry.

254 Kittrie, Nicholas N. THE RIGHT TO BE DIFFERENT; DEVIANCE AND ENFORCED THERAPY. Baltimore: Penguin, 1973. 443 p.

Presents data relating to persons whose freedom has been restricted and who have been involuntarily exposed to treatment. Emphasizes ways to minimize compulsion.

255 Koocher, G.P., and Farber, S., eds. CHILDREN'S RIGHTS AND THE MENTAL HEALTH PROFESSIONS. New York: John Wiley and Sons, 1976. 259 p.

Examines key aspects of a child's rights as a client-patient. Focuses on issues such as professional responsibility and service delivery to children, institutional responsibility, due process for children in the mental health context, and public questions in which professionals must speak on behalf of child clients.

256 *Leland, Henry; Bendekovic, John; and Feldman, Susan, eds. LAW AND ETHICS: SUPPLEMENTARY BOOKLET ON LEGAL AND ETHICAL CONSIDERATIONS IN REHABILITATION SERVICES. Columbus: Ohio State University Nisonger Center, 1976. 339 p.

Includes an annotated bibliography of over 900 references; an annotated catalog of audiovisual materials; supplementary readings, laws and codes of ethics; and a group of hypothetical cases.

257 Meisek, Alan. "Rights of the Mentally Ill: The Gulf Between Theory and Reality." HOSPITAL AND COMMUNITY PSYCHIATRY 26, no. 6 (1975): 349-53.

Reviews a number of lawsuits related to the procedural and substantive rights of mental patients. Discusses the problems of implementing the various legal decrees and the difficulties of translating into reality the rights promulgated in the courts.

258 Miller, Kent S. MANAGING MADNESS: THE CASE AGAINST CIVIL COMMITMENT. New York: Free Press, 1976. 192 p.

Develops major arguments against civil commitment; author believes that "civil commitment for mental illness is wrong."

259 Renner, K. Edward. WHAT'S WRONG WITH THE MENTAL HEALTH MOVEMENT. Chicago: Nelson Hall, 1975. 218 p.

Raises a variety of moral and ethical questions in the areas of controlling behavior, labeling patients, and involuntary hospitalization. Emphasizes the importance of an informed public.

260 Szasz, Thomas. PSYCHIATRIC SLAVERY. New York: Free Press, 1977. 159 p.

Discusses the Donaldsen vs. O'Connor case as a basis for a general discussion on commitment and involuntary hospitalization. Tries to unravel the tangled threads of the complex judicial process concerning institutionalization. Discusses how interest groups can be rallied to improve treatment, and presents a general history of American psychiatric reforms.

Chapter 3

MENTAL RETARDATION
AND DEVELOPMENTAL DISABILITIES

There seems to be a trend at this time to substitute the term "developmental disability" for the older terms of mental deficiency, mental retardation, feeblemindedness, or oligophrenia. Because most of the texts and articles chosen for this chapter have been published in the last ten years, the term "mental retardation" is the most common term used, and it is treated as synonymous with all of the terms mentioned above. Although the term "developmental disability" has not yet begun to emerge in the literature, it has appeared in much of the current legislation, both federal and state, and therefore it should be recognized that references to developmental disability, while not synonymous with mental retardation, often include mental retardation. Because we have restricted ourselves primarily to the concept of abnormal behavior, aspects of developmental disability that would include learning disabilities on the one hand or epilepsy, cerebral palsy, and other major neurological disorders on the other have not been included. This chapter is devoted primarily to the nature of mental retardation, some of the epidemiological and etiological factors as well as questions relating to prevention, treatment, and training. A newer category, the emotionally disturbed and mentally retarded person, which is beginning to emerge as an area of interest in the mental health movement, is also included. The key texts are marked with an asterisk and include numbers 265, 266, 273, 274, 282, 287, 291, 303, 313, 318, 319, 324, 325, 349, 361, 362, 398, 400, 406, 408, and 412.

GENERAL REFERENCES AND OVERVIEWS

261 Baroff, George S. MENTAL RETARDATION: NATURE, CAUSE AND MANAGEMENT. New York: Halsted, 1974. 504 p.

> A comprehensive text that attempts to address both scientific and practical aspects of mental retardation. Considers questions of normalization, the rights of the mentally retarded, and various controversial and public issues. For students and beginning professionals.

262 Begab, Michael J., and Richardson, Stephen A., eds. THE MENTALLY RETARDED AND SOCIETY: A SOCIAL SCIENCE PERSPECTIVE.

Baltimore: University Park Press, 1975. 492 p.

Includes papers involving research-oriented projects and evolving issues for social scientists. Presents research and demonstration models to guide the field into directions mandated more by scientific investigation than emotion. For research workers, students, and professionals in sociology, social work, psychology, program planning, and administration.

263 Bergsma, Daniel, and Pulver, Ann E., eds. DEVELOPMENTAL DISABILITIES: PSYCHOLOGIC AND SOCIAL IMPLICATIONS. National Foundation March of Dimes Birth Defects, Original Article Series, vol. 12, no. 4. New York: Allen R. Liss, 1976. 188 p.

Presents papers on the medical and social aspects of developmental disability and outlines the challenge to psychosocial adaptation and the special needs of the developmentally disabled child within a school setting. Considers adolescence as a particularly stressful period of life in terms of the needs of the family and the reaction of society to the integration of handicapped individuals.

264 Berkler, M.S.; Bible, G.H.; Boles, S.M.; Deitz, D.E.D.; and Repp, A.C., eds. CURRENT TRENDS FOR THE DEVELOPMENTALLY DISABLED. Baltimore: University Park Press, 1978. 232 p.

A critical review of current research and practice that discusses legal and ethical challenges to those working with the developmentally disabled. Includes a critique of the major rights won by this population and the obstacles to the realization of these rights, development of practical programs to meet these challenges, and the growing emphasis on program effectiveness and accountability. For students and professionals involved in the delivery of services to the developmentally disabled.

265 *Bialer, Irving, and Sternlicht, Manny, eds. THE PSYCHOLOGY OF MENTAL RETARDATION: ISSUES AND APPROACHES. New York: Psychological Dimensions, 1977. 680 p.

Deals with broad psychological issues of mental retardation including series of assessment, treatment, research, differential diagnosis, classification, and methodological research issues with retarded persons. Contains an excellent chapter on behavioral genetics. Represents a good interaction between practical and theoretical questions relating to programing for the mentally retarded.

266 *Blatt, Burton, and Kaplan, Fred. CHRISTMAS IN PURGATORY: A PHOTOGRAPHIC ESSAY ON MENTAL RETARDATION. Syracuse, N.Y.: Human Policy Press, 1974. 121 p.

A documentary that dramatically demonstrates through photographs the dehumanization process and the state of life in institutions for the mentally retarded. Photographs describe many present-day institutions, underlining how human beings have been and are being stripped of their dignity and basic human rights.

267 Braginsky, Dorothea D., and Braginsky, Benjamin M. HANSELS AND GRETELS: STUDIES OF CHILDREN IN INSTITUTIONS FOR THE MENTALLY RETARDED. New York: Holt, Rinehart and Winston, 1971. 212 p.

Describes a study of 177 male and female "cultural-familial" patients in two state institutions in New England, and presents a vivid account of institutional life for the mildly retarded.

268 Brown, Bertram S., and Courtless, Thomas F. "The Mentally Retarded in Penal and Correctional Institutions." AMERICAN JOURNAL OF PSYCHIATRY 124, no. 9 (1968): 1164-70.

Presents results of a nationwide survey (207 penal and correctional institutions with a combined population of 189,202) to determine the extent of mental retardation in prison populations. Includes an intensive case study that reveals significant data regarding legal issues and problems.

269 Browning, Phillip L. REHABILITATION AND THE RETARDED OFFENDER. Springfield, Ill.: Charles C Thomas, 1976. 349 p.

Presents professionals from several fields exploring the complexities associated with a population of persons who are both mentally retarded and public offenders. Addresses the identification and description of retarded offenders, their constitutional rights and litigation with respect to such rights, and the legal system and its problems and implications for this group. Includes 141 annotated references.

270 Carter, Charles H., ed. MEDICAL ASPECTS OF MENTAL RETARDATION. 2d ed. Springfield, Ill.: Charles C Thomas, 1977. 1,104 p.

Comprehensive source of information on medical aspects of mental retardation, primarily for professionals in the field.

271 Chinn, Philip C.; Drew, Clifford J.; and Logan, Don R. MENTAL RETARDATION: A LIFE CYCLE APPROACH. St. Louis: C.V. Mosby, 1975. 219 p.

An introductory text on mental retardation, using both a multidisciplinary and a human development concept.

272   Clarke, A.D.B., and Clarke, Ann M. "Mental Retardation and Be-
      havioral Change." BRITISH MEDICAL BULLETIN 30, no. 2 (1974):
      179-85.

      Discusses the psychological aspects of mental retardation in
      assessing the behavioral effects of brain damage and malfor-
      mation and extremely adverse sociocultural factors. Examines
      major views of human development and concludes that all cur-
      rent ideas need modification in light of present research re-
      sults in mental retardation. Thirty-eight references.

273   *Clarke, Ann M., and Clarke, A.D.B., eds. MENTAL DEFICIENCY:
      THE CHANGING OUTLOOK. 3d ed. New York: Free Press, 1974.
      886 p.

      Examines biosocial factors, experimental analysis of subnormal
      behavior, assessment, amelioration of mental subnormality,
      and services for the mentally subnormal and their parents.
      Emphasizes the importance of careful empirical work having
      both long- and short-term implications in the prevention and
      amelioration of mental retardation.

274   *de la Cruz, Felix F., and LaVeck, Gerald D., eds. HUMAN SEX-
      UALITY AND THE MENTALLY RETARDED. New York: Brunner/
      Mazel, 1972. 317 p.

      Offers an overview of physical, psychological, and social as-
      pects of sexual behavior of the mentally retarded. Includes
      effects of institutionalization, psycho-education, marriage and
      parenthood, sterilization, homosexuality, and masturbation.
      Addressed to professionals, but of value to all persons work-
      ing with the mentally retarded.

275   Dibenedetto, Thomas A. "Problems of the Deaf-Retarded: A Review
      of the Literature." EDUCATION AND TRAINING OF THE MENTALLY
      RETARDED 11, no. 2 (1976): 164-71.

      An overview of the problems of mentally retarded deaf per-
      sons. Forty-two references.

276   Dutton, Gordon. MENTAL HANDICAP. London: Butterworths, 1975.
      176 p. Illus.

      Treats mental handicap from the scientific standpoint, with
      particular reference to causation and remedial therapy.

277   Edgerton, Robert B., and Bercovici, Sylvia M. "The Cloak of Com-
      petence: Years Later." AMERICAN JOURNAL OF MENTAL DEFI-
      CIENCY 80, no. 5 (1976): 485-97.

      Examines the lives of thirty mentally retarded persons who

participated in a 1967 study to determine the effects of the passage of twelve to fourteen years on their community adaptation. Presents a social-anthropological review of the situation surrounding community adjustment, with emphasis on the diversity of factors that make prediction problematic, based primarily on environmental rather than personal variables. Stresses the importance of recognizing the individual's own definition of success. Thirty-eight references.

278 Fischer, Henry L., and Krajicek, Marilyn J. "Sexual Development of the Moderately Retarded Child: Level of Information and Parental Attitudes." MENTAL RETARDATION 12, no. 3 (1974): 28-30.

Discusses implications for sexual education of the retarded, and offers recommendations for decreasing the discomfort associated with sexual matters.

279 Gardner, William I. LEARNING AND BEHAVIOR CHARACTERISTICS OF EXCEPTIONAL CHILDREN AND YOUTH: A HUMANISTIC BEHAVIORAL APPROACH. Boston: Allyn and Bacon, 1977. 593 p.

280 Garrard, Sterling D., and Richmond, Julius B. "Mental Retardation: Nature and Manifestations." In ORGANIC DISORDERS AND PSYCHOSOMATIC MEDICINE, edited by Morton F. Reiser, chapter 18. American Handbook of Psychiatry, 2d ed., vol. 4. New York: Basic Books, 1974.

Discusses definition and classification of mental retardation, biomedical causation, polygenic causation, sociocultural causation, mutability of IQ, and mutability of adaptive behavior. Lists sixty-two references.

281 Gottlieb, Jay. INTRODUCTION TO MENTAL RETARDATION: SOCIAL AND BEHAVIORAL ASPECTS. Baltimore: University Park Press, 1978. 325 p.

Deals mainly with problems and issues of mild and moderate mental retardation. Considers these as primarily social problems affecting the mentally retarded person's psychological development.

282 *Haywood, H. Carl, ed. SOCIAL-CULTURAL ASPECTS OF MENTAL RETARDATION. New York: Appleton-Century-Crofts, 1970. 798 p.

Includes twenty-eight papers by well-known scientists in the field of mental retardation, with an extensive review of the state of the art introducing each section. Discusses cognition and cognitive development, cognition and language development, the impact of social institutions, education and habilitation, educational intervention and cultural deprivation, cross-cultural perspectives, mental retardation and other handicapping conditions, and culturally-related biological factors.

283   Heber, Rick F., and Stevens, Harvey A., eds. MENTAL RETARDATION: A REVIEW OF RESEARCH. Chicago: University of Chicago Press, 1964. 502 p.

Examines various research areas in the field of mental retardation. Edited by two well-respected researchers.

284   Hutt, Max L., and Gibby, Robert G. THE MENTALLY RETARDED CHILD: DEVELOPMENT, EDUCATION AND TREATMENT. 3d ed. Boston: Allyn and Bacon, 1976. 513 p.

Contains a general overview of mental retardation, focusing on children.

285   Johnston, Robert B., and Magrab, Phyllis R., eds. DEVELOPMENTAL DISORDERS: ASSESSMENT, TREATMENT, EDUCATION. Baltimore: University Park Press, 1976. 544 p.

Describes the nature of the conditions and of the roles and services formed by various intervening disciplines. Primarily for professionals dealing with developmentally handicapped children.

286   Kirman, Brian, and Bicknell, Joan. MENTAL HANDICAP. New York: Longman, 1975. 494 p.

Discusses the issues relating to the inclusion of the mentally handicapped person in the mainstream of society. Stresses the need for public, legal, and governmental support for relevant programs and financing of general human services for all handicapped individuals.

287   *Koch, Richard, and de la Cruz, Felix F., eds. DOWN'S SYNDROME: RESEARCH, PREVENTION AND MANAGEMENT. New York: Brunner/Mazel, 1973. 240 p.

Comprehensive volume discussing research, prevention, and management of Down's Syndrome.

288   Koch, Richard, and Koch, Kathryn Jean. UNDERSTANDING THE MENTALLY RETARDED CHILD: A NEW APPROACH. New York: Random House, 1974. 301 p.

An extremely comprehensive book for parents and nonprofessionals, simply written. Presents case histories to embellish the information provided, and discusses most of the relevant issues and questions surrounding the mentally retarded child.

289 Kriger, Sara Finn. LIFE STYLES OF AGING RETARDATES LIVING IN COMMUNITY SETTINGS IN OHIO. Columbus, Ohio: Psychologia Metrika, 1975. 130 p.

Attempts to identify the needs and life-styles of mildly to moderately mentally retarded aging adults.

290 _____. "On Aging and Mental Retardation." In PROCEEDINGS OF THE CONSULTATION-CONFERENCE ON THE GERONTOLOGICAL ASPECTS OF MENTAL RETARDATION, edited by J.C. Hamilton and R.M. Segal, pp. 20-32. Ann Arbor: University of Michigan, Institute of Gerontology, 1975.

Data on the life-styles of mentally retarded aging persons, indicating the need to take a closer look at this segment of the population and to establish some basic guidelines and models of care to govern their daily needs.

291 *Leland, Henry, and Smith, Daniel E. MENTAL RETARDATION: PRESENT AND FUTURE PERSPECTIVES. Belmont, Calif.: Wadsworth Publishing Co., 1974. 230 p.

Emphasizes the basic rights of the mentally retarded individual, and presents a current picture of policies relating to diagnosis, care, rehabilitation, treatment, and training of the mentally retarded. Establishes future perspectives in an attempt to formulate guidelines for developing a new orientation toward the habilitation and prevention of mental retardation. For beginning students and professionals in the field of mental retardation.

292 Levine, Michael S.; Rauh, Joseph L.; Levine, Carolyn W.; and Rubenstein, Jack H. "Adolescents with Developmental Disabilities: A Survey of Their Problems and Their Management." CLINICAL PEDIATRICS 14, no. 1 (1975): 25-32.

293 Meier, John H. DEVELOPMENTAL AND LEARNING DISABILITIES: EVALUATION, MANAGEMENT AND PREVENTION IN CHILDREN. Baltimore: University Park Press, 1976. 444 p. Glossary.

Discusses the issues and situations relating to the programs growing out of current federal and state legislation. Presents analyses of and recommendations for newly mandated programs based on ways of improving interdisciplinary understanding of and methods for dealing with the problems of children. Includes 792 references.

294 Menolascino, Frank J. CHALLENGES IN MENTAL RETARDATION: PROGRESSIVE IDEOLOGY AND SERVICES. New York: Human Sciences Press, 1977. 362 p.

Critical review of past and present definitions and treatment models. Emphasizes the personal dignity and respect which the mentally retarded person deserves. Presents developmental models of services with normalization principles as the basis. Text geared to parents and professionals.

295   Menolascino, Frank J., and Egger, M.L. MEDICAL DIMENSIONS OF MENTAL RETARDATION. Lincoln: University of Nebraska Press, 1977. 478 p.

Comprehensive, nontechnical reference on the medical aspects of mental retardation for health sciences and rehabilitation personnel, physicians lacking specialized training in the field, parents, and others who work with retarded persons.

296   Meyerowitz, Joseph H. "Sex and the Mentally Retarded." MEDICAL ASPECTS OF HUMAN SEXUALITY 5, no. 11 (1971): 94-118.

Selective review of the literature on sexuality among persons labeled as mentally retarded.

297   Meyers, C. Edward; Eyman, Richard K.; and Tarjan, George, eds. SOCIO-BEHAVIORAL STUDIES IN MENTAL RETARDATION: PAPERS IN HONOR OF HARVEY F. DINGMAN. Washington, D.C.: American Association on Mental Deficiency, 1973. 258 p.

Collection of essays from thirty-two leaders in the field of mental retardation. Addresses a wide range of subjects dealing with the sociological implications of various levels of mental retardation, from the viewpoint of the client and his or her environment.

298   Mittler, Peter, ed. RESEARCH TO PRACTICE IN MENTAL RETARDA- TION. Vol. 1: CARE AND INTERVENTION. Baltimore: University Park Press, 1977. 564 p.

Describes developments in service provision with emphasis on early intervention and multidisciplinary treatment, community and residential services, and the evaluation of such services in terms of actual needs of mentally handicapped persons.

299   _____. RESEARCH TO PRACTICE IN MENTAL RETARDATION. Vol. 2: EDUCATION AND TRAINING. Baltimore: University Park Press, 1977. 542 p.

Examines what and how to teach the mentally handicapped and how to determine individual abilities, needs, and out- comes.

300   _____. RESEARCH TO PRACTICE IN MENTAL RETARDATION. Vol.

3: BIOMEDICAL ASPECTS. Baltimore: University Park Press, 1977. 612 p.

Covers wide range of biomedical studies bearing directly upon prevention, detection, and early treatment. Examines many environmental factors related to intervention, especially those that lend themselves to treatment. Includes extensive section on malnutrition.

301 Nichtern, Sol. HELPING THE RETARDED CHILD. New York: Grosset and Dunlap, 1974. 289 p.

Describes mental retardation; attempts to explain how, why, and when it occurs; and indicates where to go for help. Excellent for laypersons and parents.

302 Polednak, A.P., and Auliffe, Jan. "Obesity in an Institutionalized Adult Mentally Retarded Population." JOURNAL OF MENTAL DEFICIENCY RESEARCH 20, no. 1 (1976): 9-15.

Presents the results of studies of 161 institutionalized mentally retarded adults. Eighteen references.

303 *Robinson, Nancy M., and Robinson, Halbert B. THE MENTALLY RETARDED CHILD: A PSYCHOLOGICAL APPROACH. 2d ed. New York: McGraw-Hill, 1976. 592 p.

An important text that covers, extensively and accurately, a broad range of topics relating to mentally retarded individuals and their families. Integrates the research of the last decade into a comprehensive historical and conceptual framework.

304 Sternlicht, Manny, and Deutsch, Martin R. PERSONALITY DEVELOPMENT AND SOCIAL BEHAVIOR IN MENTAL RETARDATION. Boston: D.C. Heath and Co., 1972. 180 p.

An account of a series of observations that attempts to explain the behavior of the mentally retarded individual within a meaningful framework. Uses an eclectic theoretical approach to review major studies and describe a system of how personality and social behavior of mentally retarded persons unfold. For students and experienced practitioners.

305 Stubbins, Joseph, ed. SOCIAL AND PSYCHOLOGICAL ASPECTS OF DISABILITY. Baltimore: University Park Press, 1977. 617 p.

Fifty-five articles for professionals.

306 Tarjan, George, and Keeran, Charles V. "An Overview of Mental Retardation." PSYCHIATRIC ANNALS 4, no. 2 (1974): 6-21.

Reviews the care, treatment, and management of mental retardation, from the viewpoint of the practicing psychiatrist. Discusses the role of the mental health center in managing mental retardation, and concludes that society has an obligation to concern itself with the retarded. Fifteen references.

307   Warren, Neil. "Malnutrition and Mental Development." PSYCHOLOGICAL BULLETIN 80, no. 4 (1973): 324-28.

Reviews retrospective studies of the relationship between malnutrition and mental deficiency, and examines the methodological problems involved. Forty-one references.

HISTORICAL PERSPECTIVES AND SOCIAL ATTITUDES

The historical question surrounding mental retardation in the United States is based almost as much on the history of social attitudes as on the actual history of work with the mentally retarded. Much of the functional history is similar to that of the mentally ill, and many of the references in chapter 2 also refer to the mentally retarded. Further, many of the general texts in the preceding portion of this chapter contain large historcial sections, so the history is fairly well covered by references already given. The following items refer to specialized studies of history and of the evolution of social attitudes as they relate to mental retardation.

308   Bogdan, Robert, and Taylor, Steven. "The Judged, Not the Judges: An Insider's View of Mental Retardation." AMERICAN PSYCHOLOGIST 31, no. 1 (1976): 47-52.

Includes edited transcripts of discussions with a twenty-six-year-old man who has been labeled as mentally retarded. Offers understanding of how diagnostic categories affect the life of the person categorized. Twenty-three references.

309   Caw, Jan, and Cleland, Charles C. "Eminence and Mental Retardation as Determined by Cattell's Space Method." MENTAL RETARDATION 13, no. 3 (1975): 20-21.

Reviews general texts and reference works published between 1908 and 1974 for specific references to mentally retarded persons. Describes well-known mentally retarded persons including Victor, the "Wild Boy of Aveyron," as written by Jean-Marc-Gaspard Itard. Thirty-one references.

310   Crissey, Marie S. "Mental Retardation: Past, Present and Future." AMERICAN PSYCHOLOGIST 30, no. 8 (1975): 800-808.

Discusses the history of the education of the retarded, the development and subsequent overuse of institutional programs,

and the current emphasis on deinstitutionalization in relation
to coincident social-political movements.

311   Gardner, James M. "Lightner Witmer: A Neglected Pioneer."
AMERICAN JOURNAL OF MENTAL DEFICIENCY 72, no. 5 (1968):
719-20.

312   Ghosh, A. "Mental Retardation: Historical Aspects." INDIAN
JOURNAL OF MENTAL RETARDATION 7, no. 2 (1974): 86-88.

Sketches the history of the treatment of mental retardation.

313   *Kugel, Robert S., and Wolfensberger, Wolf. CHANGING PATTERNS
IN RESIDENTIAL SERVICES FOR THE MENTALLY RETARDED. Presi-
dent's Committee on Mental Retardation Monograph. Washington,
D.C.: Government Printing Office, 1969. 435 p.

Major work on historical patterns in the development of institutions and residential services, with extensive reference
to the pioneers, work with the mentally retarded, and institutional data.

314   Kurtz, Richard A., and Wolfensberger, Wolf. "Separation Experience
of Residents in an Institution for the Mentally Retarded: 1910-1959."
AMERICAN JOURNAL OF MENTAL DEFICIENCY 74, no. 3 (1969):
389-96.

Provides data on institutional separation over the period studied. Thirty-seven references.

315   Lippman, Leopold. ATTITUDES TOWARD THE HANDICAPPED: A
COMPARISON BETWEEN EUROPE AND THE UNITED STATES. Springfield, Ill.: Charles C Thomas, 1972. 118 p.

316   Penrose, L.S. "Heredity, Environment and Mental Subnormality." In
ADVANCES IN THE CARE OF THE MENTALLY HANDICAPPED, edited
by Harold C. Gunzburg, chapter 1. Baltimore: Williams and Wilkins,
1973.

A classic paper in mental retardation, discussing classification
and typology of the mentally retarded dating back to the
early 1900s. Twelve references.

317   Radtke, Frederick A. "What, Then is Mercy? A Descriptive Study
of the Attitudes of Western Society Toward Mentally Retarded People
with Philosophical, Psychological and Theological Implications." DIS-
SERTATION ABSTRACTS INTERNATIONAL 36, no. 6: 3568 A. St.
Louis University, 1975. 154 p.

318   *Rosen, Marvin; Clarke, Gerald R.; and Kivitz, Marian S., eds.
       THE HISTORY OF MENTAL RETARDATION: COLLECTED PAPERS.
       Vol. 1. Baltimore: University Park Press, 1976. 400 p.

       Covers the nineteenth century; the earliest paper is from 1843.
       Papers arranged chronologically by topic, covering most of
       the pioneers of that period.

319   *_____. THE HISTORY OF MENTAL RETARDATION: COLLECTED
       PAPERS. Vol. 2. Baltimore: University Park Press, 1976. 453 p.

       Covers the early twentieth century to the present. Papers
       arranged chronologically by topic. Together with volume 1
       (see item 318), represents a thorough historical review of
       work with the mentally retarded in the United States, through
       the writings of the major persons concerned.

320   Wolfensberger, Wolf. THE ORIGIN AND NATURE OF OUR INSTI-
       TUTIONAL MODELS. Syracuse, N.Y.: Human Policy Press, 1975.
       88 p.

       Investigates the ideologies and sociological factors that led
       to the development of institutions in the United States.

EPIDEMIOLOGICAL STUDIES

321   Abramowicz, Helen D., and Richardson, Stephen A. "Epidemiology
       of Severe Mental Retardation in Children: Community Studies."
       AMERICAN JOURNAL OF MENTAL DEFICIENCY 18, no. 1 (1975):
       18-39.

       Twenty-seven epidemiological studies of severe mental retar-
       dation, showing a marked consistency in the prevalence of
       severe mental retardation in older children, a rate of about
       four per thousand (somewhat higher for males). Causes gen-
       erally not known. Forty-one references.

322   Barclay, Allan; Endres, Jan; Kelly, Tom; and Sharp, Austin R. "A
       Longitudinal Assessment of Clinical Services to the Mentally Retarded."
       MENTAL RETARDATION 14, no. 5 (1976): 10-11.

       Evaluates the impact of changes in a university child devel-
       opment clinic's services from 1966 to 1972, using data from
       1,295 cases and comparing these with data from a similar
       1960-66 study. Reveals no significant differences between
       the client populations over the twelve-year period.

323   Birch, Herbert G.; Richardson, Stephen A.; Baird, Dugald; Horobin,
       Gordon; and Illsley, Raymond. MENTAL SUBNORMALITY IN THE

COMMUNITY: A CLINICAL AND EPIDEMIOLOGIC STUDY. Baltimore: Williams and Wilkins, 1970. 200 p.

Reports a detailed examination of the prevalence and social class distribution of mental retardation in a community. Tends to relate incidence to particular antecedent health and social conditions.

324   *Conley, Ronald W. THE ECONOMICS OF MENTAL RETARDATION. Baltimore: Johns Hopkins University Press, 1973. 230 p.

Surveys the epidemiology of mental retardation, and evaluates programs designed to reintegrate the mentally retarded into society. A major work on problems relating to costs and benefits of rehabilitation and education programs.

325   *Mercer, Jane R. LABELING THE MENTALLY RETARDED. Berkeley and Los Angeles: University of California Press, 1973. 319 p.

A major epidemiological study of the mentally retarded, incorporating the adaptive behavior concept systematically into the design. Discusses in depth the processes and effects of the labeling system. Finds contrasting results, especially when ethnic group membership of the subjects is taken into consideration.

326   Stein, Zena A., and Susser, Mervyn. "The Epidemiology of Mental Retardation." In CHILD AND ADOLESCENT PSYCHIATRY, SOCIO-CULTURAL AND COMMUNITY PSYCHIATRY, 2d ed., edited by Gerald Caplan, chapter 31. American Handbook of Psychiatry, vol. 2. New York: Basic Books, 1974.

Discusses the following causes of mental retardation, from an epidemiological frame of reference: nutrition, chemical disorders, prenatal problems, and demographic problems. Also discusses the prevalence of mental retardation and the relationship between psychiatric disability and mental retardation. Includes 224 references.

ETIOLOGY

References in this and the following three sections deal with the etiology, prevention, treatment, and training of the mentally retarded under various classification systems and approaches. There is no attempt to identify specific etiological conditions, because these are extremely varied and are covered for the most part, in the classification texts already cited (see chapter 1, nos. 7, 19, 27, 35, and 437) or in the general texts on mental retardation. The items listed here, although general, will lead the reader to specific sources of descriptions of highly individualized types of disorders. Also, the reader is directed to the MANUAL ON TERMINOLOGY AND CLASSIFICA-

TION IN MENTAL RETARDATION, edited by Grossman for the American Association on Mental Deficiency (see item 35).

327 Allen, Robert M.; Cortazzo, Arnold D.; and Toister, Richard P., eds.
     THE ROLE OF GENETICS IN MENTAL RETARDATION. Coral Gables,
     Fla.: University of Miami Press, 1971. 115 p.

     Discusses clinical aspects of genetics in mental retardation,
     behavioral genetics and mental retardation, and genetic coun-
     seling. Relatively simple presentation.

328 Brown, Jason W., and Jaffe, Joseph. "Hypotheses on Cerebral Dom-
     inance." NEUROPSYCHOLOGIA 13, no. 1 (1975): 107-10.

     Discusses the hypothesis that cerebral dominance is a contin-
     uous process that evolves throughout life and accounts for the
     age-dependent forms of language difficulty and aphasia.
     Thirty-two references.

329 Clancy, Helen, and McBride, G. "The Isolation Syndrome in Child-
     hood." DEVELOPMENTAL MEDICINE AND CHILD NEUROLOGY 17,
     no. 2 (1975): 198-219.

     Proposes a new diagnostic category, "the isolation syndrome,"
     which consists of a defective social interaction and communi-
     cation between mother and baby and includes disorders of
     perceptual function and motor skills, excessive self-stimula-
     tion through stereotyped acts, and general developmental re-
     tardation, especially in language. Considered a distinct con-
     dition from infantile autism. Eighty-two references.

330 Cross, Lee, and Goin, Kennith, eds. IDENTIFYING HANDICAPPED
     CHILDREN. First Chance Series: Early Education for the Handicapped.
     New York: Walker Educational Book Corp., 1977. 127 p.

     Handbook for professionals and volunteers engaged in early
     identification of handicapped children from birth to eight
     years. Provides a listing of materials available for screening,
     diagnosis, and assessment.

331 Goldsmith, H. Hill, and Anderson, U.E. "Inherited Inadequate Uter-
     ine Environment Leading to Mental Retardation: Negative Evidence in
     Pedigree Data." BEHAVIOR GENETICS 6, no. 4 (1976): 467-71.

     Compares the frequency of mental retardation in the offspring
     of maternal aunts of retarded probands with the frequency of
     mental retardation in offspring of other aunts or uncles of the
     same probands. Does not support inherited uterine inadequacy
     as an explanatory factor in mental retardation. Reviews more
     than 6,100 cases.

332 *Holmes, Lewis B.; Moser, Hagow W.; Halldorsson, Saevar; Mack, Cornelia; Pant, Shyam S.; and Matzilevich, Benjamin T. MENTAL RETARDATION: AN ATLAS OF DISEASES WITH ASSOCIATED PHYSICAL ABNORMALITIES. New York: Macmillan, 1972. 430 p. Illus.

Attempts to survey current knowledge of disorders causing mental retardation. Presents both clinical and pathological information. Valuable for clinicians and medical personnel working in the area of mental retardation.

333 Jervis, George A. "Biomedical Types of Mental Deficiency." In ORGANIC DISORDERS AND PSYCHOSOMATIC MEDICINE, edited by Morton F. Reiser, chapter 20. American Handbook of Psychiatry, 2d ed., vol. 4. New York: Basic Books, 1974. Illus.

Discusses chromosomal abnormalities, mental deficiency caused by environmental factors, and clinical syndromes of mental retardation.

334 Lewontin, R.G. "Genetic Aspects of Intelligence." ANNUAL REVIEW OF GENETICS 9 (1975): 387-405.

Reports that problems of estimating the heritable components of variation for any human metrical character, and especially of undertaking the correlation between genetic and environmental similarity, are great and have not been understood by most behavioral geneticists. Considers that, from a scientific or social standpoint, the problem of assaying the genetic components of IQ test differences may hardly seem worth the immense effort needed to carry out decent studies. Fifty-three references.

335 Losehen, E.L. "Failure in Diagnosis and Treatment in Mental Retardation." MENTAL RETARDATION 13, no. 3 (1975): 29-31.

Reports that diagnostic errors and inadequate planning of intervention approaches are two reasons why the mentally retarded may not be responding to treatment programs. Indicates that diagnostic pitfalls include overlooking subtle physical disabilities and inadequate assessment of the client's emotional attitudes and problems.

336 Menolascino, Frank J. PSYCHIATRIC ASPECTS OF THE DIAGNOSIS AND TREATMENT OF MENTAL RETARDATION. Seattle, Wash.: Special Child Publications, 1971. 386 p.

Introductory text for psychiatrists and psychologists working in the field of mental retardation.

337 Meyers, C. Edward, and Lombardi, Thomas P. "Definition of the Mentally Retarded: Decision Time for AAMD." MENTAL RETARDATION 12, no. 2 (1974): 43.

Discusses implications of recent court decisions and legislative enactments that provided stricter definitions of the "educable mentally retarded."

338 Moore, Byron C.; Haynes, Jane D.; and Laing, Clarence R. INTRO-DUCTION TO MENTAL RETARDATION SYNDROMES AND TERMIN-OLOGY. Springfield, Ill.: Charles C Thomas, 1978. 167 p.

Provides a practical guide to mental retardation, its terminology, types of problems involved, and selected references for students, teachers, and parents.

339 Murray, Robert F., and Rosser, Earl L., eds. THE GENETIC, MET-ABOLIC, AND DEVELOPMENTAL ASPECTS OF MENTAL RETARDA-TION. Springfield, Ill.: Charles C Thomas, 1972. 343 p.

An elementary text for laypersons and students, with twenty-six contributors producing a broad framework for principles and issues in mental retardation. Provides an appreciation of the developing area of biomedical research in mental retardation.

340 Reschly, Daniel J., and Jipson, Frederick J. "Ethnicity, Geographic Locale, Age, Sex, and Urban-Rural Residence as Variables in the Prevalence of Mild Retardation." AMERICAN JOURNAL OF MENTAL DEFICIENCY 81, no. 2 (1976): 154-61.

Studies a stratified random sample of 1,040 children in grade levels 1, 3, 5, 7, and 9, and concludes that manipulation of cutoff points will partially modify disproportionate representation of minority group children in classes for the mildly retarded. Leaves the question of optimum education for these children unanswered. Twenty-seven references.

341 Schmitt, Ray, and Erickson, Marilyn T. "Early Predictors of Mental Retardation." MENTAL RETARDATION 11, no. 2 (1973): 27-29.

Examined 454 parent reports of onset of smiling and sitting alone for five-month to six-year-old children who were referred for diagnosis of developmental problems. Indicates that the two milestones predicted the same percentage of subjects subsequently diagnosed as severely retarded. Onset of smiling considered to be more useful for early prediction.

342 Smith, David W., and Simons, Estelle. "Rational Diagnostic Evalua-tion of a Child with Mental Deficiency." AMERICAN JOURNAL OF DISEASES OF CHILDREN 129, no. 11 (1975): 1285-90.

Attempts to sort the several hundred recognized disorders in which mental deficiency is a feature. Establishes four cate-gories: prenatal problems of morphogenesis, perinatal insult to

the brain, postnatal onset of brain dysfunction, and unde-
cided age at onset. Finds this type of investigation to be
more effective than "nonrational" laboratory tests. Outlines
what should be sought in the case history, particularly as it
relates to genetic counseling. Contains thirteen references.

343 Valente, Mario, and Tarjan, George. "Etiologic Factors in Mental
Retardation." PSYCHIATRIC ANNALS 4, no. 2 (1974): 23-37.

Proposes that the total evaluation of a mentally retarded child
should consider four dimensions: the intellectual, the psychiatric, the organic, and the psychosocial. Indicates that
about 20-25 percent of all mentally retarded individuals show a
definite biological etiological factor. Twenty references.

PREVENTION

344 Carter, C.O. "Prenatal Diagnosis-Prospects, Administration and Ethics." PEDIATRIC RESEARCH 7, no. 1 (1973): 56.

Discusses prenatal detection of chromosomal abnormalities, as
well as its limitations and ethical considerations.

345 Das, Jagannath P. "Cultural Deprivation and Cognitive Competence."
In INTERNATIONAL REVIEW OF RESEARCH IN MENTAL RETARDA-
TION, edited by Norman R. Ellis, pp. 1-53. New York: Academic
Press, 1973.

Reviews issues of cultural disadvantage in children, and provides a selective overview of certain areas of research with
relevant illustrations. Recommends early intervention to re-
verse the trend of intellectual retardation found in disadvantaged children at a later stage. Ninety-two references.

346 Fisher, Glenice. "Prophylactic Physiotherapy with Young Retarded
Children." AUSTRALIAN JOURNAL OF MENTAL RETARDATION 2,
no. 4 (1972): 122-26.

347 Frios, Jaime L. "Prenatal Diagnosis of Genetic Abnormalities."
CLINICAL OBSTETRICS AND GYNECOLOGY 18, no. 4 (1975):
221-36.

Reports that amniocentesis is currently the most widely used
technique for prenatal detection of fetal abnormalities. Discusses this and other methods that have been used for prenatal
detection of fetal genetic disease. Seventy references.

348 Jones, Mary B. "Antepartum Assessment in High Risk Pregnancy."

JOURNAL OF OBSTETRICS, GYNECOLOGIC AND NEONATAL NURSING 4, no. 6 (1975): 23-27.

Describes the many new techniques available within communities and resource centers for the assessment of the high-risk pregnant patient and fetus, including amniocentesis, oxytocin challenge test, Rh isoimmunization, and other specialized procedures. Reports that chromosomal abnormalities, inborn errors of metabolism involving abnormal or missing enzymes, and X-linked or sex-linked defects are the major developmental disorders that can be identified by using these techniques. Twelve references.

349 *Milumsky, Aubrey. THE PREVENTION OF GENETIC DISEASE AND MENTAL RETARDATION. Philadelphia: W.B. Saunders, 1975. 506 p.

Presents a thorough discussion of genetic and environmental contributions to mental retardation, and provides a general overview of the principles that form the basis of programs for the prevention of genetic disease. Describes a wide range of problems and approaches to their management. Includes 1,728 references.

350 Rhodes, Philip. "Obstetric Prevention of Mental Retardation." BRITISH MEDICAL JOURNAL 1, no. 5850 (1973): 399-402.

Presents a major discussion of the obstetrician's role in the prevention of mental retardation. Covers a wide range of techniques that will help to recognize and assess the presence of congenital abnormalities.

351 Rosenheim, Harold D., and Ables, Billie S. "Social Deprivation and Mental Retardation." CHILD PSYCHIATRY AND HUMAN DEVELOPMENT 4, no. 4 (1974): 216-26.

Reports a study of the effects of social deprivation that may help to understand etiological factors in mental retardation. Twenty-one references.

352 Turnbull, A.C., and Woodford, F.P., eds. PREVENTION OF HANDICAP THROUGH ANTENATAL CARE. New York: American Elsevier, 1976. 175 p.

Contains papers concerning prenatal factors known to place the fetus at risk for some physical and/or mental handicap.

TREATMENT

353 Aanes, David, and Moen, Marilyn. "Adaptive Behavior Changes of

Group Home Residents." MENTAL RETARDATION 14, no. 4 (1976): 36-40.

354   Acosta, Phyllis B., and Elsas, Louis J. DIETARY MANAGEMENT OF INHERITED METABOLIC DISEASE: PHENYLKETONURIA, GALACTO-SEMIA, TYROFINEMIA, HOMOCYSTINURIA, AND MAPLE SYRUP URINE DISEASE. Atlanta: ACELMU Publishers, 1976. 83 p.

355   Allen, Mark K. "Persistent Factors Leading to Application for Admission to a Residential Institution." MENTAL RETARDATION 10, no. 4 (1972): 25-28.

Analyzes the basic reasons or circumstances leading to application for admission to a state training school. Twenty-nine references.

356   Baran, Stanley J. "T.V. and Social Learning in the Institutionalized Mentally Retarded." MENTAL RETARDATION 11, no. 3 (1973): 36-38.

Discusses the importance of television as a medium of social learning. Presents pertinent research on observational learning, and suggests that mentally retarded children are highly likely to observationally learn social behavior from television. Forty references.

357   Bell, Nancy. "I.Q. as a Factor in Community Life Style of Previously Institutionalized Retardates." MENTAL RETARDATION 14, no. 3 (1976): 29-33.

Reports that differences in IQ appear to be related to differences in life-style, but factors other than IQ, particularly environmental support factors, may operate to cause these differences. Does not necessarily indicate that IQ scores should be used for screening.

358   Birenbaum, Arnold, and Seiffer, Samuel. RESETTLING RETARDED ADULTS IN A MANAGED COMMUNITY. New York: Praeger Publishers, 1976. 143 p.

Examines the extent to which the lives of forty-eight ex-institutionalized retarded adults had changed at three periods during their placement in community residences. Outlines assets and liabilities of the deinstitutionalization process, as demonstrated by the data.

359   Brown, Diana L. "A City's Recreation Center for the Retarded and Disabled." HOSPITAL AND COMMUNITY PSYCHIATRY 27, no. 11 (1976): 800-801.

Describes the design and operation of the first municipal recreation center designed especially for the mentally retarded and physically handicapped, located in Washington, D.C.

360 _____. "Obstacles to Services for the Mentally Retarded." SOCIAL WORK 17, no. 4 (1972): 98-100.

Discusses client and profession-related problems in the provision of services for retarded persons with brain damage or other dysfunctions. Parental problems include lack of understanding of diagnosis, insufficient information on treatment, long waiting lists, rejection of integrated services, lack of transportation, costs, language problems, substandard facilities, and lack of recreational facilities.

361 *Friedlander, Bernard Z.; Sterritt, Graham M.; and Kird, Girvin E., eds. EXCEPTIONAL INFANT: ASSESSMENT AND INTERVENTION. Vol. 3. New York: Brunner/Mazel, 1975. 668 p.

Contains research reports and articles dealing with the development of exceptional children, emphasizing assessment and treatment of developmental problems.

362 *Katz, Elias, ed. MENTAL HEALTH SERVICES FOR THE MENTALLY RETARDED. Springfield, Ill.: Charles C Thomas, 1972. 278 p.

Integrates concepts of mental illness and mental retardation, and presents them for use by practitioners. Emphasizes prevention of emotional disorders by stressing the early identification and removal of environmental elements that may generate such conditions. Discusses etiology, diagnosis, epidemiology, and treatment of mentally retarded persons.

363 Lassiter, Robert A. "Group Counseling with People Who Are Mentally Retarded." In GROUP COUNSELING AND THERAPY TECHNIQUES IN SPECIAL SETTINGS, edited by Richard E. Hardy and John G. Cull, chapter 3. Springfield, Ill.: Charles C Thomas, 1974.

Discusses issues surrounding the use of group counseling as a means of treating the mentally handicapped client. Establishes general guidelines for a systematic pattern of counseling individuals with various mentally handicapping conditions.

364 Mahoney, Michael J., and Mahoney, Katheryn. "Self-Control Techniques with the Mentally Retarded." EXCEPTIONAL CHILDREN 42, no. 6 (1976): 338-39.

Points out the advantages to the patient and staff of using the retarded individual as his or her own change agent. Outlines three components of successful self-control: self-monitoring, antecedent cue alteration, and consequence changes.

366 Muhlfelder, Warren J. "Mental Retardation and the Anatomy of Existential Therapy." PENNSYLVANIA PSYCHIATRIC QUARTERLY 9, no. 2 (1969): 25-32.

Presents the goals and methods of existential therapy as being patient centered and emphasizing the involvement of the patient. Suggests that the problem in communication with the mentally retarded is the inability of the therapist to understand rather than the inability of the retarded to communicate.

367 Roos, Philip, and Oliver, Margaret. "Evaluation for Operant Conditioning with Institutionalized Retarded Children." AMERICAN JOURNAL OF MENTAL DEFICIENCY 74, no. 3 (1969): 325-30.

Evaluates the effectiveness of operant conditioning procedures implemented by attendants of severely and profoundly retarded institutionalized young children. Nineteen references.

368 Simmons, Jane Q.; Tymchuk, Alexander J.; and Valente, Mario. "Treatment and Care of the Mentally Retarded." PSYCHIATRIC ANNALS 4, no. 2 (1974): 38-69.

Discusses three factors that may have prevented psychiatry from exerting an influence on mental retardation: an educational focus following an introduction of intelligence testing, the eugenic alarm of the nineteenth and early twentieth centuries, and the intense preoccupation of psychiatry with the intrapsychic dynamics of neuroses. Authors generally believe there is a place for psychiatry in the treatment of the mentally retarded. Forty-five references.

369 Thurman, K. Kenneth, and Gable, Robert A. "Mental Retardation Services: Social Traps and Social Senses." MENTAL RETARDATION 14, no. 5 (1976): 16-18.

Examines changes in institutional programs during the visitation of an accreditation survey team on two wards for severely retarded adults. Suggests that the percentage of programs conducted during the two-day accreditation survey was not representative of the implementation of services monitored over a nine-week period. Recommends the unannounced survey.

370 Tizard, Jack; Sinclair, Ivan; and Clarke, R.V.G., eds. VARIETIES OF RESIDENTIAL EXPERIENCE. London: Routledge and Kegan Paul, 1975. 290 p.

Presents information relating to the assessment of quality of care provided for children in residential establishments. Attempts to generate some consensus about these principles, which are significantly associated with the behavior of children after they leave the institution.

371 Townsend, W., and Flanagan, John L. "Experimental Preadmission Program to Encourage Home Care for Severely and Profoundly Retarded Children." AMERICAN JOURNAL ON MENTAL DEFICIENCY 80, no. 5 (1976): 562-69.

Reports that an experimental treatment program to reduce institutionalization of 156 severely and profoundly retarded children under the age of six found that family counseling and the development of a consensus within the family should have been sought before the children were returned home. Indicates that instructing the mother on child training procedures tended to reduce the number of instances of objectionable child behavior as well as to induce a decision to keep the child at home. Twenty-four references.

372 Uslan, Mark M. "Teaching Basic Ward Layout to the Severely Retarded Blind: An Auditory Approach." NEW OUTLOOKS OF THE BLIND 70, no. 9 (1976): 401-2.

Reports that severely retarded blind residents were taught mobility to and from the day room and dining room through the use of strategically placed auditory cues that had been associated with the presentation of food. Approach judged to be a viable technique worthy of investigation.

373 Wolf, Lucille C., and Whitehead, Paul C. "The Decision to Institutionalize Retarded Children: Comparison of Individually Matched Groups." MENTAL RETARDATION 13, no. 5 (1975): 3-7.

Study indicating that the sex of the child and the amount of disruption perceived by the family as caused by the child are significant factors in determining the course to institutionalization. Marital integration most affected by male children, who were more likely to be institutionalized than females. Twenty references.

TRAINING

374 Bateman, Barbara. "A Pilot Study of Mentally Retarded Children Attending Summer Day Camps." MENTAL RETARDATION 6, no. 1 (1968): 39-44.

Explores measurable changes in the cognitive, language, and sensory-motor functioning of mentally retarded children attending a summer camp program. Suggests that there are measurable benefits associated with camp attendance.

375 Berry, Paul, ed. LANGUAGE AND COMMUNICATION IN THE MENTALLY HANDICAPPED. Baltimore: University Park Press, 1976. 224 p.

Relates language research to practice, specifically as it affects teaching the mentally handicapped to speak and understand language. Text for teachers and other professionals working with the retarded.

376 DeMars, Patricia K. "Training Adult Retardates for Private Enterprise." AMERICAN JOURNAL OF OCCUPATIONAL THERAPY 29, no. 1 (1975): 39-42.

377 Diller, Leonard. "A Model for Cognitive Retraining and Rehabilitation." CLINICAL PSYCHOLOGIST 29, no. 2 (1976): 13-15.

Describes a model for the remediation of perceptual or cognitive problems in brain-damaged persons.

378 Doll, Edgar A. "Programs for the Adult Retardate." MENTAL RETARDATION 6, no. 1 (1968): 19-21.

379 Garner, Ralph E.; Lacy, Gene H.; and Creasy, Robert F. "Workshops: Why, What, Whether?" MENTAL RETARDATION 10, no. 3 (1972): 25-27.

Discusses the origins, development, and problem areas of workshops for the disabled and retarded.

380 Hawkins, Donald E. THE NATURAL ENVIRONMENT AND HUMAN DEVELOPMENT: IMPLICATIONS FOR HANDICAPPED CHILDREN IN URBAN SETTINGS. Washington, D.C.: U.S. Department of Agriculture, Forestry Service, 1975. 56 p.

Describes the use of the natural environment as a therapeutic modality to facilitate the development of handicapped children. Includes 180 references.

381 Hegarty, John R. "Teaching Machines for the Severely Retarded: A Review." BRITISH JOURNAL OF MENTAL SUBNORMALITY 21, no. 41 (1975): 103-14.

Presents a broad overview of the use of teaching machines with the severely mentally retarded, and discusses results and conclusions about the potential of three operant devices. Sixty-four references.

382 Karan, Irv C. "Contemporary Views on Vocational Evaluation Practices with the Mentally Retarded." VOCATIONAL EVALUATION AND WORK ADJUSTMENT BULLETIN 9, no. 1 (1976): 7-13.

Discusses the provisions and implications of the Rehabilitation Act of 1973, which gave priority to the severely handicapped,

including the mentally retarded. Emphasizes that services
may be extended to raise the general level of independence,
rather than solely for employment entry.

383 Levy, Ellen. "Designing Environments for Mentally Retarded Clients."
HOSPITAL AND COMMUNITY PSYCHIATRY 27, no. 11 (1976):
793-96.

Suggests that an environment that stimulates the auditory,
visual, and tactile senses increases appropriate behavior among
mentally retarded clients and thereby reinforces other learning actions.

384 Lloyd, Lyle L., ed. COMMUNICATION ASSESSMENT AND INTER-
VENTION STRATEGIES. Baltimore: University Park Press, 1976.
928 p.

Describes assessment and intervention strategies for the com-
municatively handicapped (hearing impaired, mentally retarded, and developmentally disabled). Reliable, up-to-date
information for clinicians, teachers, and professionals.

385 Luckey, Robert E., and Shapiro, Ira G. "Recreation: An Essential
Aspect of Habilitation Programming." MENTAL RETARDATION 12,
no. 5 (1974): 33-35.

Discusses the importance of recreation to the total system of
habilitative services for the mentally retarded. Describes
previous and current trends.

386 McEwen, J.C. "Working Conditions with Different Types of Disability." In MAN UNDER STRESS, edited by A.T. Welford, pp. 103-11.
New York: John Wiley and Sons, 1974.

Reports that the retarded tended to be found in jobs where
noise levels and demands for speed, exactness, and teamwork
were relatively high, whereas psychiatric cases were found in
jobs where all three demands were lower. Offers a model
relating performance to arousal level and the ability to with-
stand stress, in order to account for the results.

387 Morehead, Donald M., and Morehead, Ann E., eds. NORMAL AND
DEFICIENT CHILD LANGUAGE. Baltimore: University Park Press,
1976. 488 p.

A textbook on the relationship between normal and deficient
language research in child language acquisition, cognition,
and development. Presents original material by leading researchers dealing with language-deficient children.

388 O'Donnell, Patrick A., and Bradfield, Robert H., eds. MAINSTREAM-
ING: CONTROVERSY AND CONSENSUS. San Rafael, Calif.:
Academic Therapy Publications, 1976. 152 p.

Discusses the concept and practice of educational mainstream-
ing in terms of its legal, moral, and ethical evolution and
its implications for teacher training.

389 Schiefelbusch, Richard L., ed. LANGUAGE INTERVENTION STRAT-
EGIES. Baltimore: University Park Press, 1978. 350 p.

A text on language intervention, planned and written for language clinicians, teachers, specialists, supervisors, applied
researchers, and advanced students. Synthesizes and interprets
important developments in the strategies of language intervention, and serves as a resource for language practitioners.

390 Spivak, Jerry. "Normalization and Recreation for the Disabled."
JOURNAL OF LEISURABILITY 2, no. 2 (1975): 31-35.

391 Stevens, Mildred. THE EDUCATIONAL AND SOCIAL NEEDS OF
CHILDREN WITH SEVERE HANDICAP. 2d ed. Baltimore: Williams
and Wilkins, 1976. 302 p.

Describes a practical approach to training mentally handicapped children, based on the combination of creative teaching
with an evaluated program for each child. Includes 120 references.

392 Talkington, Larry W. "An Exploratory Program for Blind-Retarded."
EDUCATION OF THE VISUALLY HANDICAPPED 4, no. 2 (1972):
33-35.

Discusses the neglect of the retarded blind, including the
lack of information, techniques, facilities, and resources for
helping this handicapped group.

PARENTS AND FAMILIES OF THE MENTALLY RETARDED

393 Blodgett, Harriet. MENTALLY RETARDED CHILDREN: WHAT PARENTS
AND OTHERS SHOULD KNOW. Minneapolis: University of Minnesota Press, 1971. 165 p.

Discusses many common problems and questions that arise out
of efforts to rear mentally retarded children at home. An-
swers questions about intelligence, sexual behaviors, living
with neighbors, and other issues, and provides guidance for
parents. Recommended for parents dealing with the mentally
retarded and for family physicians or other professionals dealing with the families of the retarded.

394   Hannam, Charles. PARENTS AND MENTALLY HANDICAPPED CHIL-DREN. Hammondsworth, Engl.: Penguin, 1975. 128 p.

        Presents a discussion of interpersonal relationships of the hand-icapped child with members of the family and with others in the child's environment. Based on interviews conducted with families in which there are mentally handicapped children.

395   Heisler, Verda. A HANDICAPPED CHILD IN THE FAMILY. New York: Grune and Stratton, 1972. 160 p.

        Reports twenty years' experience dealing with handicapped children and their families, including material from parents participating in group therapy and the author's own exper-iences as a handicapped person. Stresses that the relation-ship between parent and child can be more important to the child's growth and development than specific activities or programs.

396   Hunter, Marvin; Schueman, H.; and Friedlander, George. THE RE-TARDED CHILD FROM BIRTH TO FIVE. New York: John Day Co., 1972. 250 p.

        Discusses modern trends and techniques in mental retardation, focusing on involving the family in stimulating the child's major needs and learning via participation in a multidisci-plinary program.

397   Johnson, Carol A.; Ahern, Frank M.; and Johnson, Donald C. "Level of Functioning of Siblings and Parents of Probands of Varying Degrees of Retardation." BEHAVIOR GENETICS 6, no. 4 (1976): 473-77.

        Supports the proposition that retarded of low ability levels have retarded siblings less frequently than do retarded of higher ability levels.

398   *Koch, Richard, and Dobson, James C., eds. THE MENTALLY RE-TARDED CHILD AND HIS FAMILY: MULTIDISCIPLINARY HAND-BOOK. 2d ed. New York: Brunner/Mazel, 1976. 546 p.

        Text for university students in a variety of disciplines empha-sizing multidisciplinary approaches. Presents twenty-six pro-fessionals representing seventeen disciplines discussing the causal patterns of mental retardation, its treatment, and the attendant problems of the client and family. Stresses a com-prehensive system of working with mentally retarded children and their families, including coordination and family-oriented programming on a multidisciplinary basis.

399   Morgan, Sam B. "Team Interpretation of Mental Retardation to Par-ents." MENTAL RETARDATION 11, no. 3 (1973): 10-13.

Offers suggestions for more effective interpretation of mental retardation for parents. Emphasizes team evaluations in an interdisciplinary setting, and discusses management of the information session, explanation of evaluative findings, and dealing with parental reactions.

400   *Noland, Robert L., ed. COUNSELING PARENTS OF THE MENTALLY RETARDED: A SOURCEBOOK. Springfield, Ill.: Charles C Thomas, 1970. 404 p.

Presents thirty-one articles by experts in the field of counseling parents of mentally retarded children. Includes appendixes listing major associations for parents of retarded children, clinical programs, facilities, and audiovisual materials dealing with mental retardation.

401   Twormina, J.B.; Henggeler, Scott W.; and Gayton, William F. "Age Trends in Parental Assessment of the Behavior Problems of Their Retarded Children." MENTAL RETARDATION 14, no. 1 (1976): 38-39.

Based on interviews with fifty-two mothers of retarded children. Indicates a tendency for most issues and problems to decrease with age, with the exception of social interaction, which seems to get more difficult as the child grows older. Indicates that problems related to toilet training exist across all age groups; other problems change as the retarded children grow older.

402   Tyler, Nancy B., and Kagan, Kate L. "Reduction of Stress Between Mothers and Their Handicapped Children." AMERICAN JOURNAL OF OCCUPATIONAL THERAPY 31, no. 3 (1977): 151-55.

Reports a series of behavioral instruction sessions with eighteen preschool handicapped children and their mothers, analyzing behaviors of mother and child before, immediately following, and nine months after the sessions. Indicates it is possible to reduce stressful and negative interactions and to maintain the mother's behavior of warmth and acceptance through these patterns.

403   Webster, Elizabeth J., ed. PROFESSIONAL APPROACHES WITH PARENTS OF HANDICAPPED CHILDREN. Springfield, Ill.: Charles C Thomas, 1976. 286 p.

Presents eleven professionals who deal with parents of the handicapped sharing their views and experiences on basic issues and effective approaches to parental counseling, education, and management.

LEGAL AND ETHICAL ISSUES AND THE RIGHTS OF THE MENTALLY RETARDED

404   Bass, Medora S., ed. SEXUAL RIGHTS AND RESPONSIBILITIES OF THE MENTALLY RETARDED. Santa Barbara, Calif.: Channel Lithograph, 1973. 154 p.

Selected papers dealing with the sexuality of mentally retarded individuals as well as the multifaceted aspects of their sexual rights in terms of themselves, their parents, and society.

405   Cohen, Julius S., ed. CONFRONTATION AND CHANGE: COMMUNITY PROBLEMS OF MENTAL RETARDATION AND DEVELOPMENTAL DISABILITIES. Ann Arbor: University of Michigan Publications Distribution Service, 1971. 172 p.

Papers on four major issues: labeling, child advocacy, an ecological view of mental retardation, and related disabilities and issues. Reviews some of the landmark legal cases in this area.

406   *"Declaration of General and Special Rights of the Mentally Retarded." MENTAL RETARDATION 7, no. 4 (1969): inside cover page.

Bill of seven rights established by the International League of Societies for the Mentally Handicapped in Stockholm, Sweden, on 24 October 1968 and subsequently passed by the United Nations. Article 1 states that "the mentally retarded person has the same basic rights as other citizens of the same country and the same age." Articles 2, 3, 4, 5, 6, and 7 expand this concept and lead to the general conclusion that "ABOVE ALL--THE MENTALLY RETARDED PERSON HAS THE RIGHT TO RESPECT."

407   Gardner, James M. "The Legal Rights of People in Institutions." AUSTRALIAN JOURNAL OF MENTAL RETARDATION 3, no. 2 (1974): 34-39.

Discusses the struggle to provide legal rights for people in institutions for the mentally retarded, with particular reference to recent activities in the courts of the United States. Fifteen references.

408   *Kindred, Michael; Cohen, Julius S.; Penrod, David; and Shaffer, Thomas J., eds. THE MENTALLY RETARDED PERSON AND THE LAW. New York: Free Press, 1976. 738 p.

A major reference work surveying the range of issues and problems connected with the legal rights of mentally retarded citizens. Covers concerns from narrow questions of guardianship and insurance to broad issues such as the rights to habilitation and education. For legal and citizen advocates, professionals, and parents.

409 Krishef, Curtis H. "State Laws on Marriage and Sterilization of the Mentally Retarded." MENTAL RETARDATION 10, no. 3 (1972): 36-38.

410 Mental Health Law Project. BASIC RIGHTS OF THE MENTALLY HANDICAPPED: RIGHT TO TREATMENT, RIGHT TO COMPENSATION FOR INSTITUTION-MAINTAINING LABOR, RIGHT TO EDUCATION. Washington, D.C.: 1973. 123 p.

Explains the theory behind the basic rights movement and how the cases supporting these rights were developed and presented in court.

411 Murdock, Charles W. "Civil Rights of the Mentally Retarded--Some Critical Issues." FAMILY LAW QUARTERLY 7, no. 1 (1973): 1-74.

Covers the questions of guardianship, institutionalization, and the right to education. Includes 129 references.

412 *Wolfensberger, Wolf; Nirje, Benjt; Olshansky, Simon; Perske, Robert; and Roos, Philip. THE PRINCIPLE OF NORMALIZATION AND HUMAN SERVICES. Toronto, Ontario, Canada: National Institute on Mental Retardation, 1972. 258 p.

Establishes the basic concept of normalization.

413 Wolfensberger, Wolf, and Zauha, Helen, eds. CITIZEN ADVOCACY AND PROTECTIVE SERVICES FOR THE IMPAIRED AND THE HANDICAPPED. Toronto, Ontario, Canada: National Institute on Mental Retardation, 1973. 277 p.

Presents thirty contributors describing a model citizen advocacy program based on the general concepts of normalization and deinstitutionalization.

EMOTIONALLY DISTURBED AND MENTALLY RETARDED (EDMR)

With the increasing importance given to the development of community mental health services, a new area has emerged, an overlapping area of individuals who are judged to be both emotionally disturbed (or mentally ill) and mentally retarded. Historically, a great deal of time has been spent on aspects of differential diagnosis, and these questions are still considered important, but it is now generally recognized that, at least in terms of the delivery of services and the fuller understanding of the conditions, a category of emotionally disturbed and mentally retarded (EDMR) persons must be served without trying to divide them into separate groups. Thus, the notion of treating the whole person regardless of label becomes paramount. The following items approach this issue from a variety of viewpoints.

414   Balthazar, Earl E., and Stevens, Harvey A. THE EMOTIONALLY DISTURBED/MENTALLY RETARDED: A HISTORICAL AND CONTEMPORARY PERSPECTIVE. Englewood Cliffs, N.J.: Prentice-Hall, 1975. 288 p.

> Presents a general description and critique of the literature related to emotional adjustments in the mentally retarded population. Offers an in-depth historical background and overview, and discusses differential diagnosis and treatment approaches as well as aspects of psychotherapy and related remediation procedures.

415   Berman, Merrill I. "Mental Retardation and Depression." MENTAL RETARDATION 5, no. 6 (1967): 19-21.

416   Chess, Stella, and Hassibi, Mahin. "Behavior Deviation in Mentally Retarded Children." JOURNAL OF THE AMERICAN ACADEMY OF CHILD PSYCHIATRY 9, no. 2 (1970): 282-97.

> Describes treatment and management of children with mental retardation and behavior disorders. Discusses various aspects of problems relating to appropriate diagnosis and to understanding of the relationship between mental retardation and maladaptive behavior. Eleven references.

417   DeMyer, Marian K.; Barton, Sandra; and Norton, James A. "A Comparison of Adaptive, Verbal and Motor Profiles of Psychotic and Non-Psychotic Subnormal Children." JOURNAL OF AUTISM AND CHILDHOOD SCHIZOPHRENIA 2, no. 4 (1972): 359-77.

> Offers an experimental analysis to evaluate intellectual, verbal, motor, perceptual-motor, and perceptual task performance levels of preschool psychotic children compared with mentally subnormal children. Reports that primary autistic subjects were better at stair climbing than were schizophrenic subjects whose motor performance profiles proved similar to those of lower functioning autistic children. Discusses the etiological implications of the results. Thirty references.

418   Menolascino, Frank J. "Emotional Disturbances in Mentally Retarded Children." AMERICAN JOURNAL OF PSYCHIATRY 126, no. 2 (1969): 168-76.

> Describes experiences of a multidisciplinary team with 256 emotionally disturbed mentally retarded children. Presents diagnostic findings for several types of emotional disturbance,

along with treatment-management considerations. Seventeen references.

419 _____. "Primitive, Atypical and Abnormal Psychotic Behavior in Institutionalized Mentally Retarded Children." JOURNAL OF AUTISM AND CHILDHOOD SCHIZOPHRENIA 3, no. 1 (1972): 49-64.

Discusses administrative implications and guidelines for implementing specific diagnostic and treatment approaches with emotionally disturbed young patients. Fifteen references.

420 _____. "Symposium on the Treatment of Behavioral Problems II. Three Frequent Types of Behavioral Disturbances in Institutionalized Retarded." BRITISH JOURNAL OF MENTAL SUBNORMALITY 28, no. 35, part 2 (1972): 71-80.

Describes the types of primitive, atypical, and abnormal behaviors that may be shown by mentally disturbed retarded patients. Presents treatment and management guidelines for the emotionally disturbed and mentally retarded.

421 _____, ed. PSYCHIATRIC ASPECTS OF THE DIAGNOSIS AND TREATMENT OF MENTAL RETARDATION. Seattle: Special Child Publications, 1971. 386 p.

Sourcebook of papers dating from 1959 to 1967, including many classics in the field. Covers broad areas of the relationship between mental retardation and child psychopathology, and emphasizes the basis for psychiatric participation.

422 Menolascino, Frank J., and Eaton, Louise. "Psychoses of Childhood: A Five Year Follow-Up of Experiences in a Mental Retardation Clinic." AMERICAN JOURNAL OF MENTAL DEFICIENCY 72, no. 3 (1967): 370-80.

Reports a study following thirty-two psychotic mentally retarded children, charting the general pattern of growth and development in a clinic. Summarizes other follow-up studies from the literature. Twenty-two references.

423 Metzger, Helen L. "Early Recognition of Emotional Difficulties." NEW YORK STATE JOURNAL OF MEDICINE 68, no. 5 (1968): 638-42.

Emphasizes that there is a tendency for disturbed children (who may be recognized as young as three years of age) to reach the age of nine years before they are admitted to a service. Stresses the importance of mother-child relationships at an early age. Sixteen references.

424   Mordock, John B. THE OTHER CHILDREN: AN INTRODUCTION TO EXCEPTIONALITY. New York: Harper and Row, 1975. 734 p.

Uses a multidisciplinary approach in examining selected types of exceptionality, including schizophrenia, early infantile autism, and mild retardation. Six pages of references.

425   Payne, Rudolph. "The Psychotic Subnormal." JOURNAL OF MENTAL SUBNORMALITY 14, no. 1 (1968): 25-34.

Reports a study of 216 male mentally defective inpatients, of whom 22 adults were found to be psychotic. Finds specific correlations with the degree of subnormality or the age of onset. Notes that ignoring psychosis in subnormal individuals may be dangerous to the individual and to society. Twenty references.

426   Phillips, Irving, and Williams, Nancy. "Psychopathology and Mental Retardation: A Study of 100 Mentally Retarded Children I. Psychopathology." AMERICAN JOURNAL OF PSYCHIATRY 132, no. 12 (1975): 1265-71.

Reports a study of one hundred mentally retarded children referred to a psychiatric clinic. Twenty-two references.

427   Pilkington, Thomas L. "Symposium on the Treatment of Behavioral Problems: I. Psychiatric Needs of the Subnormal." BRITISH JOURNAL OF MENTAL SUBNORMALITY 28, no. 35, part 2 (1972): 66-70.

Presents data from four studies on the incidence of mental illness in the subnormal population that indicate that from 10 to 50 percent might benefit from some psychiatric contact. Twenty-three references.

428   Reid, A.H., and Naylor, G.J. "Short-Cycle Manic Depressive Psychosis in Mental Defectives: A Clinical and Physiological Study." JOURNAL OF MENTAL DEFICIENCY RESEARCH 20, no. 1 (1976): 67-76.

429   Revill, M.G. "Symposium on the Treatment of Behavioral Problems: IV Manic Depressive Illness in Retarded Children." BRITISH JOURNAL OF MENTAL SUBNORMALITY 28, no. 35, part 2 (1972): 89-93.

Reviews the literature on the incidence of manic depressive illness in children and in mentally retarded patients. Fifteen references.

430   Smith, Edith; McKinnon, Rosemary; and Kessler, Jane W. "Psychotherapy with Mentally Retarded Children." PSYCHOANALYTIC STUDY OF THE CHILD 31 (1976): 493-514.

Discusses the applicability of modified psychoanalytic psychotherapy to the treatment of mentally retarded children with
neurotic symptoms. Twenty-seven references.

Chapter 4

THE ORGANIC PSYCHOSES

Organic brain disorders are among the most complex psychiatric diagnostic problems. The basic descriptions establish various types of prototypic symptoms, but because of the very nature of an organic brain disorder the prototypic symptoms rarely relate clearly to specific cases. Minor personality changes and depression often serve to mask the more definitive symptoms of brain lesions. No specific group of abnormal behaviors better illustrates the individuality of persons than the organic brain dysfunctions. These problems result in both a delay in diagnosis and treatment and the possibility of using treatments that may be harmful. In this regard, the basic classification systems (DSM II and the proposed DSM III--see item 29) are generally considered to be inadequate to these diagnostic problems. The major difficulty centers around the fact that a wide variety of somatic disorders have an inseparable interaction with the brain. The results may be dementia or psychotic-like behaviors which result either from the direct effect of the somatic condition or from the attempts of the individual to adapt to the physical changes. The adaptations occur within the body organization and within a broad relationship to society.

This chapter contains four groups of items: general references on organic brain dysfunction, and specific references in terms of those dysfunctions associated with (1) intracranial infections, (2) other cerebral conditions, specifically brain trauma, and (3) other physical conditions such as endocrine disorders; metabolic or nutritional disorders; systemic infections; drug, alcohol, or poison intoxication; and childbirth. Our intention is to highlight each condition rather than to describe it. We have adopted this approach both because of the complex diagnostic problems and because the broader lines of classification in this area are covered by the general references in chapter 2 and the more specific classification and sourcebook material in chapter 1. The most important works in this area are starred: numbers 447, 468, 479, 490, 501, and 504.

ORGANIC PSYCHOSES—GENERAL

431   Ban, Thomas A. "Psychopathology, Psychopharmacology, and the Organic Brain Syndrome: I." PSYCHOSOMATICS 17, no. 2 (1976): 77-82.

432 _____. Psychopathology, Psychopharmacology, and the Organic
Brain Syndrome: II." PSYCHOSOMATICS 17, no. 3 (1976): 131-
37.

Reviews a wide range of topics relating to the use of psychopharmacological agents in organic brain syndromes.

433 Chess, Stella. "Neurological Dysfunction and Childhood Behavioral
Pathology." JOURNAL OF AUTISM AND CHILDHOOD SCHIZOPHRE-
NIA 2, no. 3 (1972): 299-311.

Examines the relationship between neurological dysfunction
and childhood behavioral pathology in 1,400 patients (838
boys and 562 girls) ranging in age from thirteen weeks to
nineteen years.

434 Colbert, J., and Harrow, M. "Depression and Organicity." PSY-
CHIATRIC QUARTERLY 40, no. 1 (1966): 93-103.

Reports that, because depression and organicity are not mutu-
ally exclusive, the relative usefulness of a number of traditional indicators must be questioned.

435 de la Cruz, Felix F.; Fox, Bernard M.; and Roberts, Richard H., eds.
MINIMAL BRAIN DYSFUNCTION. New York: Academy of Sciences,
1973. 396 p.

Contains thirty-five papers dealing with various aspects of
minimal brain dysfunction and learning disability.

436 Eisenson, Jon, and Ingram, David. "Childhood Aphasia: An Up-Dated
Concept Based on Recent Research." ACTA SYMBOLICA 3, no. 2
(1972): 108-16.

Describes how asphasic children are impaired in their perceptual ability for the auditory events that constitute speech.

437 Elisco, Thomas S. "Three Examples of Hypnosis in the Treatment of
Organic Brain Syndrome with Psychosis." INTERNATIONAL JOURNAL
OF CLINICAL AND EXPERIMENTAL HYPNOSIS 22, no. 1 (1974):
9-19.

438 Fauman, M.A. "A Diagnostic System for Organic Brain Disorders:
Critique and Suggestion." PSYCHIATRIC QUARTERLY 49, no. 3
(1977): 173-86.

Proposes a new diagnostic system with examples that should
fit present systems (DSM II and the proposed DSM III--see
item 29) and still be flexible enough to overcome their problems.

439   Graham, Phillip, and Rutter, Michael. "Organic Brain Dysfunction and Child Psychiatric Disorders." BRITISH MEDICAL JOURNAL 3 (September 1968): 695-700.

Notes that psychiatric disorders in children with neuro-epileptic conditions are five times as common as in the general population and three times as common as in children with chronic physical handicaps not involving the brain. Thirty-eight references.

440   Heath, Robert G. "Brain Function and Behavior, I. Emotion and Sensory Phenomena in Psychotic Patients and Experimental Animals." JOURNAL OF NERVOUS AND MENTAL DISEASE 160, no. 3 (1975): 159-75.

Discusses psychoses of patients and how frontal lobe operations do not correct effective emotional mechanisms of the psychotic individual.

441   Ketai, R. "Psychotropic Drugs in the Management of Psychiatric Emergencies." POST GRADUATE MEDICINE 58, no. 4 (1975): 87-93.

States that although antipsychotic drugs are "agents of choice" for the management of acute functional psychoses, they should be avoided in many organic psychoses.

442   Lezak, Muriel Deutsch. NEUROPSYCHOLOGICAL ASSESSMENT. New York: Oxford University Press, 1976. 549 p.

Major textbook for professionals on neuropsychological assessment processes.

443   Messert, Bernard; Kurlanzik, Arthur E.; and Thorning, David R. "Adult Failure-to-Thrive Syndrome." JOURNAL OF NERVOUS AND MENTAL DISEASE 162, no. 6 (1976): 401-9.

Describes the analogy between the failure-to-thrive syndrome of childhood and a symptom complex seen in adult neurology. Thirty-eight references.

444   Perlman, B.B. "Schizophrenia: A Postulated Animal Model." MEDICAL HYPOTHESES 2, no. 6 (1976): 238-40.

Suggests that psychiatric concomitants of epilepsy and brain injury show that these may be based on which side the injury occurs.

445   Praag, H.M. "The Harold E. Himwich Memorial Lecture. Significance of Biochemical Parameters in the Diagnosis, Treatment and Prevention of Depressive Disorders." BIOLOGICAL PSYCHIATRY 12, no. 1 (1977): 101-31.

446 Praag, H.M.; Korf, J.; Lakke, J.P.W.F.; and Schut, T. "Dopamine Metabolism in Depression, Psychoses, and Parkinson's Disease: The Problem of the Specificity of Biological Variables in Behavior Disorders." PSYCHOLOGICAL MEDICINE 5, no. 2 (1975): 138-46.

447 *Reitan, Ralph M. "Neurological and Physiological Bases of Psychopathology." ANNUAL REVIEW OF PSYCHOLOGY 27 (1976): 189-216.

Presents an overview of data on the biological bases of adverse psychological functions. Emerging trends are identified and consideration is given to psychological deficits resulting from known structural cerebral lesions as well as those related to minimal brain dysfunction and learning disabilities. Includes 140 references.

448 Rutter, Michael. "Brain Damage Syndromes in Childhood: Concepts and Findings." JOURNAL OF CHILD PSYCHOLOGY AND PSYCHIATRY 18, no. 1 (1977): 1-21.

449 Scheinberg, I. Herbert. "Psychosis Associated with Hereditary Disorders." In ORGANIC DISORDERS AND PSYCHOSOMATIC MEDICINE, edited by Morton F. Reiser, chapter 16. American Handbook of Psychiatry, 2d ed., vol. 4. New York: Basic Books, 1974.

Discusses Huntington's chorea, Wilson's disease, acute intermittent porphyria, and genetic patterns. Twenty-one references.

450 Schwab, J.J. "Comprehensive Medicine and the Concurrence of Physical and Mental Illness." PSYCHOSOMATICS 11, no. 6 (1970): 591-95.

Discusses the relationship between minor personality changes and depression and the more definitive symptoms of organic brain dysfunction and tumors. Indicates that the symptoms of one often mask the other, resulting in delayed diagnosis and treatment.

451 Shaffer, D.; McNamara, Nancy; and Pincus, J.H. "Controlled Observations on Problems of Activity, Attention and Impulsivity in Brain Damaged and Psychiatrically Disturbed Boys." PSYCHOLOGICAL MEDICINE 4 (February 1974): 4-18.

Suggests that overactivity is a function of psychiatric disturbance rather than abnormality of the central nervous system. Two pages of references.

452 Shagass, Charles; Gershon, Samuel; and Friedhoff, Arnold J., eds.

PSYCHOPATHOLOGY AND BRAIN DYSFUNCTION. New York: Raven Press, 1977. 400 p.

Reviews recent developments in psychology, biochemistry, and neurophysiology that relate psychopathology to altered brain structure and function.

543 Shevitz, S.A.; Silberfarb, P.M; and Lipowski, Z.J. "Psychiatric Consultations in a General Hospital: A Report of One Thousand Referrals." DISEASES OF THE NERVOUS SYSTEM 37, no. 5 (1976): 295-300.

An epidemiological report.

454 Small, Leonard. NEUROPSYCHODIAGNOSIS IN PSYCHOTHERAPY. New York: Brunner/Mazel, 1976. 315 p.

Attempts to integrate the skills of systematically trained psychodiagnosticians and therapists with the added dimensions of neuropsychodiagnosis.

455 Smith, J.S.; Kiloh, L.G.; Ratnavale, G.S.; and Grant, D.A. "The Investigation of Dementia: The Results in 100 Consecutive Admissions." MEDICAL JOURNAL OF AUSTRALIA 2, no. 11 (1976): 403-5.

An epidemiological report.

456 Sweet, William; Obrador, Sixto; and Martin-Rodriquez, Jose G., eds. NEUROLOGICAL TREATMENT IN PSYCHIATRY, PAIN AND EPILEPSY. Baltimore: University Park Press, 1977. 768 p.

Proceedings of the fourth World Congress of Psychiatric Surgery, held in Madrid, Spain, in 1975.

457 Tiller, J.W. "Psychiatric Consultations in a Children's Hospital." MEDICAL JOURNAL OF AUSTRALIA 1, no. 10 (1978): 532-35.

An epidemiological report of 191 consecutive referrals between one and fourteen years of age.

458 Weiss, Jules M., and Kaufman, Herbert S. "A Subtle Organic Component in Some Cases of Mental Illness. A Preliminary Report of Cases." ARCHIVES OF GENERAL PSYCHIATRY 25 (July 1971): 74-78.

Discusses a syndrome found in individuals who have a family history of allergic symptoms and a history of carbohydrate-related metabolic disease.

459 Young, Laures D.; Taylor, Inga; and Holmstrom, Valerie. "Lithium

Treatment of Patients with Affective Illness Associated with Organic Brain Symptoms." AMERICAN JOURNAL OF PSYCHIATRY 134, no. 12 (1977): 1405-7.

Describes how the treatment controlled manic symptoms and did not seem to cause further organic deterioration.

PSYCHOSIS ASSOCIATED WITH INTRACRANIAL INFECTION

460 Brill, Henry. "Postencephalitic States or Conditions." In ORGANIC DISORDERS AND PSYCHOSOMATIC MEDICINE, edited by Morton F. Reiser, chapter 6. American Handbook of Psychiatry, 2d ed., vol. 4. New York: Basic Books, 1974.

Discusses general postencephalitic states and their treatment, encephalitis lethargico (Von Economo's disease), and other postencephalitic states. Twenty-nine references.

461 Bruetsch, Walter L. "Neurosyphilitic Conditions: General Paralysis, General Paresis, Dementia Paralytica." In ORGANIC DISORDERS AND PSYCHOSOMATIC MEDICINE, edited by Morton F. Reiser, chapter 5. American Handbook of Psychiatry, 2d ed., vol. 4. New York: Basic Books, 1974.

Discusses the etiology, mental symptoms, psychiatric syndromes, and senile form of syphilitic-related organic disease. Seventy-six references.

462 Chess, Stella; Korn, Sam J.; and Fernandez, Paulina B. PSYCHIATRIC DISORDERS OF CHILDREN WITH CONGENITAL RUBELLA. New York: Brunner/Mazel, 1971. 154 p.

Reviews experiences with 243 preschool-aged children who were examined at the Rubella Birth Defect Evaluation Project at New York University Medical Center. Also reviews the literature concerning the general and behavioral dimensions of rubella-affected children.

463 Hierons, R.; Janota, I.; and Corsellis, J.A. "The Late Effects of Necrotizing Encephalitis of the Temporal Lobes and Limbic Areas: A Clinico-Pathological Study of Ten Cases." PSYCHOLOGICAL MEDICINE 8, no. 1 (1978): 21-42.

464 Hotson, J.R., and Pedley, T.A. "The Neurological Complications of Cardiac Transplantation." BRAIN 99, no. 4 (1976): 673-94.

Reports that Central Nervous System infection is the single most frequent cause of neurological complications, often misdiagnosed as "intensive care unit psychosis."

465 Segal, B.M. "Dysthymia: An Atypical Protracted Depression. A Preliminary Report." PSYCHOTHERAPY AND PSYCHOSOMATICS 27, no. 2 (1976-77): 76-85.

Describes a special group of symptoms usually following somatic disease.

466 Wilson, L.G. "Viral Encephalopathy Mimicking Functional Psychosis." AMERICAN JOURNAL OF PSYCHIATRY 133, no. 2 (1976): 165-70.

467 Wilson, W.P.; Musella, L.; and Short, M.J. "The Electroencephalogram in Dementia." CONTEMPORARY NEUROLOGICAL SERVICES 15 (1977): 205-21.

Describes the EEG in normal aging and in dementia caused by a variety of cerebral diseases.

PSYCHOSIS ASSOCIATED WITH CEREBRAL CONDITIONS AND BRAIN TRAUMA

468 *Goldstein, Kurt. "Functional Disturbances in Brain Damage." In ORGANIC DISORDERS AND PSYCHOSOMATIC MEDICINE, edited by Morton F. Reiser, chapter 8. American Handbook of Psychiatry, 2d ed., vol. 4. New York: Basic Books, 1974.

Reviews historical notes regarding brain damage, and discusses the effect of impairment on the abstract attitudes owing to brain damage. Covers material concerning the general aspects of brain damage, its effect on general mental functions, specific symptoms, and examination methods. Forty-three references.

469 Heintel, Helmut. "Traumatic Psychoses in Childhood." ACTA PAEDOPSYCHIATRICA 39, no. 6 (1973): 126-31.

Discusses twenty-three traumatic psychoses occurring in five-to fourteen-year-old children. Twenty-one references.

470 Kiloh, L.G., and Smith, J.S. "The Neural Basis of Aggression and Its Treatment by Psycho-Surgery." AUSTRALIA AND NEW ZEALAND JOURNAL OF PSYCHIATRY 12, no. 1 (1978): 21-28.

Discusses the social and ethical questions surrounding psychosurgical procedures.

471 Lippen, Steven, and Tuchman, Michael M. "Treatment of Chronic Post-Traumatic Organic Brain Syndrome with Dextroamphetamine: First Reported Case." JOURNAL OF NERVOUS AND MENTAL DISEASE 162, no. 5 (1976): 366-71.

472 Lishman, W.A. "The Psychiatric Sequelae of Head Injury: A Review." PSYCHOLOGICAL MEDICINE 3, no. 3 (1973): 304-18.

Discusses the etiology and common clinical pictures of post-traumatic psychiatric disability. Fifty-six references.

473 Luria, Aleksandr R. THE MAN WITH A SHATTERED WORLD: THE HISTORY OF A BRAIN WOUND. New York: Basic Books, 1972. 165 p.

A twenty-five-year diary written by a man who suffered extensive destruction of the posterior portion of his brain.

474 Peterson, G.C. "Psychiatric Aspects of Chronic Organic Brain Syndrome." POST-GRADUATE MEDICINE 60, no. 5 (1976): 162-68.

Reports that in chronic OBS (or dementia) the patient generally retreats to simple, familiar situations and resists involvement with others. Indicates that these symptoms represent both deficits due to brain damage and psychological reactions to the deficits.

475 Schulman, Jerome L.; Kaspar, Joseph C.; and Throne, Frances M. BRAIN DAMAGE AND BEHAVIOR. Springfield, Ill.: Charles C Thomas, 1965. 165 p.

Discusses the relationship between brain damage and general behavior.

476 Serofetinides, E.A., and Cherlow, Diana G. "Psychiatric Test Assessment of Patients with Psychomotor Epilepsy." AMERICAN JOURNAL OF PSYCHIATRY 133, no. 7 (1976): 844-47.

Reports a study of thirty-one patients with temporal lobectomies and six with implantation of depth electrodes for relief of epileptic seizures. Notes general postoperative improvement, but depression tended to recur with time.

477 Shaffer, David. "Psychiatric Aspects of Brain Injury in Childhood: A Review." DEVELOPMENTAL MEDICINE AND CHILD NEUROLOGY 15, no. 2 (1973): 211-20.

Reviews known psychiatric sequelae to readily diagnosable CNS (central nervous system) disease. Three pages of references.

478 Taylor, D.C. "Factors Influencing the Occurrence of Schizophrenia-Like Psychosis in Patients with Temporal Lobe Epilepsy." PSYCHOLOGICAL MEDICINE 5, no. 3 (1975): 249-54.

Reports on 255 patients with temporal lobectomies.

479   *Tueretz, Kenneth; Fish, Irving; and Ransohoff, Joseph. "Head In-
       jury." In ORGANIC DISORDERS IN PSYCHOSOMATIC MEDICINE,
       edited by Morton F. Reiser, chapter 7. American Handbook of Psy-
       chiatry, 2d ed., vol. 4. New York: Basic Books, 1974.

       Discusses significant head trauma, concussion, post-traumatic
       syndrome, mental change associated with structural injury,
       focal injury, and a wide variety of other problems related to
       the head injury. Forty-four references.

PSYCHOSIS ASSOCIATED WITH OTHER PHYSICAL CONDITIONS

As we indicated in the introduction to this chapter, organic brain disorders
are among the most complex psychiatric diagnostic problems. This is underlined when one begins to examine organic brain dysfunction associated with
other physical conditions. Here, the general rule that emerges is that almost
any form of physical disease or malfunction can carry with it the potential
for emotional disturbance, and if the physical disorder is sufficiently traumatic, the associated emotional disorder may become severe enough to be
described as a neuropsychiatric disorder or a psychosis. Therefore, this section will cover endocrine, metabolic, and nutritional disorders; systemic infections; drug, alcohol, or poison intoxication; and childbirth. Many of the
articles selected represent a vast group of articles, which are typically single
case studies and whose inclusion would make this section unwieldy. The omis-
sion of individual studies is in no way a value judgment, but rather supports
our emphasis on broader review articles involving a large number of cases.
Exceptions are made where the condition is rare or may be considered prototypic of the types of problems that emerge.

480   Asch, Stuart S., and Rubin, Lowell J. "Post-Partum Reactions: Some
       Unrecognized Variations." AMERICAN JOURNAL OF PSYCHIATRY
       131, no. 8 (1974): 870-74.

       Describes types of postpartum syndromes that are not often
       identified, including infanticide and child battering, the
       grandmother reaction, the adoptive mother reaction and the
       father reaction. Twenty-one references.

481   Ascher, Edward. "Motor Syndromes of Functional or Undetermined
       Origin: Tics, Cramps, Gilles de la Tourette's Disease and Others."
       In ADULT CLINICAL PSYCHIATRY, edited by Silvano Arieti and Eu-
       gene Brody, chapter 35. American Handbook of Psychiatry, 2d ed,
       vol. 3. New York: Basic Books, 1974.

       Describes the etiology, manifestations, and treatment of these
       conditions. Seventy-eight references.

482   Bowers, Malcolm B., Jr., and Freedman, Daniel X. "Psychoses As-
       sociated with Drug Use." In ORGANIC DISORDERS AND PSYCHO-
       SOMATIC MEDICINE, edited by Morton F. Reiser, chapter 14.

American Handbook of Psychiatry, 2d ed., vol. 4. New York: Basic Books, 1974.

Deals with the genesis of psychotic behavior in which intake of a pharmacologic compound plays a significant role. Includes 110 references.

483   Brambilla, F.; Viani, F.; and Rossotti, V. "Endocrine Aspects of Child Psychosis." DISEASES OF THE NERVOUS SYSTEM 30, no. 9 (1969): 627-32.

Reports the results of a study that demonstrated that the endocrine glands are impaired in child psychosis and that the most striking alterations effect in progressive order the early primary destructuring, schizophrenic-like, and symbolic psychoses. Twenty-four references.

484   Cutting, J. "A Reappraisal of Alcoholic Psychoses." PSYCHOLOGICAL MEDICINE 8, no. 2 (1978): 285-95.

Notes that the phenomena of this illness correspond poorly with classical descriptions of alcoholic hallucinosis, delirium tremens, and alcoholic paranoia. Indicates that symptoms and syndromes seem to change with the environment and the times.

485   Freed, Earl V. "Alcoholism and Schizophrenia: The Search for Perspectives: A Review." JOURNAL OF STUDIES IN ALCOHOL 36, no. 7 (1975): 835-81.

Reviews the historical search for meaningful relationships between alcoholism and schizophrenia. Includes 186 references.

486   Friel, Patrick B. "Familial Incident of Gilles de la Tourette's Disease: Observations on Etiology and Treatment." BRITISH JOURNAL OF PSYCHIATRY 122, no. 571 (1973): 655-58.

Summarizes information on Gilles de la Tourette's disease, and discusses possible causes and treatment. Seventeen references.

487   Glaser, G.H. "Epilepsy, Hysteria and 'Possession': A Historical Essay." JOURNAL OF NERVOUS AND MENTAL DISEASE 166, no. 4 (1978): 268-74.

488   Gupta, V.P., and Ehrlich, G.E. "Organic Brain Syndrome in Rheumatoid Arthritis Following Corticosteroid Withdrawal." ARTHRITIS AND RHEUMATISM 19, no. 6 (1976): 1333-38.

489   Hafken, Louis; Leichter, Steven; and Reich, Theodore. "Organic Brain Dysfunction as a Possible Consequence of Post-Gastrectomy Hypoglycemia." AMERICAN JOURNAL OF PSYCHIATRY 132, no. 12 (1975): 1321-24.

490   *Hatotani, N., ed. PSYCHONEUROENDOCRINOLOGY. Basel: S. Karger, 1974. 312 p.

      Contains papers on the relationships between body hormones, circadian rhythms, and such abnormal behaviors as schizophrenia and other psychoses.

491   Herington, R.N., ed. CURRENT PROBLEMS IN NEURO-PSYCHIATRY: SCHIZOPHRENIA, EPILEPSY AND THE TEMPORAL LOBE. BRITISH JOURNAL OF PSYCHIATRY.Special Publication No. 4. Ashford, Kent, Engl.: Headley Brothers, 1969. 184 p.

492   Herzog, Alfred, and Detre, Thomas. "Psychotic Reactions Associated with Child Birth." DISEASES OF THE NERVOUS SYSTEM 37, no. 4 (1976): 229-38.

      Reviews the literature on postpartum psychoses. Discusses psychological and physiological precipitants of postpartum psychoses, and proposes a "stress summation theory" to explain the etiology of these reactions. Sixty-one references.

493   Horowitz, I.; Klingenstein, R.J.; Levy, R.; and Zimmerman, M.J. "Fat Embolism Syndrome in Delirium Tremens." AMERICAN JOURNAL OF GASTROENTEROLOGY 68, no. 5 (1977): 476-80.

      Discusses DTs followed by FES asterixis and Korsakoff's psychosis.

494   Johnson, G.F. "Lithium Neurotoxicity." AUSTRALIA AND NEW ZEALAND JOURNAL OF PSYCHIATRY 10, no. 1 (1976): 33-38.

      Indicates that lithium may cause permanent CNS toxicity.

495   Kaplan, Eugene H., and Blackman, Lionel H. "The Husband's Role in Psychiatric Illness Associated with Child Bearing." PSYCHIATRIC QUARTERLY 43, no. 3 (1969): 396-409.

496   Kristensen, O., and Sindrup, E.H. "Psychomotor Epilepsy and Psychosis I. Physical Aspects." ACTA NEUROLOGICA SCANDINAVICA 57, no. 5 (1978): 361-69.

      Studies ninty-six patients with paranoid-hallucinatory psychosis and ninty-six controls, both groups diagnosed with the same type of epilepsy.

497   Kruger, G.; Thomas, D.J.; Weinhardt, F.; and Hoger, S. "Disturbed
       Oxidative Metabolism in Organic Brain Syndrome Caused by Bismuth
       in Skin Creams." LANCET 1, no. 7984 (1976): 485-87.

498   Lamprecht, F. "Epilepsy and Schizophrenia: A Neurochemical Bridge."
       JOURNAL OF NEURAL TRANSMISSION 40, no. 2 (1977): 159-70.

       Reviews literature suggesting neurochemical processes by which
       the regulation of seizure thresholds and the onset of schizo-
       phrenic-like symptoms are interrelated.

499   Merrill, R.H., and Collins, J.L. "Acute Psychosis in Chronic Renal
       Failure: Case Reports." MILITARY MEDICINE 139, no. 8 (1974):
       622-24.

500   Packard, R.C. "The Neurologic Complications of Alcoholism."
       AMERICAN FAMILY PHYSICIAN 14, no. 3 (1976): 111-15.

       Reports that common syndromes are polyneuropathy, withdrawal
       syndromes, and a combination of Wernick's encephalopathy
       and Korsakoff's psychosis. Notes also cerebellar ataxia,
       convulsions, acute hallucinosis, myopathy, and coma.

501   *Sacher, Edward J. "Psychiatric Disturbances Associated with Endo-
       crine Disorders." In ORGANIC DISORDERS AND PSYCHOSOMATIC
       MEDICINE, edited by Morton F. Reiser, chapter 12. American Hand-
       book of Psychiatry, 2d ed., vol. 4. New York: Basic Books, 1974.

       Discusses adrenal disorders, Klinefelter's syndrome, farathyroid
       disorders, thyroid disorders, pancreatic disorders, menstrual
       disorders, and the failure-to-grow syndrome. Ninty-five ref-
       erences.

502   _____, ed. HORMONES, BEHAVIOR, AND PSYCHOPATHOLOGY.
       New York: Raven Press, 1976. 307 p.

503   Scheiber, S.C., and Zieset H., Jr. "Dementia Dialytica: A New
       Psychotic Organic Brain Syndrome." COMPREHENSIVE PSYCHIATRY
       17, no. 6 (1976): 781-85.

504   *Shapiro, A.; Shapiro, E.; Bruun, R.; and Sweet, R. GILLES DE LA
       TOURETTE SYNDROME. New York: Raven Press, 1978. 437 p.

       Basic work and review of this rare syndrome, which involves
       multiple motor tics and an irresistable compulsion to swear.

505   Simopoulos, V. "Amphetamine Psychosis: Review and a Hypothesis."
       DISEASES OF THE NERVOUS SYSTEM 36, no. 6 (1975): 336-39.

Reviews the clinical features and the varied proposed pathogenetic mechanisms of amphetamine psychosis. Twenty-six
references.

506   Thacore, Vinod R., and Shukla, S.R. "Cannabis Psychosis and Paranoid Schizophrenia." ARCHIVES OF GENERAL PSYCHIATRY 33,
no. 3 (1976): 383-86.

Reports a study attempting to compare twenty-five cases of
cannabis psychosis with twenty-five cases of paranoid schizophrenia. Finds substantial differences between the two types.
Twenty-seven references.

507   Treadway, Richard C.; Kane, Francis J., Jr.; Jarrahi-Zadeh, Ali;
and Lipton, Morris A. "A Psycho Endocrine Study of Pregnancy and
Puerperium." AMERICAN JOURNAL OF PSYCHIATRY 125, no. 100
(1969): 1380-86.

Speculates that the increased incidence of clinically significant disorders among women in the postpartum period may be
due to the increased environmental stresses of maternal responsibilities in association with lack of rebound from the
biochemical changes of pregnancy. Fifty-two references.

508   Trimble, M. "The Relationship Between Epilepsy and Schizophrenia:
A Biochemical Hypothesis." BIOLOGICAL PSYCHIATRY 12, no. 2
(1977): 299-304.

509   Wells, C.E. "Transient Ictal Psychosis." ARCHIVES OF GENERAL
PSYCHIATRY 32, no. 9 (1975): 1201-3.

Notes that episodes of continuous cerebral epileptiform discharges may mimic depressive, hysterical, and schizophrenic
psychosis and delirium.

510   Whittier, John R.; Roizin, Leon; and Kaufman, Mavis A. "Mental
Disorders with Huntington's Chorea." In ORGANIC DISORDERS AND
PSYCHOSOMATIC MEDICINE, edited by Morton F. Reiser, chapter
17. American Handbook of Psychiatry. 2d ed., vol. 4. New York:
Basic Books, 1974.

Covers clinical aspects and neuropathology. Ninty-two references.

511   Whybrow, P.C.; Prange, A.J.; and Treadway, C.R. "Mental Changes
Accompanying Thyroid Gland Dysfunction." ARCHIVES OF GENERAL
PSYCHIATRY 20 (January 1969): 48-63.

512   Woodrow, Kenneth M. "Gilles de la Tourettes Disease--A Review."
AMERICAN JOURNAL OF PSYCHIATRY 131, no. 9 (1974): 1000-
1003. Two pages of references.

Chapter 5

PSYCHOSES AND PSYCHOTIC BEHAVIOR

The historical nosology of abnormal behavior centers primarily around the functional observation of individuals who are doing things considered different or peculiar and who, in a broad sense, seem to have a life of their own different from that of everybody else. The word "psychosis" has evolved from the Greek word meaning "the giving of life." Thus, a psychotic individual is one who has been given a "special" life, independent from the rest of us. The classification used in this chapter is the familiar one based on functioning, so references will be easily found. The chapter presents first the general works, both adult- and child-oriented, and each subsection is broken down into special references for adults and children. There are two special sections included: one on genetics and one on the role of language. These two areas have created particular interest in the broad questions of the cause and identification of psychotic behavior. The most important references are starred, and these include numbers 534, 596, 598, 609, 614, 621, 631, 633, 655, 667, 678, and 680.

GENERAL PSYCHOSES

513   Anderson, William H., and Kuehnle, John C. "Strategies for the Treatment of Acute Psychosis." JOURNAL OF THE AMERICAN MEDICAL ASSOCIATION 229, no. 14 (1974): 1884-89.

Discusses the management of acute-onset psychosis. Authors believe that the cornerstone of appropriate initial management is the use of high-potency antipsychotic chemotherapy. Sixteen references.

514   Andreasen, Nancy J., and Powers, Pauline S. "Creativity and Psychosis: An Examination of Conceptual Style." ARCHIVES OF GENERAL PSYCHIATRY 32, no. 1 (1975): 70-73.

Compares the performance of fifteen creative writers with that of fifteen manic and schizophrenic patients. Reports that the conceptual style of writers seems to resemble mania more than schizophrenia, and, if overinclusiveness is accepted as an index for thought disorder, manics have a more florid thought disorder than schizophrenics. Twenty-five references.

515 Appleton, William S. "A Guide to the Use of Psychoactive Agents." DISEASES OF THE NERVOUS SYSTEM 28, no. 9 (1967): 609-13.

Outlines the use of phenothiazines, antidepressants, minor tranquilizers, and miscellaneous drugs. Includes classification, differences, potency, dosage, efficacy, side effects, and treatment of side effects. Offers a bibliography of review articles.

516 Astrup, Christian. "Studies of Higher Nervous Activity in Functional Psychoses." PAVLOVIAN JOURNAL OF BIOLOGICAL SCIENCE 10, no. 4 (1975): 194-215.

Suggests that psychiatric illnesses be conceived of as experiments of nature, providing a variety of psychopathological mechanisms that may elucidate normal psychological processes. Two pages of references.

517 Becker, Ernest. THE REVOLUTION IN PSYCHIATRY: THE NEW UNDERSTANDING OF MAN. New York: Free Press, 1974. 276 p.

Presents a behavioral theory of two major mental illnesses (schizophrenia and depression). Examines the idea that mental illness is not a medical problem but rather a problem related to development in general. Proposes a behavioral theory of human action. Sixteen pages of references.

518 Bowers, Malcolm B. RETREAT FROM SANITY: THE STRUCTURE OF EMERGING PSYCHOSIS. New York: Human Sciences Press, 1974. 275 p.

Presents a collection of case studies and interview data to document the characteristic process and states of developing psychosis. Ten pages of references.

519 Chiland, Collette, ed. LONG TERM TREATMENTS OF PSYCHOTIC STATES. New York: Human Sciences Press, 1977. 696 p.

English edition of papers from conferences in Montreal (1969) and Paris (1972). Emphasizes what professionals do, and covers general problems, therapeutic experiences and experiments, epidemiological and transcultural studies, and the role of the psychiatrist in the community.

520 Cooper, A.F. "Deafness and Psychiatric Illness." BRITISH JOURNAL OF PSYCHIATRY 129 (September 1976): 216-26.

Reviews the literature concerning the relationship between deafness and psychiatric disorder. Sixty-one references.

521 Heath, Robert G. "Brain Function and Behavior: I. Emotion and Sensory Phenomena in Psychotic Patients and in Experimental Animals." JOURNAL OF NERVOUS AND MENTAL DISEASE 160, no. 3 (1975): 159-75.

Describes the twenty-five-year research program at Tulane University's Department of Psychiatry and Neurology, which has devised a variety of techniques based on the development of specific biological methods for the treatment of behavioral disorders. Forty-four references.

522 Janov, Arthur. "On Psychosis." JOURNAL OF PRIMAL THERAPY 1, no. 4 (1974): 331-34.

Describes the use of primal therapy with psychotic patients.

523 Kassorla, Irene C. "A New Approach to Mental Illness." SCIENCE JOURNAL 5, no. 6 (1969): 68-74.

Discusses the use of operant conditioning to treat "neurotic, psychotic or other deviant behaviors."

524 Krakowski, Adam J. "General Principles of Chemotherapy of Mental Illness." PSYCHOSOMATICS 10, no. 2 (1969): 82-87.

Discusses chemotherapy as one method in the total approach to the management of mental illness. Forty references.

525 Levy, Linda L. "Movement Therapy for Psychiatric Patients." AMERICAN JOURNAL OF OCCUPATIONAL THERAPY 28, no. 6 (1974): 354-57.

Discusses movement as an approach to the treatment of severely disorganized psychotic patients.

526 McNeil, Elton B. THE PSYCHOSES. Englewood Cliffs, N.J.: Prentice-Hall, 1970. 194 p.

General text dealing with functional and organic psychosis.

527 Magaro, Peter A. THE CONSTRUCTION OF MADNESS: EMERGING CONCEPTIONS AND INTERVENTIONS INTO THE PSYCHOTIC PROCESS. New York: Pergamon Press, 1976. 240 p.

Attempts to define "madness" and provide understanding of the treatments used. Presents social, behavioral, psychoanalytic, religious, and mystical models of madness.

528   Pauling, Linus. "On the Orthomolecular Environment of the Mind:
       Orthomolecular Theory." AMERICAN JOURNAL OF PSYCHIATRY
       131, no. 11 (1974): 1251-57.

       Defines orthomolecular psychiatry as the achievement and
       preservation of good mental health by the provision of the
       optimum molecular environment for the mind through the con-
       centrations of substances normally present in the human body
       (i.e, vitamins). Thirty-five references.

529   Procci, Warren R. "Schizo-Affective Psychoses: Fact or Fiction? A
       Survey of the Literature." ARCHIVES OF GENERAL PSYCHIATRY
       33, no. 10 (1976): 1167-78.

       Reports that classification of functional psychoses has tradi-
       tionally been dichotomous, with schizophrenia and manic-
       depressive disorders considered as separate entities, but the psy-
       chiatric literature is replete with descriptions of psychoses
       with mixed features. Includes 127 references.

530   Wolpert, Arthur. "Psychopharmacology: An Overview." PSYCHI-
       ATRIC QUARTERLY 42, no. 3 (1968): 444-51.

       Discusses the place of psychopharmacology in the treatment
       of mental illness. Eighteen references.

Children

531   Adams, Kathryn A. "The Child Who Murders: A Review of Theory
       and Research." CRIMINAL JUSTICE AND BEHAVIOR 1, no. 1
       (1974): 51-61.

       Reviews the literature on child murderers: their character,
       modeling, victim precipitation, reaction to stress as cause of
       homicide by children, legal considerations, and prediction
       and prevention procedures. Twenty-three references.

532   Cain, Albert C. "Special 'Isolated' Abilities in Severely Psychotic
       Young Children." PSYCHIATRY: JOURNAL FOR THE STUDY OF
       INTER-PERSONAL PROCESSES 32, no. 2 (1969): 137-49.

       Offers observations and reflections relevant to childhood psy-
       chosis, especially that strikingly advanced, seemingly isolated
       special abilities are found in some young "preschool or latency
       age" severely psychotic children. Two pages of references.

533   Eveloff, Herbert H. "Psychopharmacologic Agents in Child Psychiatry:
       A Survey of the Literature Since 1961." ARCHIVES OF GENERAL
       PSYCHIATRY 14, no. 5 (1966): 472-81.

Surveys the use of agents in the pediatric and adolescent age range. Sixty-six references.

534 *Goldfarb, William. "Childhood Psychosis." In CARMICHAEL'S MANUAL OF CHILD PSYCHOLOGY, edited by Paul H. Mussen, vol. 2, pp. 667-764. New York: John Wiley and Sons, 1970.

Offers an integrated and comprehensive review of the state of knowledge on childhood psychosis, with emphasis on research and development from 1960 to 1970.

535 Gratton, Laurent, and Rizzo, Aldolfo E. "Group Therapy with Young Psychotic Children." INTERNATIONAL JOURNAL OF GROUP PSYCHOTHERAPY 19, no. 1 (1969): 63-71.

Discusses the validity of the hypothesis that psychotic children show their problems in a group situation.

536 Knoblock, Hilda, and Pasamanick, Benjamin. "Some Etiologic and Prognostic Factors in Early Infantile Autism and Psychosis." PEDIATRICS 55, no. 2 (1975): 182-91.

Reports a study of fifty infants and young preschool children seen in a pediatric developmental service and diagnosed as autistic. Indicates that all had evidence of organic brain disease but did not differ in any respect from a comparison group of patients with central nervous system dysfunction unassociated with autism. Eleven references.

537 Lockyer, Linda, and Rutter, Michael. "A 5-to-15 Year Follow-Up Study of Infantile Psychoses: III. Psychological Aspects." BRITISH JOURNAL OF PSYCHIATRY 115, no. 525 (1969): 865-82.

Describes a study of sixty-three psychotic children matched with nonpsychotic controls and reexamined at the mean age of 15 1/2 years. Reports psychiatric, neurological, social, and psychological assessments. Forty-five references.

538 McDermott, John F., Jr.; Harrison, Saul I.; Schrager, Jules; Lindy, Janet; and Killins, Elizabeth. "Social Class and Mental Illness in Children: The Question of Childhood Psychosis." AMERICAN JOURNAL OF ORTHOPSYCHIATRY 37, no. 3 (1967): 548-57.

Presents data from psychiatric evaluations of children diagnosed as psychotic and divided into groups according to social class. Nineteen references.

539 Masagatani, Gladys N. "Hand Gesturing Behavior in Psychotic Children." AMERICAN JOURNAL OF OCCUPATIONAL THERAPY 27, no. 1 (1973): 24-29.

Reviews the literature on hand movements in the human fetus and newborn, and suggests that movements may be manifestations of delayed or irregular development and of psychological problems.

540   Rock, Nicholas L. "Childhood Psychoses and Long Term Chemo- and Psychotherapy." DISEASES OF THE NERVOUS SYSTEM 35, no. 7 (1974): 303-8.

Describes a multidisciplinary approach to the problem of childhood psychosis which involves individual and group psychotherapy with children and parents as well as adjunct chemotherapy.

541   Rutter, Michael; Greenfield, David; and Lockyer, Linda. "A 5-15 Year Follow-Up Study of Infantile Psychosis: II." BRITISH JOURNAL OF PSYCHIATRY 113 (November 1968): 1183-99.

See item 537.

542   Rutter, Michael, and Lockyer, Linda. "A 5-15 Year Follow-Up Study of Infantile Psychosis: I." BRITISH JOURNAL OF PSYCHIATRY 113 (November 1968): 1169-82.

See item 537.

543   Schopler, Eric. "Changes of Direction with Psychotic Children." In CHILD PERSONALITY AND PSYCHOPATHOLOGY: CURRENT TOPICS I, edited by Anthony Davids, chapter 6. New York: John Wiley and Sons, 1974.

Discusses recent changes in thinking about research and theory in childhood psychosis or autism, emphasizing the shift from theoretical to empirical thinking in the areas of classification, theories of causation, roles of parents, treatment interventions, and social and ecological considerations. Two pages of references.

544   Silberstein, Richard M.; Mandell, Wallace; Dallack, John D.; and Cooper, Allen. "Avoiding Institutionalization of Psychotic Children." ARCHIVES OF GENERAL PSYCHIATRY 19 (July 1968): 17-21.

Reports a study to determine whether programs of drug therapy and parental counseling are effective for maintaining psychotic children in the community and enabling them to function successfully. Eleven references.

545   Szurek, Stanislaus A., and Berlin, Irving N., eds. CLINICAL STUDIES IN CHILDHOOD PSYCHOSIS. New York: Brunner/Mazel, 1972. 780 p.

A comprehensive text of the therapeutic team approach to childhood psychoses, based on twenty-five years of experimental work in treatment, training, and research.

546   Zrull, Joel P.; Westman, Jack C.; Arthur, Bettie; and Rice, Dale L. "An Evaluation of Methodology Used in the Study of Psychiatric Drugs for Children." JOURNAL OF THE AMERICAN ACADEMY OF CHILD PSYCHIATRY 5, no. 2 (1966): 384-91.

Families and Parents

547   Akerley, Mary S. "The Invulnerable Parent." JOURNAL OF AUTISM AND CHILDHOOD SCHIZOPHRENIA 5, no. 3 (1975): 275-81.

Discusses the invulnerable parent of an autistic child. Applies the concept of "invulnerability" to persons who seem totally unaware of or unaffected by the illness of a member of their family.

548   Anthony, E. James. "A Clinical Evaluation of Children with Psychotic Parents." AMERICAN JOURNAL OF PSYCHIATRY 126, no. 2 (1969): 177-84.

Reports that children of psychotic parents were found to have a variety of disturbance indicators that might be considered predictive of later problems as adults.

549   _____ . "Comment: The Invulnerable Parent." JOURNAL OF AUTISM AND CHILDHOOD SCHIZOPHRENIA 5, no. 3 (1975): 281-82.

Makes several points concerning invulnerability: (1) "good" environments may carry certain hazards producing disturbed children, (2) "well" children may come from "bad" environments and not only survive but thrive, and (3) the invulnerable parent or child should not be made to feel guilty.

550   Cicchetti, Domenic V. "Critical Review of the Research Relating Mother Dominance to Schizophrenia." PROCEEDINGS OF THE 77TH ANNUAL CONVENTION OF THE AMERICAN PSYCHOLOGICAL ASSOCIATION 4 (1969): 557-58.

Reviews the major studies that support the relationship between mother dominance and etiology of schizophrenia.

551   Hartman, Carol C. "Psychotic Mothers and Their Babies." NURSING OUTLOOK 16, no. 12 (1968): 32-36.

Reports preliminary findings of an investigation of joint admission of eleven psychotic mothers and their children over a two-year period.

552 Reed, Sheldon C.; Hartley, Carl; Anderson, V. Elving; Phillips, Vivian P.; and Johnson, Nelson A. THE PSYCHOSES: FAMILY STUDIES. Philadelphia: W.B. Saunders Co., 1973. 578 p.

Describes a fifty-year study of over eighteen thousand descendants of 118 psychotic patients. Attempts to answer questions concerning heritable and congenital risks of developing functional psychoses in families with at least one seriously ill member.

553 Rosenthal, David; Wender, Paul H.; Kety, Seymour S.; Schulsinger, Fini; Welner, Joseph; and Rieder, Ronald O. "Parent-Child Relationships and Psychopathological Disorders in the Child." ARCHIVES OF GENERAL PSYCHIATRY 32, no. 4 (1975): 466-76.

Uses naturally occurring adoptions to separate the effects of heredity and rearing on the development of psychopathological disorders in the child. Assesses the quality of relationships between the child and adoptive parents in four groups, with a total of 258 adoptees and foster children. Correlates the degree of illness in the child with the quality of the parent-child relationship. Twenty-two references.

554 Schopler, Eric, and Reichler, Robert J. "Parents As Co-Therapists in the Treatment of Psychotic Children." JOURNAL OF AUTISM AND CHILDHOOD SCHIZOPHRENIA 1, no. 1 (1971): 87-102.

Describes a treatment program for psychotic and autistic children in which parents are helped to function as primary developmental agents. Twenty-six references.

555 Serban, George. "Parental Stress in the Development of Schizophrenic Offspring." COMPREHENSIVE PSYCHIATRY 16, no. 1 (1975): 23-36.

Analyzes influence of parental mental illness on schizophrenic offspring in 641 hospitalized schizophrenics. Reports that disturbed family relationships contributed to the etiology only to the degree to which the patient perceived that family interaction was disturbed. Nineteen references.

556 Woodmansey, A.C. "The Common Factor in Problems of Adolescents." BRITISH JOURNAL OF MEDICAL PSYCHOLOGY 42, no. 4 (1969): 353-70.

Analyzes the hypothesis that childhood psychogenic illness can be regarded as the result of fear, retaliation, or self-attack in response to the hostility of parental figures. Fifty-three references.

Special Study Areas

Because of the amount of research material available, two special fields of study in the area of psychosis have been singled out. These are (1) general discussions of the relationship of genetic considerations to the development of various types of psychotic disorders and (2) references on the growth and development of language as part of a psychotic disorder. Also, because of the nature of the research in these areas, the usual separation between studies of adults and of children has not been made.

GENETIC CONSIDERATIONS

557 Abe, K., and Coppen, Alec. "Personality and Body Composition in Monozygotic Twins with an Affective Disorder." BRITISH JOURNAL OF PSYCHIATRY 115, no. 524 (1969): 777-80.

> Reports a study of seven sets of twins and the analysis of physiological and psychological variables.

558 Allen, Martin G. "Twin Studies of Affective Illness." ARCHIVES OF GENERAL PSYCHIATRY 33, no. 12 (1976): 1476-78.

> Summarizes major twin studies of affective illness, and notes significant differences between monozygotic and dizygotic concordance rates for both unipolar and bipolar illness. Thirty-eight references.

559 Debray, J. "The Genetic Etiology of Schizophrenia." INFORMA-TION PSYCHIATRIQUE 48, no. 9 (1972): 907-16.

> Explores hereditary factors connected with schizophrenia. Notes that a genetic sickness is not always evident at birth, nor are hereditary illnesses always transmitted according to the laws of Mendel. Twenty-five references.

560 Farley, John D. "Phylogenetic Adaptations and the Genetics of Psychosis." ACTA PSYCHIATRICA SCANDINAVICA 53, no. 3 (1976): 173-92.

> Suggests that many social skills and responses that are of adaptive value are under a significant degree of genetic control. Sixty-five references.

561 Fulker, D.W. "A Biometrical Genetic Approach to Intelligence and Schizophrenia." SOCIAL BIOLOGY 20, no. 3 (1973): 266-75.

> Describes a method that permits reanalysis of existing data on schizophrenia, and suggests that biometrical genetics could

easily be applied to the analysis of human behavior. Twenty-nine references.

562   Gershon, Elliot S. "The Inheritance of Affective Disorders: A Review of Data and Hypotheses." BEHAVIOR GENETICS 6, no. 3 (1976): 227-61.

Reports that twin and family history studies of genetic factors in affective disorders suggest that the form of disorder (bipolar or unipolar) is transmitted within families, that early onset of affective disorders is associated with increased morbid risk of the disorder, and that female relatives have higher prevalence of illness, although the sex of the ill person does not appear to be a factor in transmission. Five pages of references.

563   Goetzl, Ugo; Green, Ronald; Whybrow, Peter; and Jackson, Rebecca. "X-Linkage Revisited: A Further Family Study of Manic-Depressive Illness." ARCHIVES OF GENERAL PSYCHIATRY 31, no. 5 (1974): 665-72.

Reports a family study of thirty-nine individuals with proven manic-depressive disorder. Twenty-seven references.

564   Gottesman, Irving L., and Shields, James. "Genetic Theorizing and Schizophrenia." BRITISH JOURNAL OF PSYCHIATRY 122, no. 566 (1973): 15-30.

Discusses a genetic basis for schizophrenia, which rests on the compatibility of the pattern of elevated risks to relatives with certain genetic models and the continued exclusion of any particular environmental factor as a sufficient cause. Sixty-four references.

565   _____. SCHIZOPHRENIA AND GENETICS: A TWIN STUDY VANTAGE POINT. New York: Academic Press, 1972. 433 p.

Presents a detailed account of classic twin studies and a balanced summary of twin and adoption studies with regard to schizophrenia.

566   Kidd, K.K., and Cavalli-Sforza, L.L. "An Analysis of the Genetics of Schizophrenia." SOCIAL BIOLOGY 20, no. 3 (1973): 254-65.

Summarizes observations on the inheritance of schizophrenia, presenting what both the genetics and the environment contribute to the disease. Twenty-seven references.

567   Kraus, Robert F. "Schizophrenia as a Genetic Polymorphism." PSYCHIATRIC QUARTERLY 47, no. 4 (1973): 546-58.

Reviews the literature that reveals convincing evidence for
a genetic factor in the etiology of schizophrenia. Twenty-
five references.

568 Loranger, Armand W. "X-Linkage and Manic-Depressive Illness."
BRITISH JOURNAL OF PSYCHIATRY 127 (November 1975): 482-88.

Describes a theory based on four hundred parents of one hundred male and one hundred female bipolar manic-depressive
probands. Indicates that it is premature to invoke sex-linked
heredity as a general explanation for manic-depression, although there is evidence that it may account for the illness
in some families. Eighteen references.

569 McCabe, Michael A. "Psychiatric Illness on Paternal and Maternal
Sides of Reactive Psychoses." COMPREHENSIVE PSYCHIATRY 16,
no. 6 (1975): 525-28.

570 Rich, Walter. "The Schizophrenia Spectrum: A Genetic Concept."
JOURNAL OF NERVOUS AND MENTAL DISEASE 162, no. 1 (1976):
3-12.

Describes a spectrum concept of schizophrenia that hypothesizes that (1) classical schizophrenia results at least in part
from a genetic diathesis; (2) certain other usually milder psychopathological states, which do not satisfy the classical criteria for the diagnosis of schizophrenia, represent varying
clinical expressions of the same diathesis; and (3) all of these
states constitute a genetically based spectrum of schizophrenic
disorders.

571 Stabereau, James R., and Pollin, William. "Early Characteristics of
Monozygotic Twins Discordant for Schizophrenia." ARCHIVES OF
GENERAL PSYCHIATRY 17 (December 1976): 723-34.

Describes eighty-six cases reported worldwide. Sixty-one references.

572 Wohl, Otto F. "Monozygotic Twins Discordant for Schizophrenia: A
Review." PSYCHOLOGICAL BULLETIN 83, no. 1 (1976): 91-106.

Describes these approaches using monozygotic twins discordant
for schizophrenia. Notes that comparisons of discordant with
concordant pairs have yielded conflicting results concerning
the possibility of both genetic and environmentally induced
forms of schizophrenia. Thirty-three references.

LANGUAGE STUDIES

573 Andreasen, Nancy J.C., and Pfohl, Bruce. "Linguistic Analysis of Speech in Affective Disorders." ARCHIVES OF GENERAL PSYCHIATRY 33, no. 11 (1976): 1361-67.

Compares various aspects of speech and language using psycholinguistic techniques on fifteen depressed patients and sixteen manic patients. Twenty-six references.

574 Baltaxe, Christiane A., and Simmons, James Q. "Language and Childhood Psychosis: A Review." ACTA SYMBOLICA 49, no. 4 (1975): 439-58.

Reviews the literature on language and childhood psychosis, covering the general characteristics of linguistic deficits, the importance of language in diagnosis and prognosis, mother-child linguistic interaction, and intervention programs. Four pages of references.

575 Chaika, Elaine. "A Linguist Looks at Schizophrenic Language." BRAIN AND LANGUAGE 1, no. 3 (1974): 257-76.

Notes that the language of some patients diagnosed as schizophrenic is apparently caused by a disruption in the ability to order linguistic elements into meaningful structures. Thirty-one references.

576 Churchill, Dan W. "The Relation of Infantile Autism and Early Childhood Schizophrenia to Developmental Language Disorders of Childhood." JOURNAL OF AUTISM AND CHILDHOOD SCHIZOPHRENIA 2, no. 2 (1972): 182-97.

Presents evidence to support a thesis that central language deficits related to those found in children with developmental aphasia, but more severe, may be the necessary and sufficient cause of behavior that marks the children as autistic and schizophrenic. Seventy-one references.

577 Cohen, D.J.; Caparulo, B.; and Shaywitz, B. "Primary Childhood Aphasia and Childhood Autism: Clinical, Biological and Conceptual Observations." JOURNAL OF THE AMERICAN ACADEMY OF CHILD PSYCHIATRY 15, no. 4 (1976): 604-45.

Reviews behavioral and physiological correlates of aphasia and autism, comparing and contrasting the two syndromes. Includes 130 references.

578 Fay, Warren H., and Schuler, Adriana Luce. EMERGING LANGUAGE IN AUTISTIC CHILDREN. Baltimore: University Park Press, 1978. 300 p.

Explores the dimensions of language and language-related

behaviors in autistic children. Clarifies the extent to which autistic children are limited in the areas of speech, language, communication, and cognition, and discusses the implications of these limitations with respect to conventional intervention strategies as well as alternative approaches.

579   Goldfarb, William; Goldfarb, Nathan; Braunstein, Patricia; and Scholl, Hannah. "Speech and Language Faults of Schizophrenic Children." JOURNAL OF AUTISM AND CHILDHOOD SCHIZOPHRENIA 2, no. 3 (1972): 219-33.

Analyzes data from tape recordings of directed speech activities and nondirected conversation of twenty-five schizophrenic children in residential treatment and twenty-five normal public school children matched for age.

580   Lecours, Andre R., and Vanier-Clement, Marie. "Schizophasia and Jargonaphasia: A Comparative Description with Comments on Chaika's and Fromkin's Respective Looks at 'Schizophrenic' Language." BRAIN AND LANGUAGE 3, no. (1976): 516-65.

Defines and analyzes varieties of deviant spoken language segments and different forms of deviant spoken language behaviors at morphological and syntactic levels. Three pages of references. (See item no. 575.)

581   Mugckari, Loras H., and Kames, Edna. "The Effects of Video Tape Feedback and Modeling on the Behavior of Chronic Schizophrenics." JOURNAL OF CLINICAL PSYCHOLOGY 29, no. 3 (1973): 313-16.

Investigates the effects of videotape feedback and videotaped modeling on the verbal performance of chronic psychotics. Reports that videotape feedback was effective in increasing task-oriented verbal behavior, with no effect noted for performance behavior.

582   Reilly, Frank E.; Harrow, Martin; and Tucker, Gary G. "Language and Thought Content in Acute Psychosis." AMERICAN JOURNAL OF PSYCHIATRY 130, no. 4 (1973): 411-17.

Reports that during the acute phase, subjects tended to get lost in a vivid, overwhelming flood of details; during a partial recovery phase, they took more distance and were not so involved.

583   Stein, Johanna, and Tompson, Samuel V. "Crazy Music: Theory." PSYCHOTHERAPY: THEORY, RESEARCH AND PRACTICE 8, no. 2 (1971): 137-45.

Studies the musical output of hospitalized psychotic adults and the patients' perceptions of it.

THE SCHIZOPHRENIAS

The greatest amount of literature in the area of mental abnormality or abnormal behavior refers to the psychotic condition described as "schizophrenia." Here we are faced with a situation where everybody knows it's there, but nobody is sure what it is. We have included a number of items earlier in this chapter, under the general headings of psychoses and the subtopics of genetics and language. The items in this section focus directly on the condition itself or on the relationship between schizophrenia and other psychotic conditions. We are not dividing this section into the usual subparts (catatonia, hebephrenia, and paranoia), because most of the major descriptions of these conditions are included in the general references on schizophrenia itself. Therefore, we have integrated the references on these subcategories into one section. We also present sections on childhood schizophrenia and childhood autism; the latter is an area of growing interest. Here it is recognized that there is a great deal of disagreement concerning the differences between "childhood schizophrenia" and "autism," and we have made no effort to reconcile the arguments. Rather, we have chosen to present a series of references from each category and to categorize the works under the headings used by the authors.

584 Arieti, Silvano. "Acting Out and Unusual Behavior in Schizophrenia." AMERICAN JOURNAL OF PSYCHOTHERAPY 28, no. 3 (1974): 333-42.

Views acting out among schizophrenic patients as connected with special cognitive processes such as active concretization, delusional thinking, and hallucinations. Seventeen references.

585 _____. "Anxiety and Beyond in Schizophrenia and Psychotic Depression." AMERICAN JOURNAL OF PSYCHOTHERAPY 27, no. 3 (1973): 338-45.

Discusses various aspects of anxiety in psychiatric disorders in terms of whether the anxiety maintains its basic form or becomes a major ingredient in schizophrenia or depression.

586 _____. "Individual Psychotherapy and Schizophrenia." In ADULT CLINICAL PSYCHIATRY, edited by Silvano Arieti and Eugene Brody, chapter 27. American Handbook of Psychiatry, 2d ed., vol. 3. New York: Basic Books, 1974.

Offers a historical survey and indications for psychotherapy in current practice. Ninty references.

587 _____. INTERPRETATION OF SCHIZOPHRENIA. 2d rev. ed. New York: Basic Books, 1974. 800 p.

Covers various aspects of schizophrenia in terms of Arieti's basic theory, which involves both genetic and psychodynamic factors.

588   Bar, Thomas A. "Pharmacotherapy of Schizophrenia: Facts, Specula-
       tions, Hypotheses and Theories." PSYCHOSOMATICS 15, no. 4
       (1974): 178-87.

       Reviews drugs used in the treatment of schizophrenia. Ninety
       references.

589   _____. RECENT ADVANCES IN THE BIOLOGY OF SCHIZOPHRE-
       NIA. Springfield, Ill.: Charles C Thomas, 1973. 119 p.

       Reflects major directions of current research in the area.
       Provides historical approaches, and reviews experimental find-
       ings and treatment modalities.

590   Beaver, W. Robert. "Schizophrenia and Despair." COMPREHENSIVE
       PSYCHIATRY 13, no. 6 (1972): 561-72.

       Reviews concepts of schizophrenia, and concludes that "schiz-
       ophrenia is neither an intrusion from the outside world nor a
       simple biochemical aberration." Reports that it is a manifes-
       tation of a profound life crisis with a sense of aloneness, loss
       of self, and despair caused by a disparity between the indi-
       vidual's essential needs and the ability to satisfy those needs.
       Thirty-nine references.

591   Belford, Barbara. "Electrophysiological Basis for a Dichotomy in
       Schizophrenia." PSYCHOLOGICAL REPORTS 39, no. 2 (1976):
       591-99.

       Presents an overview of the electrophysiological basis for the
       traditional process/reactive or typical/atypical distinction in
       schizophrenia. Fifty-three references.

592   Bemporad, Jules R., and Pinsker, Henry. "Schizophrenia: The Man-
       ifest Symptomatology." In ADULT CLINICAL PSYCHIATRY, edited by
       Silvano Arieti and Eugene Brody, chapter 23. American Handbook of
       Psychiatry, 2d ed., vol. 3. New York: Basic Books, 1974.

       Presents a historical review and approaches to diagnosis, prog-
       nosis, and differential diagnosis. Ninety-two references.

593   Cancro, Robert; Fox, Norma; and Shapiro, Lester, eds. STRATEGIC
       INTERVENTION IN SCHIZOPHRENIA. New York: Human Sciences
       Press, 1974. 326 p.

       Reviews the present state of knowledge in regard to schizo-
       phrenia, delineating current developments in the management
       of the disorder.

594   Carpenter, William T.; Bartko, John J.; Carpenter, Carol L.; and

Strauss, John S. "Another View of Schizophrenia Subtypes: A Report from the International Pilot Study of Schizophrenia." ARCHIVES OF GENERAL PSYCHIATRY 33, no. 4 (1976): 508-16.

Describes work based on sign and symptom data from the international pilot study of schizophrenia, which addresses questions on traditional subtype diagnosis applied across cultures. For example, are the various traditional subtypes symptometrically distinguishable, and can cluster analytic techniques define a more distinctive set of schizophrenic subgroups? Twenty-four references.

595   Cash, Thomas F. "Methodological Problems and Progress in Schizophrenia Research: A Survey." JOURNAL OF CONSULTING AND CLINICAL PSYCHOLOGY 40, no. 2 (1973): 278-86.

Classified a sample of 166 research studies in schizophrenia on the basis of their adequacy in dealing with problems of methodology and utility. Thirty-two references.

596   *Chapman, Loren J., and Chapman, Jean P. DISORDERED THOUGHT IN SCHIZOPHRENIA AND RESEARCH. Englewood Cliffs, N.J.: Prentice-Hall, 1973. 359 p.

Provides a comprehensive account of schizophrenia, with a good summary of Kraepelin's description of schizophrenia (see item no. 64). Defines schizophrenia from a historical viewpoint, discusses methodological problems, and emphasizes various theories that explain schizophrenia.

597   Cromwell, Rue L. "Assessment of Schizophrenia." ANNUAL REVIEW OF PSYCHOLOGY 26 (1975): 593-619.

Presents a historical review of the concept of schizophrenia, to illustrate how early issues have a direct bearing on contemporary problems of investigation. Eighty-one references.

598   *Davis, John M. "Overview: Maintenance Therapy in Psychiatry: I, Schizophrenia." AMERICAN JOURNAL OF PSYCHIATRY 132, no. 12 (1975): 1237-45.

Notes that hospital psychiatry has evolved from long-term "treatment" programs that were primarily custodial to the successful pharmacological treatment of acute psychotic episodes. Suggests that drugs have provided the potential for truly preventive psychiatry. Sixty-two references.

599   Dempsey, G. Michael; Tsuang, Ming T.; Struss, Andra; and Dvoredsky-Wortsman, Ana. "Treatment of Schizo-Affective Disorder." COMPREHENSIVE PSYCHIATRY 16, no. 1 (1975): 55-59.

Attempts to classify schizo-affective disorders, as a basis for providing guidelines for treatment. Eighteen references.

600 Durell, Jack, and Archer, Ellen G. "Plasma Proteins in Schizophrenia: A Review." SCHIZOPHRENIA BULLETIN 2, no. 1 (1976): 147-49.

Reviews research since 1970 on the autoimmune hypothesis of schizophrenia, which indicates that there is only fragmentary and uncorroborated data showing specific alterations in blood proteins, and there are reasonably consistent data suggesting that a pattern of change resembling the "acute phase reaction" occurs in schizophrenic patients. Four pages of references.

601 Falek, Arthur, and Moser, Atanna M. "Classification in Schizophrenia." ARCHIVES OF GENERAL PSYCHIATRY 32, no. 1 (1975): 59-67.

Considers that schizophrenia has been defined as an identifiable disorder based on phenomenologic classification. Seventy-one references.

602 Frohiman, Charles E., and Gottlieb, Jacques S. "The Biochemistry of Schizophrenia." In ADULT CLINICAL PSYCHIATRY, edited by Silvano Arieti and Eugene Brody, chapter 26. American Handbook of Psychiatry, 2d ed., vol. 3. New York: Basic Books, 1974.

603 Gruenberg, Ernest M. "The Epidemiology of Schizophrenia." In CHILD AND ADOLESCENT PSYCHIATRY, SOCIO-CULTURAL AND COMMUNITY PSYCHIATRY, 2d ed., edited by Gerald Caplan, chapter 3. American Handbook of Psychiatry, vol. 2. New York: Basic Books, 1974.

Uses epidemiological knowledge to plan effective treatment, based on historical trends, community diagnosis, individual risks, the identification of syndromes, and the working of health services. Thirty-eight references.

604 Gunderson, John G.; Autry, Joseph H.; Mosher, Loren R.; and Buchsbaum, Sherry. "Special Report: Schizophrenia 1974." SCHIZOPHRENIA BULLETIN, no. 9, 1974, pp. 15-54.

Reviews ongoing research on schizophrenia, concentrating on studies conducted by National Institute of Mental Health grantees. Six pages of references.

605 Hagen, Richard L. "Behavioral Therapies and the Treatment of Schizophrenics." SCHIZOPHRENIA BULLETIN, no. 13, 1975, pp. 70-96.

Provides a behavioral definition of schizophrenia, and discusses the goals of behavioral therapy and specific treatment modalities. Six pages of references.

606 Hawkins, David R. "Diagnosing the Schizophrenic." JOURNAL OF ORTHOMOLECULAR PSYCHIATRY 6, no. 1 (1977): 18–26.

Discusses types of studies that have been done on the various forms of schizophrenia, and outlines the procedures used in diagnosing the illness. Twenty references.

607 Heffner, Peggy A.; Strauss, Milton E.; and Grisell, James. "Rehospitalization of Schizophrenics as a Function of Intelligence." JOURNAL OF ABNORMAL PSYCHOLOGY 84, no. 6 (1975): 735-36.

Reports that brighter schizophrenic subjects were rehospitalized three and five years after discharges less often than were subjects of less than midian IQ.

608 Hoenig, J. "The Schizophrenic Patient at Home." ACTA PSYCHIATRICA SCANDINAVICA 50, no. 3 (1974): 297-308.

Reports a four-year follow-up study to assess the progress of 120 schizophrenic patients, all first admissions to hospitals, who are managed extramurally and live at home.

609 *Holzman, Phillip S. "Theoretical Models and the Treatment of the Schizophrenias." PSYCHOLOGICAL ISSUES 9, no. 4 (Monograph 36) (1976): 134-57.

Discusses the conflict between metapsychological and clinical theory in the description of schizophrenic phenomena, and urges a systems view which would incorporate data on genetic, biochemical, neurological, sociological, and other variables as well as clinical observations. Thirty-seven references.

610 Jacobs, S.C.; Prusoff, B.A.; and Paykel, E.S. "Recent Life Events in Schizophrenia and Depression." PSYCHOLOGICAL MEDICINE 4, no. 4 (1974): 444-53.

Compares fifty depressives and fifty matched first-admission schizophrenics on life events experienced in the six months before the onset of the illness. Indicates that depressives reported more events than schizophrenics, but this involves only certain types of events. Also indicates that depressives reported more exits from the social field and a variety of undesirable events. Twenty references.

611 Kodman, Frank, and Sparks, Charles. "Sleep Deprivation in Schizophrenic Patients." JOURNAL OF CLINICAL PSYCHOLOGY 25,

no. 4 (1969): 365-67.

Analyzes EEG sleep patterns on schizophrenics and normal subjects, all under a sleep deprivation schedule. Classifies findings in seven categories.

612 Lehmann, H.E. "Physical Therapies of Schizophrenia." In ADULT CLINICAL PSYCHIATRY, edited by Silvano Arieti and Eugene Brody, chapter 28. American Handbook of Psychiatry, 2d ed., vol. 3. New York: Basic Books, 1974.

Discusses pharmacological treatment, metabolic treatment, hypoglycemic coma treatment, and psychiatric surgery. Includes 134 references.

613 Liberman, Robert P. "Behavioral Modification of Schizophrenia: A Review." SCHIZOPHRENIA BULLETIN, no. 6, 1972, pp. 32-48.

Reviews applications of behavior modification technology to a variety of schizophrenic behaviors, including social interaction, delusions, hallucinations, self-help and grooming skills, and instrumental work behavior. Forty-one references.

614 *Lidz, Theodore. THE ORIGIN AND TREATMENT OF SCHIZOPHRENIC DISORDERS. New York: Basic Books, 1973. 145 p.

Summarizes Lidz's work on the importance of critically studying and emphasizing the relationship between family psychodynamics and schizophrenia. Of historical and clinical importance.

615 Marshall, W.L. "Cognitive Functioning in Schizophrenia: I. Stimulus Analyzing and Response Selection Processes." BRITISH JOURNAL OF PSYCHIATRY 123, no. 575 (1973): 413-23.

Indicates that defective cognitive functioning in schizophrenics may result from difficulties in stimulus analysis or response selection or in difficulty in holding material in short-term memory, retrieving from memory, transferring information, or associating at a central level.

616 _____. "Cognitive Functioning in Schizophrenia: II. Conceptual Performance under Unpaced, Speeded and Slowed Conditions." BRITISH JOURNAL OF PSYCHIATRY 123, no. 575 (1973): 423-28.

617 Mednick, Sarnoff A. "Breakdown in Individuals at High Risk for Schizophrenia: Possible Predispositional Prenatal Factors." MENTAL HYGIENE 54, no. 1 (1970): 50-63.

Notes a distinctive premorbid pattern of behavior in a group of adolescents who suffered psychiatric breakdowns. Fifty-seven references.

618   Meltzer, Herbert Y. "Biochemical Studies in Schizophrenia." SCHIZOPHRENIA BULLETIN 2, no. 1 (1976): 10-18.

Provides a general review of recent research on biochemical factors in the etiology and cause of schizophrenia, emphasizing four major areas. Three pages of references.

619   _____. "Neuromuscular Dysfunction in Schizophrenia." SCHIZOPHRENIA BULLETIN 2, no. 1 (1976): 106-35.

Reviews evidence from studies of the incidence of various types of neuromuscular dysfunction in patients with schizophrenic and affective illness. Five pages of references.

620   Mitchell, Alexander R. SCHIZOPHRENIA: THE MEANINGS OF MADNESS. New York: Taplinger, 1972. 158 p.

Briefly interprets the meaning of madness in history and in current thought and art, and discusses the importance of madness to insanity and to psychiatry.

621   *Nell, Renee. "A New Type of Milieu Therapy." JOURNAL OF CONTEMPORARY PSYCHOTHERAPY 1, no. 1 (1968): 37-42.

Describes the type of milieu therapy that works in an isolated rural home with borderline schizophrenics, in an attempt to bring them back to a state of mental health in which they can live constructively, enjoy their natural endowments, and accept their limitations.

622   *O'Brien, Charles P. "Group Therapy for Schizophrenia: A Practical Approach." SCHIZOPHRENIA BULLETIN, no. 13, 1975, pp. 119-30.

Notes that the literature indicates that group therapy may have therapeutic advantages for outpatient schizophrenics. Twenty-nine references.

623   Pasamanick, Benjamin; Scarpitti, Frank R.; and Dinitz, Simon. SCHIZOPHRENICS IN THE COMMUNITY: AN EXPERIMENTAL STUDY IN THE PREVENTION OF HOSPITALIZATION. New York: Appleton-Century-Crofts, 1967. 448 p.

Provides impressive evidence that most of the incarceration in state hospitals is unnecessary and perhaps destructive.

624   Pope, Alfred. "Problems of Interpretation in the Chemical Pathology of Schizophrenia." JOURNAL OF PSYCHIATRIC RESEARCH 11 (1974): 265-72.

Describes postmortem studies of brains from schizophrenic subjects, from the viewpoint of the neuropathologist. Twenty references.

625 Rieder, Ronald O.; Rosenthal, David; Wender, Paul; and Blumenthal, Helene. "The Offspring of Schizophrenics: Fetal and Neonatal Deaths." ARCHIVES OF GENERAL PSYCHIATRY 32, no. 2 (1975): 200-211.

Reports on the neurological development among the offspring of schizophrenics. Twenty-two references.

626 Rolf, Jon E., and Harig, Paul T. "Etiological Research in Schizophrenia and the Rationale for Primary Intervention." AMERICAN JOURNAL OF ORTHOPSYCHIATRY 44, no. 4 (1974): 538-54.

Reviews theories, methods, and general findings of etiological research in schizophrenia and the primary prevention literature. Four pages of references.

627 Serban, George. "Functioning Ability in Schizophrenic and 'Normal' Subjects: Short-Term Prediction of Rehospitalization of Schizophrenics." COMPREHENSIVE PSYCHIATRY 16, no. 5 (1975): 447-56.

Examines the social and interpersonal adjustment of 125 acute and 516 chronic schizophrenic patients, by comparing their levels of functioning with those of normal subjects. Twenty-two references.

628 _____. "Stress in Schizophrenics and Normals." BRITISH JOURNAL OF PSYCHIATRY 126 (May 1975): 397-407.

Describes findings related to the measurement of stress in 641 schizophrenics and 95 comparable normals. Twenty-one references.

629 Steiner, Jerome. "The Group Therapy of Schizophrenics." GROUPS: A JOURNAL OF GROUP DYNAMICS AND PSYCHOTHERAPY 7, no. 1 (1975-76): 25-29.

Discusses the dilemma of schizophrenics who need guidance but fear engulfment and loss of self. Fifteen references.

630 Strahilevitz, Meir. "Interaction of Environmental and Biological Factors in the Etiology of Schizophrenia: Review and Integration." CANADIAN PSYCHIATRIC ASSOCIATION JOURNAL 19, no. 2 (1974): 207-17.

Suggests that environmental pressures or other biochemical/physiological alterations may be etiologically related to the development of acute schizophrenic psychoses. Includes 112 references.

631 *Usdin, Gene, ed. SCHIZOPHRENIA: BIOLOGICAL AND PSYCHO-LOGICAL PERSPECTIVES. New York: Brunner/Mazel, 1975. 144 p.

Presents an overview of research and conceptualization in this area.

632 Varsamis, J.; Adamson, J.D.; and Sigurdson, W.F. "Schizophrenics with Delusions of Poisoning." BRITISH JOURNAL OF PSYCHIATRY 121, no. 565 (1972): 673-75.

633 *Wynne, Lyman C.; Cromwell, Rue L.; and Matthysse, Steven, eds. THE NATURE OF SCHIZOPHRENIA: NEW APPROACHES TO RESEARCH AND TREATMENT. New York: Wiley-Interscience, 1978. 726 p.

Discusses genetic, biochemical, and sociocultural aspects of schizophrenia.

Specific Subcategories of Schizophrenia

634 Cameron, Norman A. "Paranoid Conditions and Paranoia." In ADULT CLINICAL PSYCHIATRY, edited by Silvano Arieti and Eugene Brody, chapter 29. American Handbook of Psychiatry, 2d ed., vol. 3. New York: Basic Books, 1974.

Discusses paranoid conditions, persecution complex, other psychotic paranoid reactions, psychodynamics and early childhood, and treatment. Eighty references.

635 Clark, Robert A. "The Outpatient Treatment of Paranoid Reactions." PENNSYLVANIA PSYCHIATRIC QUARTERLY 7, no. 2 (1967): 3-9.

Outlines the feasibility of successful treatment of milder paranoid reactions in the psychiatric outpatient department.

636 Gjessing, Leiv R. "A Review of Periodic Catatonia." BIOLOGICAL PSYCHIATRY 8, no. 1 (1974): 23-45.

Reviews the clinical features, laboratory findings, etiology, pathogenesis, diagnoses, and treatment of periodic catatonic stupor and excitement. Five pages of references.

637 _____. "The Switch Mechanism in Periodic Catatonia and Manic-Depressive Disorder." CHRONOBIOLOGIA 2, no. 4 (1975): 307-16.

638   Hudson, Wayne C. "Play Therapy in the Treatment of Hebephrenia."
PSYCHOTHERAPY AND PSYCHOSOMATICS 26, no. 5 (1975): 286-
93.

Outlines a multiple technique therapy for the treatment of
hebephrenia. Twenty-one references.

639   Lester, David. "The Relationship Between Paranoid Delusions and
Homosexuality." ARCHIVES OF SEXUAL BEHAVIOR 4, no. 3 (1975):
285-94.

Reviews the literature on Freud's theory that paranoid delusions are motivated by unconscious homosexual impulses. Does
not support this prediction. Thirty-five references.

640   McDowell, David; Reynolds, Brian; and Magaro, Peter. "The Integration Defect in Paranoid and Nonparanoid Schizophrenia." JOUR-
NAL OF ABNORMAL PSYCHOLOGY 84, no. 6 (1975): 629-36.

Views the central defect as an inadequate integration of perceptual and cognitive processes. Thirty-four references.

641   Maher, Brendan. "Delusional Thinking and Cognitive Disorder." In
THOUGHT AND FEELING: COGNITIVE ALTERATION OF FEELING
STATE, edited by H. London and R.E. Nisbett, chapter 7. Chicago:
Aldine-Atherton, 1974.

Suggests that there is a group of patients who suffer from primary perceptual disorder, fundamentally biological but influ-
enced by stress, and that these disorders involve vivid and
intense sensory input. Twenty-four references.

642   Morrison, James R. "Catatonia: Diagnosis and Management." HOS-
PITAL AND COMMUNITY PSYCHIATRY 26, no. 2 (1975): 91-94.

Notes a general decline in this type of schizophrenia, and
describes the types that are still seen, including the excited
and withdrawn, as well as some organic and psychiatric conditions that resemble catatonia. Makes suggestions for differential diagnosis.

643   _____. "Catatonia: Prediction of Outcome." COMPREHENSIVE
PSYCHIATRY 15, no. 4 (1974): 317-24.

Reports the outcome of 250 patients diagnosed as having catatonic schizophrenia or catatonic syndrome. Includes 170 references.

644   Retterstol, Nils. PROGNOSIS IN PARANOID PSYCHOSIS. Springfield, Ill.: Charles C Thomas, 1971. 173 p.

Describes a follow-up study of paranoid psychotics from 1958 to 1967.

645 Swanson, David W.; Bohnert, Philip J.; and Smith, Jackson A. THE PARANOID. Boston: Little, Brown, 1970. 523 p.

Discusses the nature of paranoid disorders, and gives detailed considerations of biological, psychological, and social factors.

646 Winokur, George; Morrison, James; Clancy, John; and Crowe, Raymond. "Iowa 500: The Clinical and Genetic Distinction of Hebephrenic and Paranoid Schizophrenia." JOURNAL OF NERVOUS AND MENTAL DISEASE 159, no. 1 (1974): 12-19.

Studied 115 consecutively-admitted hebephrenic and 62 paranoid schizophrenics, using hospital records, interview transcripts, and clinical observations and assessments.

CHILDHOOD SCHIZOPHRENIA

647 Baron, Miron, and Stern, Max. "Familial Concordance in Schizophrenia: A Comparative Study of Pairs of Sibs." COMPREHENSIVE PSYCHIATRY 17, no. 3 (1976): 461-67.

Reports a study with thirty-six pairs of schizophrenic siblings. Computes significant concordant rates for isolated symptoms, regardless of diagnosis, for pairs resembling in paranoid delusions, hallucinations, cyclothymic traits, and sexual preoccupation. Twenty-two references.

648 Bender, Lauretta. "The Life Course of Children with Schizophrenia." AMERICAN JOURNAL OF PSYCHIATRY 130, no. 7 (1973): 783-86.

Describes the background, heredity data, history of organic stress, and intellectual development of one hundred children diagnosed as schizophrenics from 1935 to 1952.

649 Carter, Ronald D., and Poeschel, Susan M. "Programming for Severely Disturbed Youngsters in a Public School." SALT: SCHOOL APPLICATIONS OF LEARNING THEORY 6, no. 3 (1974): 39-42.

Details a program for autistic or schizophrenic children, based on behavior modification theories.

650 Fish, Barbara, and Hagin, Ross. "Visual-Motor Disorders in Infants at Risk for Schizophrenia." ARCHIVES OF GENERAL PSYCHIATRY 28, no. 6 (1973): 900-904.

Measured visual-motor development from birth to two years of age in infants born to schizophrenic mothers. Twenty-five references.

651 Frankel, Fred, and Simmons, James Q. "Self-Injurious Behavior in Schizophrenic and Retarded Children." AMERICAN JOURNAL OF MENTAL DEFICIENCY 80, no. 5 (1976): 512-22.

Reports that self-injurious behavior is a problem with children who are primarily nonverbal and low functioning. Examines possible operant and respondent paradigms. Sixty references.

652 Garmezy, Norman. "Children at Risk: The Search for the Antecedents of Schizophrenia: II. On-Going Research Programs, Issues, and Interventions." SCHIZOPHRENIA BULLETIN, no. 9, 1974, pp. 55-122.

Reviews the status of a number of ongoing or recently completed investigations of children vulnerable to schizophrenia. Discusses various issues in risk research. Nine pages of references.

653 Goldfarb, William. "Distinguishing and Classifying the Individual Schizophrenic Child." In CHILD AND ADOLESCENT PSYCHIATRY, SOCIO-CULTURAL AND COMMUNITY PSYCHIATRY, 2d ed., edited by Gerald Caplan, chapter 5. American Handbook of Psychiatry, vol. 2. New York: Basic Books, 1974.

Describes historical sources of the construct "childhood schizophrenia" and gives diagnosis of childhood schizophrenia and various subclassifications. Ninety-nine references.

654 _____. GROWTH AND CHANGE OF SCHIZOPHRENIC CHILDREN: A LONGITUDINAL STUDY. Washington, D.C.: V.H. Winston and Sons, 1974. 271 p.

Reports findings of a three-year study on psychological growth and self-regulative behavior in seven- to ten-year-old schizophrenic children in a residential facility. Forty-three references.

655 *Hingtgen, Joseph N., and Bryson, Carolyn Q. "Recent Developments in the Study of Early Childhood Psychoses: Infantile Autism, Childhood Schizophrenia and Related Disorders." SCHIZOPHRENIA BULLETIN, no. 5, 1972, pp. 8-53.

Reports a descriptive study of various types of early childhood psychosis. Sixteen pages of references.

656 Katz, Phillip. "The Therapy of Adolescent Schizophrenia." AMERICAN JOURNAL OF PSYCHIATRY 27, no. 2 (1970): 132-37.

Describes the relationship between adolescents and schizophrenia, emphasizing the importance of developmental evaluation in formulating a therapeutic program.

657 Miller, Robert T. "Childhood Schizophrenia: A Review of Selected Literature." INTERNATIONAL JOURNAL OF MENTAL HEALTH 3, no. 1 (1973): 3-46.

Reviews various aspects of the literature on childhood schizophrenia. Seven pages of references.

658 Piggott, Leonard R., and Gottlieb, Jacques S. "Childhood Schizophrenia: What is It?" JOURNAL OF AUTISM AND CHILDHOOD SCHIZOPHRENIA 3, no. 2 (1973): 96-103.

Presents diagnostic criteria and follow-up findings on groups of children diagnosed by various investigators as childhood schizophrenic, autistic, or atypical. Thirty references.

659 Rinsley, Donald. "A Contribution to the Nosology and Dynamics of Adolescent Schizophrenia." PSYCHIATRIC QUARTERLY 46, no. 2 (1972): 159-86.

Reviews the literature and disputes the "turmoil" view of adolescence, which characterizes this period as one of behavioral stress. Suggests that this applies only to a minority suffering from major psychopathological problems. Eighty-four references.

CHILDHOOD AUTISM

660 Axline, Virginia M. DIBS: IN SEARCH OF SELF. Boston: Houghton Mifflin, 1970. 220 p.

Presents an account of how play therapy helped a severely disturbed (if not autistic) child rehabilitate himself.

661 Bender, Lauretta. "A Longitudinal Study of Schizophrenic Children with Autism." HOSPITAL AND COMMUNITY PSYCHIATRY 20 (August 1969): 28-35.

Analyzes the life course of thirty children who meet the criteria of infantile autism described by Kanner (see item nos. 61 and 62). Twenty-two references.

662 Bosch, Gerlhard. INFANTILE AUTISM. New York: Springer-Verlag, 1970. 158 p.

Contains a phenomenological attempt to describe the world as seen by autistic children.

663 Chess, Stella. "Autism in Children with Congenital Rubella." JOURNAL OF AUTISM AND CHILDHOOD SCHIZOPHRENIA 1, no. 1 (1971): 33-47.

Identifies the syndrome of autism in 10 out of 243 preschool children with congenital rubella. Twenty-five references.

664 Churchill, Don W.; Alpern, Gerald D.; and DeMyer, Marian K., eds. INFANTILE AUTISM: PROCEEDINGS OF THE INDIANA UNIVERSITY COLLOQUIUM. Springfield, Ill.: Charles C Thomas, 1971. 340 p.

Contains a symposium focused on diagnostic, etiological, and therapeutic aspects of infantile autism.

665 Creak, Mildred. "Reflections on Communication and Autistic Children." JOURNAL OF AUTISM AND CHILDHOOD SCHIZOPHRENIA 2, no. 1 (1972): 1-8.

Stresses the significance of the fact that a major defect of autistic children is their inability to communicate. Suggests that the study of human communication and how it is established may provide a key to the treatment of autism.

666 DeMyer, Marian K. "Research in Infantile Autism: A Strategy and Its Results." BIOLOGICAL PSYCHIATRY 10, no. 4 (1975): 433-52.

Reports twelve years of research testing of the nurture theory, the nature theory, and nature-nurture interaction theories of autism. Reports that data from major studies show strong support for the nature causation theory. Three pages of references.

667 *DesLauriers, Austin M., and Carlson, C.F. YOUR CHILD IS ASLEEP: EARLY INFANTILE AUTISM. Homewood, Ill.: Dorsey Press, 1969. 403 p.

Presents various aspects of infantile autism and their treatment.

668 Erskine, Richard G., ed. AUTISM AND CHILDHOOD PSYCHOSES: ANNOTATED BIBLIOGRAPHY, 1969-1974. Urbana, Ill.: Special Education Department, University of Illinois, 1975. 175 p.

669 Everard, Margaret P., ed. AN APPROACH TO TEACHING AUTISTIC CHILDREN. Oxford, Engl.: Pergamon Press, 1976. 158 p.

Offers advice on the day-to-day behavior management and teaching of autistic children. Fifty-five references.

670 Gold, Mark S., and Gold, Janice R. "Autism and Attention: Theoretical Considerations and a Pilot Study Using Set Reaction Time." CHILD PSYCHIATRY AND HUMAN DEVELOPMENT 6, no. 2 (1975): 68-80.

Describes research on an intentional reaction time model that proposes that infantile autism results from a malfunction in basic alerting and attentional mechanisms. Fifty-one references.

671 Isaev, D.N., and Kagan, V.E. "Autistic Syndromes in Children and Adolescents." ACTA PAEDOPSYCHIATRICA 40, no. 15 (1974): 182-89.

Discusses several variants of autism, stressing the specificity of the organization of cognitive processes, the inconsistency of behavior, and the strange nature of interest and communications characteristic of autistic psychopathic problems.

672 Kanner, Leo; Rodriquez, Alejandro; and Ashenden, Barbara. "How Far Can Autistic Children Go in Matters of Social Adaptation?" JOURNAL OF AUTISM AND CHILDHOOD SCHIZOPHRENIA 2, no. 1 (1972): 9-33.

Discusses case histories of one female and eight male autistic children selected from a total of 96 diagnosed prior to 1953; children are presently in their 20s and 30s. Draws attention to differences between this group and other autistic patients, to maturation and environmental issues, and to past and present matters of behavior and personality structure.

673 Kugelmass, I. Newton. THE AUTISTIC CHILD. Springfield, Ill.: Charles C Thomas, 1970. 341 p.

Presents a study of autism, its language, and clinical considerations.

674 Lovaas, O. Ivar. THE AUTISTIC CHILD. New York: Halsted, 1976. 246 p.

Describes a behaviorally oriented program of treatment.

675 Margolies, Paul J. "Behavioral Approaches to the Treatment of Early Infantile Autism: A Review." PSYCHOLOGICAL BULLETIN 84, no. 2 (1977): 249-64.

Examines and evaluates behavioral approaches to the treatment of early infantile autism. Ninety-one references.

676 Ornitz, Edward M., and Ritvo, Edward R. "Perceptual Inconsistency in Early Infantile Autism." ARCHIVES OF GENERAL PSYCHIATRY 18 (January 1968): 79-98.

Describes pathologic process common to early infantile autism, certain cases of childhood schizophrenia, and atypical children. Forty-seven references.

677 _____. "The Syndrome of Autism: A Critical Review." AMERICAN
JOURNAL OF PSYCHIATRY 133, no. 6 (1976): 609-21.

Reviews the clinical features and behavioral characteristics
of autism, differential diagnosis of the syndrome, and clinical neurophysiological and biochemical research. Includes
151 references.

678 *Rimland, Bernard. INFANTILE AUTISM. New York: Appleton-
Century-Crofts, 1964. 282 p.

Contains an important presentation of the theory and management of autism.

679 Ritvo, Edward R.; Cantwell, Dennis; Johnson, Edith; Clements, Martha;
Benbrook, Fay; Slagle, Sandra; Kelly, Patricia; and Ritz, Michael.
"Social Class Factors in Autism." JOURNAL OF AUTISM AND
CHILDHOOD SCHIZOPHRENIA 1, no. 3 (1971): 297-310.

Studies social class factors in families of 148 patients hospitalized from 1961 to 1970. Twelve references.

680 *Ritvo, Edward R.; Freeman, Betty Jo; Ornitz, Edward M.; and Tang-
uay, Peter E., eds. AUTISM: DIAGNOSIS, CURRENT RESEARCH
AND MANAGEMENT. New York: Spectrum Publications, 1976.
302 p.

Discusses current studies regarding infantile autism, including
genetic, operant, neurobiochemical, language, clinical, and
management aspects of research.

681 Rutter, Michael. "Concepts of Autism: A Review of Research."
JOURNAL OF CHILD PSYCHOLOGY AND PSYCHIATRY 9 (October
1968): 1-25.

Reviews trends in work on terminology, on autism as a variety
of mental subnormality, on autism as a type of schizophrenia,
and on the possible genetic basis of autism. Five pages of
references.

682 _____. "The Development of Infantile Autism." PSYCHOLOGICAL
MEDICINE 4, no. 2 (1974): 147-63.

Describes research over the last thirty years in the genesis of
the behavior covered by the term "infantile autism." Four
pages of references.

683 Schechter, Marshall D.; Shurley, Jay T.; Sexauer, Jane D.; and
Toussieng, Paul W. "Perceptual Isolation Therapy: A New Experimental Approach in the Treatment of Children Using Infantile Autistic

Defenses: A Preliminary Report." JOURNAL OF AMERICAN ACAD-
EMY OF CHILD PSYCHIATRY 8, no. 1 (1969): 97-139.

Presents a hypothesis that children use autism as a defensive
stance against incoming stimuli experienced as overwhelming
and noxious. Four pages of references.

684   Treffert, Harold A. "Epidemiology of Infantile Autism." ARCHIVES
OF GENERAL PSYCHIATRY 22, no. 5 (1970): 431-38.

Identifies 280 unduplicated cases of childhood schizophrenia
and infantile autism in a five-year survey to establish epidemiological parameters in a variety of behavioral areas.
Twenty-one references.

685   Tustin, Frances. AUTISM AND CHILDHOOD PSYCHOSIS. New
York: Jason Aronson, 1973. 200 p.

Presents evidence of autism supporting the environmentalist
position.

686   Ward, Alan J. CHILDHOOD AUTISM AND STRUCTURAL THERAPY:
SELECTED PAPERS ON EARLY CHILDHOOD AUTISM. Chicago, Ill.:
Nelson Hall, 1976. 236 p.

Describes the implementation of a new treatment approach
for childhood autism, using techniques that employ an active
intervention on the part of the therapist and require early
identification and an ongoing program of day care and hospitalization.

687   Whittaker, James K. "Causes of Childhood Disorders: New Findings."
SOCIAL WORK 21, no. 2 (1976): 91-96.

Examines the status of the "family etiology hypothesis" in
view of recent research in autism and learning disability.

688   Williams, Sara, and Harper, Juliet. "A Study of Etiological Factors
at Critical Periods of Development in Autistic Children." AUSTRA-
LIAN AND NEW ZEALAND JOURNAL OF PSYCHIATRY 7, no. 3
(1973): 163-68.

Describes a ten-year study of ninety-seven autistic children
seen along with their families in an effort to determine etiological factors.

689   Wing, J.K., ed. EARLY CHILDHOOD AUTISM: CLINICAL, EDU-
CATIONAL AND SOCIAL ASPECTS. London: Pergamon Press, 1966.
333 p.

Contains essays and perspectives in this area.

690   Wing, Lorna. "The Handicaps of Autistic Children: A Comparative Study." JOURNAL OF CHILD PSYCHOLOGY AND PSYCHIATRY AND ALLIED DISCIPLINES 10, no. 1 (1969): 1-40.

Reviews the behavior of a variety of autistic children, as reported by their parents. Forty-two references.

AFFECTIVE DISORDERS

The other major group of psychotic disorders comes under the broad heading of affective disorders or bipolar psychoses. Here we include the manic-depressive illnesses, involutional melancholia, and depression, again distinguishing between the usual forms and those found in children. At the end of this section we present works on rare psychotic disorders, included primarily for classification purposes, since there is not a great deal of material available that is appropriate for this volume.

691   Angst, Jules. "The Etiology and Nosology of Endogenous Depressive Psychoses: A Genetic, Sociological, and Clinical Study." FOREIGN PSYCHIATRY 2, no. 1 (1973): 108 p.

Describes the etiological significance of physical and psychological factors in precipitory endogenous depression, the frequency of psychosis in relatives of a depressed patient and the nature of the genetic factors involved. Includes 194 references.

692   Becker, Joseph. AFFECTIVE DISORDERS. Morristown, N.J.: General Learning Press, 1977. 244 p.

Discusses the major investigative approaches to depression: psychodynamic, cognitive-behavioral, and biological. Includes experiments and case studies of numerous psychologists and educators as well as major psychosocial research.

693   Bruder, G.E., and Yozawitz, A. "Application of Psycho-physical and Psycho-motor Measures in the Study of Affective Disorders." RESEARCH COMMUNICATIONS IN PSYCHOLOGY, PSYCHIATRY AND BEHAVIOR 1, no. 1 (1976): 1-14.

Describes the use of psychophysical and psychomotor measurement of twenty-six newly admitted male psychiatric patients and thirty-three non-patient controls. Reports that subjects diagnosed as affective psychotic were less sensitive in detecting an auditory transient than were schizophrenics or nonpatients. Twenty-three references.

694   Cole, Jonathan O.; Schatzberg, Alan F.; and Frazier, Shervert H., eds. DEPRESSION: BIOLOGY, PSYCHODYNAMICS AND TREATMENT. New York: Plenum Publishing Corp., 1978. 262 p. Illus.

Contains a major overview of current knowledge.

695   Gattozzi, Antoinette A.   LITHIUM IN THE TREATMENT OF MOOD
DISORDERS. Washington, D.C.: Department of Health, Education and
Welfare, 1970.   90 p.

Presents a history of lithium; describes its use with manic,
depressive, and other disorders; and reviews relevant literature.

696   Goodwin, Frederick K., and Bunney, William E.   "Psycho-biological
Aspects of Stress and Affective Illness."   In SEPARATION AND DE-
PRESSION: CLINICAL AND RESEARCH ASPECTS, edited by J.P.
Scott and E.C. Sinay, pp. 91-113.   American Association for the
Advancement of Science, no. 94.   Washington, D.C.:   1973.

697   Kashiwagi, Tetereo; McClure, James N.; and Wetzel, Richard D.
"Pre-menstrual Affective Syndrome and Psychiatric Disorder."   DIS-
EASES OF THE NERVOUS SYSTEM   37, no. 3 (1976):   116-19.

Investigates the relationship between premenstrual affective
syndromes and psychiatric disorders in eighty-one women at
a neurology clinic.   Fifteen references.

698   Maas, James W.   "Biogenic Amines and Depression: Biochemical and
Pharmachological Separation of Two Types of Depression."   ARCHIVES
OF GENERAL PSYCHIATRY   32, no. 11 (1975):   1357-61.

Presents research findings indicating that depressive disorders
may be divided into two groups, using specific biochemical
and pharmacological criteria.   Eighty-nine references.

699   McGlashan, Thomas H., and Carpenter, William T., Jr.   "An Investigation of the Post-Psychotic Depressive Syndrome."   AMERICAN
JOURNAL OF PSYCHIATRY   133, no. 1 (1976):   14-19.

Examines the frequency of the syndrome, predictive variables,
and its prognostic implications, from the data of thirty 18- to
60-year-old schizophrenic patients.

700   _____.   "Post-Psychotic Depression in Schizophrenia."   ARCHIVES
OF GENERAL PSYCHIATRY   33, no. 2 (1976):   231-39.

Presents a review and reformulation of the syndrome.   Sixty-
two references.

701   Mendels, J.   "Biological Aspects of Affective Illness."   In ADULT
CLINICAL PSYCHIATRY, edited by Silvano Arieti and Eugene Brody,
chapter 22.   American Handbook of Psychiatry, 2d ed., vol. 3.
New York: Basic Books, 1974.

Discusses the biological changes associated with depressive illness, some of the related genetic aspects, biogenic amines, and neuro-endocrine studies. Includes 372 references.

702   Pull, C., and Pichot, P. "On the Concept of Involutional Melancholia: An Historical Study." ANNALES MEDICO-PSYCHOLOGIQUES 2, no. 3 (1975): 571-82.

Traces the history of the syndrome of involutional melancholia since its introduction by Kraepelin in 1896. Includes 129 references.

703   Rosenthal, Saul H. "Involutional Depression." In ADULT CLINICAL PSYCHIATRY, edited by Silvano Arieti and Eugene Brody, chapter 30. American Handbook of Psychiatry, 2d ed., vol. 3. New York: Basic Books, 1974.

Gives a classical picture of the condition, including its controversy and early history. Discusses the premorbid personality and the relationship of menopause to involutional depression. Seventy-three references.

704   Schaller, J.P. "Melancholia and Depression." VIA MEDICALE AU CANADA FRANCAISE 4, no. 8 (1975): 997-1005.

Presents the views of physicians and theologians since ancient times on the causes, characteristics, and treatment of melancholia.

705   Schildkraut, Joseph J. "Neuropsychopharmacology and the Affective Disorders: I." NEW ENGLAND JOURNAL OF MEDICINE 281, no. 4 (1969): 197-201.

Discusses variations in classification of affective disorders. Fifty-nine references.

705a   _____. "Neuropsychopharmacology and the Affective Disorders: II." NEW ENGLAND JOURNAL OF MEDICINE 281, no. 5 (1969): 248-55.

Discusses three major psychopharmacological agents in the clinical treatment of affective disorders. Three pages of references.

706   _____. "Neuropsychopharmacology and the Affective Disorders: III." NEW ENGLAND JOURNAL OF MEDICINE 281, no. 6 (1969): 302-6.

Discusses metabolic mechanisms responsible for action of various drugs, and reviews biogenic amine metabolism in connection with the administration of psychoactive drugs.

Twenty-one references.

707   Winokur, George. "Diagnostic and Genetic Aspects of Affective Ill-
       ness." PSYCHIATRIC ANNALS 3, no. 2 (1973): 6-15.

       Examines data on a number of illnesses under the general
       rubric of affective disorders. Twenty references.

708   Zubin, Joseph, and Freyhan, Fritz A., eds. DISORDERS OF MOOD.
       Baltimore: Johns Hopkins Press, 1972. 200 p.

       Deals with the psychopharmacological aspects of depression
       and the classification of depressive disorders.

Affective Disorders—Children

709   Cytryn, Leon; McKnew, Donald H.; Toque, Mayada; and Desai,
       Remesh E. "Biochemical Correlates of Affective Disorders in Chil-
       dren." ARCHIVES OF GENERAL PSYCHIATRY 31, no. 5 (1974):
       659-61.

       Reports a preliminary study of six- to twelve-year-old chil-
       dren with affective disorders during a two to three week hos-
       pitalization. Eighteen references.

710   Feinstein, Sherman C. "Diagnostic and Therapeutic Aspects of Manic-
       Depressive Illness in Early Childhood." EARLY CHILD DEVELOPMENT
       AND CARE 3, no. 1 (1973): 1-12.

       Provides short case descriptions of children who suffered from
       juvenile manic-depressive illness that had its onset during
       early childhood.

711   McKnew, Donald H., and Cytryn, Leon. "Historical Background in
       Children with Affective Disorders." AMERICAN JOURNAL OF PSY-
       CHIATRY 130, no. 11 (1973): 1278-80.

       Provides the histories of children with affective disorders,
       revealing that certain environmental factors were present
       either singly or in combination in every case. Fifteen ref-
       erences.

712   Warneke, L. "A Case of Manic-Depressive Illness in Childhood."
       CANADIAN PSYCHIATRIC ASSOCIATION JOURNAL 20, no. 3
       (1975): 195.

713   Weinberg, Warran A., and Brumback, Roger A. "Mania in Child-
       hood." AMERICAN JOURNAL OF DISEASES OF CHILDREN 130,

no. 4 (1976): 380-85.

Establishes criteria for mania in children on the basis of criteria for mania in adults. Reports that mania in children is an episodic disorder characterized by marked irritability or agitation, a considerable increase in activity level, and noticeable mood instability that persists for longer than one month. Forty-two references.

Manic-Depressive Disorders—Bipolar Psychoses

714   Abrams, Richard; Taylor, Michael A.; and Gaztanage, Pedro. "Manic-Depressive Illness and Paranoid Schizophrenia: A Phenomenologic Family History and Treatment-Response Study." ARCHIVES OF GENERAL PSYCHIATRY 31, no. 5 (1974): 640-42.

715   Arieti, Silvano. "Affective Disorders: Manic-Depressive Psychosis and Psychotic Depression. Manifests Symptomatology, Psycho-Dynamics, Sociological Factors, and Psychotherapy." In ADULT CLINICAL PSYCHIATRY, edited by Silvano Arieti and Eugene Brody, chapter 21. American Handbook of Psychiatry, 2d ed., vol. 3. New York: Basic Books, 1974.

Contains historical notes and discussion of classical depression, manic attacks, manic varieties, and psychotic depression. Describes psychodynamic mechanisms in adulthood and childhood and therapy choice. Eighty-one references.

716   Fieve, Ronald R. "New Developments in Manic-Depressive Illness." In NEW DIMENSIONS IN PSYCHIATRY: A WORLD VIEW, edited by Silvano Arieti and G. Chrzonowski, chapter 1. New York: John Wiley and Sons, 1975.

717   Geatzel, J. "Psychopathological Aspects of Cyclothymic Depressive Courses." PSYCHIATRICA CLINICA 7, no. 2 (1974): 120-28.

718   Gordon, Malcolm W., and Van der Velde, Christian D. "Metabolic Adaptation in the Manic-Depressive." NATURE 247, no. 5437 (1974): 160-62.

Reports on a study testing the ability of five manic-depressives to reorganize their hormonal balance during fasting, which in a healthy person provokes a diabetic-like response to a glucose load. Twenty-three references.

719   Harp, Peter. "Etiological Factors in Manic-Depressive Psychoses." ARCHIVES OF GENERAL PSYCHIATRY 33, no. 10 (1976): 1187-88.

Reviews work with fifty consecutive patients with bipolar affective psychoses. Reports that this syndrome appeared etiologically heterogeneous, in that some patients had an early onset and prominent genetic determinance, while in others without apparent hereditary predisposition, the illness started later and showed EEG evidence of cerebral dysfunction.

720 Himmelhoch, Jonathan M.; Mulla, Dawood; Neil, John F.; Detre, Thomas P.; and Kupfer, David J. "Incidence and Significance of Mixed Affective States in a Bipolar Population." ARCHIVES OF GENERAL PSYCHIATRY 33, no. 9 (1976): 1062-66.

Reports that the simultaneous existence of manic and depressive symptoms in a manic-depressive patient was first described by Kraepelin. Presents an investigation showing a mixed state to be the initial episode in 31 percent of eighty-four manic-depressive outpatients. Thirty-four references.

721 Morrison, James R. "The Family Histories of Manic-Depressive Patients with and without Alcoholism." JOURNAL OF NERVOUS AND MENTAL DISEASE 160, no. 3 (1975): 227-29.

Reports that an investigation of family histories of thirty-eight bipolar affective disorder patients with and without an additional diagnosis of alcoholism showed that affective disorder was seen with equal frequency in both populations of relatives. Indicates that alcoholism was significantly more prevalent in the relatives of the alcoholic probands than in the relatives of those who did not have alcoholism.

722 Platman, S.R., and Fieve, Ronald R. "Sleep in Depression and Mania." BRITISH JOURNAL OF PSYCHIATRY 116, no. 531 (1970): 218-20.

Compares depressive and hypomanic or manic patients. Reports that all measures except one (awake in bed, not attempting to sleep) significantly differentiated sleep patterns in depression and mania.

723 Winokur, George, and Tsuang, Ming. "The Iowa 500: Suicide in Mania, Depression, and Schizophrenia." AMERICAN JOURNAL OF PSYCHIATRY 132, no. 6 (1975): 650-51.

Reports that long-term (thirty to forty year) follow-up data for 76 manic patients, 182 depressives, 170 schizophrenics, and 109 controls showed that 10 percent of the schizophrenics, 8.5 percent of the manics, and 10.6 percent of the depressives who were deceased had died by suicide.

Rare Psychotic Conditions

724   Arieti, Silvano, and Bemporad, Jules R. "Rare, Unclassified and Collective Psychiatric Syndromes." In ADULT CLINICAL PSYCHIATRY, edited by Silvano Arieti and Eugene Brody, chapter 31. American Handbook of Psychiatry, 2d ed., vol. 2. New York: Basic Books, 1974.

Lists symptoms for Gansel's syndrome, Capgras's syndrome, autoscopic syndrome, Cotard's syndrome, psychosis passionale of Clerombault, Munchausen's syndrome, and collective psychoses. Sixty-two references.

725   Bankier, Robert G. "Capgras' Syndrome: The Illusion of Double." CANADIAN PSYCHIATRIC ASSOCIATION JOURNAL 11, no. 5 (1966): 426-29.

Reports that patients suffering from psychotic illness having paranoid features may display the Capgras illusion, in which the patient misidentifies a close relative and believes instead that a double of the relative has been created. Reviews the literature and gives a detailed account of one unusual case recently observed.

726   Buchanan, Denton C.; Abram, Harry S.; Wells, Charles; and Teschan, Paul. "Psychosis and Pseudo Dementia Associated with Hemodialysis." INTERNATIONAL JOURNAL OF PSYCHIATRY AND MEDICINE 8, no. 1 (1977-78): 85-97.

Discusses a case in relation to dialysis dementia, which may be fatal.

727   Lazarus, Herbert R., and Hogens, Jerome H. "Prevention of Psychosis Following Open Heart Surgery." AMERICAN JOURNAL OF PSYCHIATRY 124, no. 9 (1968): 1190-95.

Reports that the high risk of postoperative psychotic reaction occurring in patients who have undergone open heart surgery has been attributed to several factors. Studies the preoperative psychological state of the patient and environment in the recovery room, to determine their influence upon the incidence of postoperative reaction of heart surgery patients.

728   Meth, Johannes M. "Exotic Psychiatric Syndromes." In ADULT CLINICAL PSYCHIATRY, edited by Silvano Arieti and Eugene Brody, chapter 32. American Handbook of Psychiatry, 2d ed., vol. 3. New York: Basic Books, 1974.

Describes somatic pathology and psychopathology of various conditions, such as Letah, Amok, Koro, Whitico Psychosis, Susto/Espanto, and Voodoo. Includes 159 references.

729 Rosenstock, Harvey A., and Vincent, Ken R. "Capgras Syndrome: A Case Report of an Adolescent and Review of the Literature." JOURNAL OF CLINICAL PSYCHIATRY 39, no. 7 (1978): 629-30.

Presents a case report of an adolescent with Capgras syndrome in the absence of organic brain syndrome. Reviews seventy-five case reports from the standpoint of differential diagnosis, especially with respect to organic brain syndrome and schizophrenia.

730 Vogel, B. Frank. "The Capgras Syndrome and Its Psychopathology." AMERICAN JOURNAL OF PSYCHIATRY 131, no. 8 (1974): 922-24.

Presents case reports that indicate that the Capgras syndrome is far less rare than has been commonly accepted.

Chapter 6

NEUROSES

As we analyze various aspects of human development, it becomes apparent that in any given situation a variety of things may go wrong. One source of difficulty is a group of behaviors that broadly comes under the heading of "mental illness," however, other difficulties have been variously grouped under other headings, such as neuroses, personality disorders, or behavior disorders. This chapter deals with those behaviors often brought together under the heading of "neuroses." Again, the classifications are not clear; different schools of psychological and psychiatric thought evolve different labels for the same behaviors, and various classification manuals and descriptions often label different behaviors with a common name. We have made some effort to group those labels and behaviors that seem, in a general sense, to reflect some communality, but again we have made no effort to define the "right" or "wrong" terms. We present those works that have proven useful in defining and describing abnormal behaviors which may broadly be classified as neurotic or related to severe anxiety reactions of an acute or chronic nature. In some instances (for example, depression), the reactions are judged to be neurotic in comparison with similar reactions thought to be psychotic, as discussed in previous chapters. In other instances (for example, phobias), they seem to be a class of behaviors which may occur with some psychotic persons or with other diagnosable conditions, but nonetheless stand out by themselves as a problem behavior. All of these are brought together under the broad rubric of neuroses and are presented in the terms chosen by the authors of the articles and books.

We group the neuroses first under the broad heading of general neuroses, which touches on the history, etiology, prevention, epidemiology, and potential treatment of the behaviors so described. Other sections of the chapter cover the phobias, hysterical symptoms and conditions, depressive neuroses, obsessive-compulsive reactions, neuroses in childhood, and a group of behaviors (touched on in chapter 4) that seem to result directly from physical illness or function as the etiological basis of physical illness. It is not entirely clear where the latter should be classified; we have chosen to classify them with the neuroses, but in a separate section titled "Psychosomatic and Somatopsychic Manifestations and Conditions." The major works on neuroses are starred and include numbers 734, 736, 740, 746, 773, 779, 790, 804, 807, 809, 822, 840, 851, 872, 879, 883, 900, and 907.

GENERAL NEUROSES

731 Angyal, Andras. NEUROSES AND TREATMENT. Rev. ed. New York: Viking Press, 1973. 328 p.

An updated version of Angyal's theory of personality (1941), specifically related to neurotic behavior and ways to treat it.

732 Blos, Peter. "The Epigenesis of the Adult Neuroses." PSYCHOAN-ALYTIC STUDY OF THE CHILD 27 (1972): 106-35.

Advances the thesis that late adolescence is the decisive period for the formation of adult neuroses. Twenty-seven references.

733 Cautela, Joseph. "A Behavior Therapy Approach to Pervasive Anxiety." BEHAVIOR RESEARCH AND THERAPY 4, no. 2 (1966): 99-109.

Discusses pervasive anxiety and presents a method for its treatment which combines reassurance, relaxation along with implicit verbal behavior, a modification of Wolpe's desensitization technique, and assertiveness training.

734 *Chang, Suk C. "Morita Therapy." AMERICAN JOURNAL OF PSY-CHOTHERAPY 28, no. 2 (1974): 208-21.

Describes Morita therapy, a psychotherapeutic technique developed in Japan that resembles meditation.

735 Clancy, John, and Noyes, Russell. "Anxiety Neurosis: A Disease for the Medical Model." PSYCHOSOMATICS 17, no. 2 (1976): 90-93.

Discusses problems of diagnosis of anxiety neurosis, making the point that much time and money is lost because of an attempt to fit the diagnosis of neurosis into a standard medical model.

736 *Ellis, Albert. HOW TO LIVE WITH A 'NEUROTIC' AT HOME AND AT WORK. Rev. ed. New York: Crown, 1975. 159 p.

Describes a program for helping and understanding neurotic individuals at home or on the job, including methods to channel criticisms of such persons and to deal with the symptoms. Ten pages of references.

737 Fellion, G.; Duflot, J.P.; and Cailleteau, Y. "Prison Environment and Psychoneurotic Disturbances." ANNALES MEDICO-PSYCHOLOG-IQUES 2, no. 1 (1972): 94-105.

Describes the noxious elements, from a psychological point of view, that are found in most prisons today.

738 Gnepp, Eric H. "Learning and Anxiety Neurosis." PSYCHOLOGY 12, no. 2 (1975): 27-31.

Applies learning theory to explain how the anticipatory response to anxiety becomes dysfunctional.

739 Goldstein, Michael J., and Palmer, James O. THE EXPERIENCE OF ANXIETY: A CASE BOOK. 2d ed. New York: Oxford University Press, 1975. 294 p.

A textbook for abnormal psychology that includes unanalyzed reports designed to increase student skill in diagnosis and treatment.

740 *Gray, Melvin. NEUROSES: A COMPREHENSIVE AND CRITICAL VIEW. New York: Van Nostrand Reinhold, 1978. 341 p.

Surveys neurotic disorders from historical, philosophical, and clinical perspectives. Clarifies terminology, introduces a practical method of organizing data for diagnostic purposes, and describes the history, classification, etiology, diagnosis, course progress, and treatment for eight types of neurotic behaviors.

741 Greden, John F. "Anxiety or Caffeinism: A Diagnostic Dilemma." AMERICAN JOURNAL OF PSYCHIATRY 131, no. 10 (1974): 1089-92.

Reports that a high intake of caffeine can produce symptoms that are indistinguishable from those of anxiety neurosis. Twenty-nine references.

742 Ibor, J.J. Lopez. "Basic Anxiety as the Core of Neurosis." ACTA PSYCHIATRICA SCANDINAVICA 41, no. 3 (1965): 329-32.

Discusses a different view of anxiety, which postulates the existence of endothymic anxiety based on a pathological state in the endothymic layer of the personality.

743 Inouye, Eiji. "Genetic Aspect of Neurosis: A Review." INTERNATIONAL JOURNAL OF MENTAL HEALTH 6, nos. 1 and 2 (1972): 176-89.

Reviews biological, particularly genetic, studies of neuroses. Seventy-one references.

744 Isenberg, Morris. "Responsibility and the Neurotic Patient." AMERICAN JOURNAL OF PSYCHOANALYSIS 34, no. 1 (1974): 43-50.

Analyzes the concept of responsibility in the context of psychoanalytic treatment of neuroses. Seventeen references.

745 Kraines, S.H. "The Neurophysiologic Basis of the Neuroses." PSYCHOSOMATICS 10, no. 5 (1969): 285-88.

Presents the neurotic symptom as resulting from the integration of an emotional component including the physiologic reaction to a stimulus and emotion-free concepts from the cerebral cortex.

746 *Kubie, Lawrence S. "The Nature of the Neurotic Process." In ADULT CLINICAL PSYCHIATRY, edited by Silvano Arieti and Eugene Brody, chapter 1. American Handbook of Psychiatry, 2d ed., vol. 3. New York: Basic Books, 1974.

Tries to spell out the complexity and range of variables that enter into all processes of psychological development, both normal and neurotic. Thirty-three references.

747 Lader, Malcolm, and Marks, Isaac M. CLINICAL ANXIETY. New York: Grune and Stratton, 1972. 202 p.

Presents summary statements of relevant research. Focuses on treatment, with strong coverage of pharmacological issues, and on other aspects of work with the neurotic.

748 Lazarus, Arnold A. "Broad-Spectrum Behavior Therapy and the Treatment of Agoraphobia." BEHAVIOR RESEARCH AND THERAPY 4, no. 2 (1966): 95-97.

Discusses a broad spectrum approach to the treatment of neurotic conditions, from a behavior therapy point of view.

749 McNeil, Elton B. NEUROSES AND PERSONALITY DISORDERS. Englewood Cliffs, N.J.: Prentice Hall, 1970. 176 p.

General textbook written from a psychoanalytic frame of reference.

750 Marks, Isaac M. "Research in Neurosis: A Selective Review I. Causes and Courses." PSYCHOLOGICAL MEDICINE 3, no. 4 (1973): 436-54.

Reviews research in neurosis, from the standpoint of genetics, phylogenesis, physiology, epidemiology, and prognosis. Includes 118 references.

751 Marks, Isaac M., and Lader, Malcolm. "Anxiety States (Anxiety Neurosis): A Review." JOURNAL OF NERVOUS AND MENTAL

DISEASE 156, no. 1 (1973): 3-18.

Defines anxiety states as a question of symptoms based on fear, the source of which is not recognized by the patient. Seventy-three references.

752 May, Rollo. THE MEANING OF ANXIETY. New York: Norton, 1977. 425 p.

Reviews the cultural, historical, biological, and physiological dimensions of every major theory of anxiety.

753 Merin, Joseph H., and Nagler, Simon H., eds. THE ETIOLOGY OF NEUROSES. Palo Alto, Calif.: Science and Behavior Books, 1966. 164 p.

754 Milman, Donald S., and Goldman, George D., eds. THE NEUROSES OF OUR TIME: ACTING OUT. Springfield, Ill.: Charles C Thomas, 1973. 365 p.

Contains twenty papers on neuroses.

755 Miner, Gary D. "The Evidence for Genetic Components in the Neurosis: A Review." ARCHIVES OF GENERAL PSYCHIATRY 29, no. 1 (1973): 111-18.

Reviews family and twin studies, and addresses the genetic components of specific types of neuroses. Fifty-six references.

756 Nemiah, John C. "Anxiety: Signal, Symptom and Syndrome." In ADULT CLINICAL PSYCHIATRY, edited by Silvano Arieti and Eugene Brody, chapter 5. American Handbook of Psychiatry, 2d ed., vol. 3. New York: Basic Books, 1974.

Discusses clinical aspects of anxiety, the nature of anxiety, differential diagnosis, and treatment. Fifty references.

757 Rickels, Karl; Downing, Robert W.; and Downing, Mildred H. "Personality Differences Between Somatically and Psychologically Oriented Neurotic Patients." JOURNAL OF NERVOUS AND MENTAL DISEASE 142, no. 1 (1966): 10-18.

Compares sixty-five primarily somatizing patients treated in a medical setting with patients predominantly of psychological orientation treated in a psychiatric setting. Finds that there were group differences even when social class variables were similar.

758 Salzman, Leon. "Modern Psychoanalytic Theory and Practice in the

Neuroses: A Review." JOURNAL OF THE AMERICAN ACADEMY OF PSYCHOANALYSIS 2, no. 3 (1974): 261-68.

Examines the current status of psychoanalysis, emphasizing those aspects of traditional psychoanalytic theory open to theoretical and practical revision.

759 Shagass, Charles. "Experimental Neuroses." In HUMAN BEHAVIOR: BIOLOGICAL, PSYCHOLOGICAL AND SOCIOLOGICAL, edited by A.M. Freedman and H.I. Kaplan, chapter 23. New York: Atheneum, 1972.

Reviews the work of Hebb, Gantt, Liddell, Masserman, Mahl, and Pavlov in studying the experimental animal neuroses and psychosomatic disorders. Thirty-five references.

760 Shapiro, David. "Dynamic and Holistic Ideas of Neurosis and Psychotherapy." PSYCHIATRY 38, no. 3 (1975): 218-26.

761 Sollod, Robert N. "A Step Wise In Vivo Approach to Extinction of Neurotic Anxiety Based on Projection." NEWSLETTER FOR RESEARCH IN MENTAL HEALTH AND BEHAVIORAL SCIENCES 16, no. 1 (1974): 14-15.

Describes a method in which a sequential process is taught so that the patient learns to discriminate between real and neurotic anxiety.

762 Sugarman, Daniel A., and Freeman, Lucy. THE SEARCH FOR SERENITY: UNDERSTANDING AND OVERCOMING ANXIETY. New York: Macmillan, 1970. 355 p.

Enumerates the essential causes of anxieties.

763 Uhlenhuth, E.H., and Paykel, Eugene S. "Symptom Configuration and Life Events." ARCHIVES OF GENERAL PSYCHIATRY 28, no. 5 (1973): 744-48.

Reports that symptom configuration, derived from symptom self-reports in a sample of 167 mainly neurotic patients, was not related to the amount or qualitative character of recent life stress. Fifteen references.

764 Welz, Werner K. "Traumatic Neurosis and Compensation Neurosis." PENNSYLVANIA PSYCHIATRIC QUARTERLY 8, no. 4 (1968-69): 3-15.

Links the etiology of traumatic and compensation neurosis, and stresses predisposition in conjunction with morbid or secondary gain as precipitating factors. Thirty-nine references.

PHOBIC BEHAVIOR

765 Agras, Stewart; Sylvester, David; and Oliviau, Donald. "The Epidemiology of Common Fears and Phobias." COMPREHENSIVE PSYCHIATRY 10, no. 2 (1969): 151-56.

Reports that the frequency of mild phobia based on the probability sample of the general population is 76.9/1000 and of severe phobia is 2.2/1000.

766 Allen, David W. THE FEAR OF LOOKING, OR SCOPOPHILIC-EXHIBITIONISTIC CONFLICTS. Charlottesville: University Press of Virginia, 1974. 134 p.

Describes the historical and clinical background of scopophilia and exhibitionism. Four pages of references.

767 Ambrosino, Salvatore V. "Phobic-Anxiety-Depersonalization Syndrome." NEW YORK STATE JOURNAL OF MEDICINE 73, no. 3 (1973): 419-25.

Describes the syndrome's three common courses: phobic avoidances, depersonalization-derealization, and a myriad of somatic complaints. Thirty-one references.

768 Farmer, R.G., and O'Gorman, J.G. "The Role of Disinhibition in the Etiology, Maintenance, and Relapse of Phobias: Implications for Behavior Therapy." AUSTRALIAN PSYCHOLOGIST 8, no. 3 (1973): 203-12.

Presents data in opposition to the generally accepted notion that it is sufficient to focus on the presenting fear in recurring phobic behaviors and to ignore nonphobic factors in treatment. Forty-six references.

769 Friedman, Paul, and Goldstein, Jacob. "Phobic Reactions." In ADULT CLINICAL PSYCHIATRY, edited by Silvano Arieti and Eugene Brody, chapter 6. American Handbook of Psychiatry, 2d ed., vol. 3. New York: Basic Books, 1974.

Describes experimental studies of acquired fears, differential considerations, pathogenesis, repression/displacement, identification/regression, symbolism in phobias, and phobias in children and adults. Includes 136 references.

770 Kirchner, John H., and Hogon, Robert A. "The Therapist Variable in the Implosion of Phobias." PSYCHOTHERAPY: THEORY, RESEARCH AND PRACTICE 3, no. 3 (1966): 102-4.

Reports that after listening to taped therapy, significantly more experimental than control patients lost their fear of rats.

771 Leifer, Ronald. "Avoidance and Mastery: An Interactional View of Phobias." JOURNAL OF INDIVIDUAL PSYCHOLOGY 22, no. 1 (1966): 80-93.

Suggests that the concept of instinctual basis of behavior unduly stresses the organism at the expense of its relationship to the environment.

772 Lewis, Aubrey. "A Note on Classifying Phobia." PSYCHOLOGICAL MEDICINE 6, no. 1 (1976): 21-22.

Presents a historical look at the confusion long present in classifying phobic states, stressing the need for greater clarity in the definition and the determination of phobias.

773 *Marks, Isaac M. LIVING WITH FEAR. New York: McGraw-Hill, 1978. 320 p.

Describes behavioral methods for managing fear and phobic reactions, and for understanding and coping with anxiety.

774 Mathews, Andrew H. "Psychophysiological Approaches to the Investigation of Desensitization and Related Procedures." PSYCHOLOGICAL BULLETIN 76, no. 2 (1971): 73-91.

Reviews and evaluates all available studies concerning desensitization which utilize measurement. Two pages of references.

775 Nichols, Keith A. "Severe Social Anxiety." BRITISH JOURNAL OF MEDICAL PSYCHOLOGY 47, no. 4 (1974): 301-6.

Discusses the classification and definition of phobic disorders, and questions whether the category of social phobias should be included in such a classification. Eighteen references.

776 Robinson, Craig, and Suinn, Richard M. "Group Desensitization of a Phobia in Massed Sessions." BEHAVIOR RESEARCH AND THERAPY 7, no. 3 (1969): 319-21.

777 Scrignar, Chester B.; Swanson, William C.; and Bloom, William A. "Use of Systematic Desensitization in the Treatment of Airplane Phobic Patients." BEHAVIOR RESEARCH AND THERAPY 11, no. 1 (1973): 129-31.

778 Watson, J.P.; Gaind, R.; and Marks, Isaac M. "Physiological Habituation to Continuous Phobic Stimulation." BEHAVIOR RESEARCH

AND THERAPY 10, no. 3 (1972): 269-79.

Reports a study of ten phobic patients monitored physiologically during treatment by prolonged exposure to their phobic situations in fantasy and in practice.

HYSTERICAL CONDITIONS—CONVERSION AND DISSOCIATIVE REACTIONS

779 *Abse, Wilfred D. "Hysterical Conversion and Dissociative Syndromes and the Hysterical Character." In ADULT CLINICAL PSYCHIATRY, edited by Silvano Arieti and Eugene Brody, chapter 8. American Handbook of Psychiatry, 2d ed., vol. 3. New York: Basic Books, 1974.

Discusses the terminology and symptoms of hysteria. Gives brief history and clinical manifestations, the nature of the symptoms, psychopathology, prognosis, management, and treatment. Includes 107 references.

780 Alarcon, Renato D. "Hysteria and Hysterical Personality: How Come One Without the Other?" PSYCHIATRIC QUARTERLY 47, no. 2 (1973): 258-75.

Presents a review of the recent literature on hysteria and hysterical personality which reveals a persistent relationship between the two concepts beyond their common semantics. Fifty-five references.

781 Alarcon, Renato D., and Covi, Lino. "Hysterical Personality and Depression: A Pathogenetic View." COMPREHENSIVE PSYCHIATRY 14, no. 2 (1973): 121-32.

Surveys the literature on hysterical personality and depression in the last two decades, to achieve some degree of agreement among conflicting approaches. Forty-five references.

782 Celani, David. "An Interpersonal Approach to Hysteria." AMERICAN JOURNAL OF PSYCHIATRY 133, no. 2 (1976): 1414-18.

Defines hysteria in terms of specific observable classes of interpersonal behaviors, and examines the impact of these behaviors on the receiver. Sixteen references.

783 Chodoff, Paul. "The Diagnosis of Hysteria: An Overview." AMERICAN JOURNAL OF PSYCHIATRY 131, no. 10 (1974): 1073-78.

Outlines three predominant conceptualizations of hysteria: that described by Briquet in 1859 and reviewed by current researchers; hysteria as a conversion symptom; and the idea of the hysterical personality. Forty-six references.

784 Chrzanowski, Gerard. "Neurasthenia and Hypochondriasis." In ADULT CLINICAL PSYCHIATRY, edited by Silvano Arieti and Eugene Brody, chapter 7. American Handbook of Psychiatry, 2d ed., vol. 3. New York: Basic Books, 1974.

Discusses neurasthenia and hypochondriasis in terms of etiological concepts, considerations for social psychiatry, management, and therapy. Forty references.

785 Davis, David, and Weiss, James. "Malingering and Associated Syndromes." In ADULT CLINICAL PSYCHIATRY, edited by Silvano Arieti and Eugene Brody, chapter 13. American Handbook of Psychiatry. 2d ed., vol. 3. New York: Basic Books, 1974.

Offers definitions and historical aspects of malingering. Discusses symptomatology, etiology, and additional syndromes such as Ganser syndrome and Munchausen's syndrome. Ninety-three references.

786 Diggle, G.E. "Severe Forms of Hysteria. A Review." ASSOCIATION OF EDUCATIONAL PSYCHOLOGISTS JOURNAL 3, no. 7 (1974): 24-26.

Suggests that hysterical illness represents a reaction, either unconscious or preconscious, which develops to afford relief from emotional conflict and results in symptoms and sometimes in specific signs.

787 Dorfman, Wilfred. "Hypochondriasis-Revisited: A Dilemma and Challenge to Medicine and Psychiatry." PSYCHOSOMATICS 16, no. 1 (1975): 14-16.

Presents a brief historical synopsis of concepts of hypochondriasis, which is today viewed as a syndrome in which both inherent and environmental factors play a part.

788 Forrest, A.D. "The Differentiation of Hysterical Personality from Hysterical Psychopathy." BRITISH JOURNAL OF MEDICAL PSYCHOLOGY 40, no. 1 (1967): 65-77.

Reports on sixty-two patients with diagnoses of hysteria or anxiety states. Twenty-five references.

789 Frank, Richard L. "Conversion and Disassociation." NEW YORK STATE JOURNAL OF MEDICINE 69, no. 13 (1969): 1872-77.

Suggests that the individual suffering from the psychoneurosis "hysteria" has a high degree of basic confidence and only transient disturbances of reality testing.

790   *Horowitz, Mardi J. HYSTERICAL PERSONALITY. New York: Jason Aronson, 1977. 441 p.

Describes formation and manifestation of the hysterical personality along with treatment strategies.

791   Howland, John S. "The Use of Hypnosis in the Treatment of a Case of Multiple Personality." JOURNAL OF NERVOUS AND MENTAL DISEASE 161, no. 2 (1975): 138–42.

792   Krashner, L.A. "Dissociative Reactions: A Historical Review and Clinical Study." ACTA PSYCHIATRICA SCANDINAVICA 49, no. 6 (1973): 694–711.

Reviews writings on dissociative reactions, to illustrate the diversity of clinical data and theory on the subject. Twenty-five references.

793   Lader, Malcolm. "The Psychophysiology of Hysterics." JOURNAL OF PSYCHOSOMATIC RESEARCH 17, no. 4 (1973): 265–69.

Reviews the arousal mechanisms of conversion hysterics, and suggests that acute hysterics are under-aroused, whereas chronic patients are over-aroused. Twenty-two references.

794   Lewis, William C. "Hysteria: The Consultant's Dilemma: 20th Century Demonology, Pejorative Epithet, or Useful Diagnosis?" ARCHIVES OF GENERAL PSYCHIATRY 30, no. 2 (1974): 145–51.

Reports that consultant psychiatrists are often asked to evaluate patients on the dimension of "hysteria," while the term continues to suffer erosion through recent changes in definition. Indicates that labeling is a dangerous as well as useful procedure, and that recently acquired information suggests that changes in diagnostic criteria are necessary to promote constructive use of the term. Thirty-two references.

795   Luisada, Paul V.; Peele, Roger; and Patard, Elizabeth A. "The Hysterical Personality in Men." AMERICAN JOURNAL OF PSYCHIATRY 131, no. 5 (1974): 518–22.

Forty-nine references.

796   Mayon, Richard. "The Social Setting of Hysteria." BRITISH JOURNAL OF PSYCHIATRY 127, no. 4 (1975): 466–69.

Contends that previous reviews of hysteria have emphasized the most severe and disabling forms and ignored the evidence from a variety of sources. Twenty-five references.

797   Micklem, Niel. "On Hysteria: The Mythical Syndrome." SPRING, 1974, pp. 147-65.

Discusses various aspects of hysteria as it has been regarded throughout the centuries from the earliest mythology, when Dionysus was thought to be the archetype of hysteria, through the feasts called "the hysteria" honoring the mother-goddess, to present times.

798   Nicol, Charles F. "Masks of Hysteria: Medical and Neurologic." NEW YORK STATE JOURNAL OF MEDICINE 69, no. 13 (1969): 1883-87.

Elaborates ways in which hysterical symptoms can be distinguished from neurological ones.

799   Powers, Henry P. "Psychotherapy for Hysterical Individuals." SOCIAL CASEWORK 53, no. 7 (1972): 435-40.

Describes therapeutic techniques, such as psychoanalysis, transactional analysis, ego psychology, crisis intervention, social casework, and systems theory, for women with the diagnosis of hysterical personality.

800   Scharfman, Melvin A. "Psychotherapeutic Approaches." NEW YORK STATE JOURNAL OF MEDICINE 69, no. 13 (1969): 1887-92.

Describes two main categories of psychotherapeutic approaches to the treatment of hysteria: the symptom-oriented approach and the approach which treats the symptom as part of the whole personality.

801   Schiffer, Irvine. "Psychotherapy with Patients with Hysterical Disorders." In THE THEORY AND PRACTICE OF PSYCHOTHERAPY WITH SPECIFIC DISORDERS, edited by Max Hammer, chapter 6. Springfield, Ill.: Charles C Thomas, 1972.

Presents a detailed discussion of historical developments in the treatment of hysterical patients. Seventeen references.

802   Sirois, Francois. "Epidemic Hysteria." ACTA PSYCHIATRICA SCANDINAVICA, Supplement 252 (1974): 44 p.

Presents a historical survey and a comprehensive review of the world literature on epidemic hysteria. Examines some variables relevant to the spreading of psychopathology within the group. Compares epidemic hysteria with other forms of socially shared psychopathology. Includes 204 references.

803 Small, S. Mouchly. "Hysteria: Concepts of Hysteria: History and Re-evaluation." NEW YORK STATE JOURNAL OF MEDICINE 69, no. 13 (1969): 1866-72.

> Briefly traces the reporting of hysteria from 1900 B.C. to the twentieth century. Thirty-five references.

804 *Templer, Donald I., and Lester, David. "Conversion Disorders: A Review of Research Findings." COMPREHENSIVE PSYCHIATRY 15, no. 4 (1974): 285-94.

> Reviews data on the validity of conversion disorder diagnoses, prevalence of conversion disorders, conversion disorders as extraverted neuroses, conversion disorders and antisocial behavior, genetic factors, families of persons with conversion disorders, execessive surgery and hospitalization, birth order, personality characteristics, follow-up studies and prognoses, conversion disorders in children, and group conversion reactions. Two pages of references.

805 Woolsey, Robert M. "Hysteria: 1875 to 1975." DISEASES OF THE NERVOUS SYSTEM 37, no. 7 (1976): 379-86.

> Discusses hysteria as an ancient disorder whose clinical symptoms have changed through the years and whose modern definition and interpretation has been substantially influenced by the works of Charcot and Freud. Fifty-seven references.

DEPRESSION

Depression is a highly generalized and widely used category. We discussed some types of depression in the chapters on general psychoses and organic psychoses, and here again in the chapter on neuroses. There is genuine professional disagreement on what kinds of symptoms should be labeled as "depression." Also, the depressive symptoms upon which most professionals are able to agree vary in intensity and in their effect on the overall personality and behavior of the individual. One can talk about depression of a psychotic nature, indicating that the individual has become so depressed that loss of functional contact with the reality of the environment occurs. One may also speak of depression which, while it takes on the same elements as other psychotic depressions, seems to have a direct relationship to an organic process. In this chapter, we talk about those depressions which do not seem to separate individuals from the reality of the environment, but nonetheless so overwhelm them that they cannot function appropriately. Thus, they exhibit a variety of "depressed" behavioral characteristics, though they do function within a minimal level of social tolerance. This type of depression comes under the heading of "general neuroses," and the items in this section refer more specifically to this type of depression, recognizing that there is a great amount of overlap and that the diagnosis is not always clearcut.

806   Akeskal, Hagop S., and McKinney, William T. "Overview of Recent Research in Depression: Integration of Ten Conceptual Models into a Comprehensive Clinical Frame." ARCHIVES OF GENERAL PSYCHIATRY 32, no. 3 (1975): 285-305.

Reports that disciplinary fragmentation and nosological and semantic controversies have obscured the advances made in the area of depressive disorders during the past decade. Authors review several theoretical models and present a new theoretical model of depression. Includes 267 references.

807   *Anthony, E. James, and Benedek, Therese, eds. DEPRESSION AND HUMAN EXISTENCE. Boston: Little, Brown, 1975. 568 p.

Examines in detail various aspects of depression, from a clinical frame of reference.

808   Beck, Aaron T. DEPRESSION: CAUSES AND TREATMENT. Philadelphia: University of Pennsylvania Press, 1973. 147 p.

Text for graduate students, clinicians, and researchers on the cognitive organization underlying self-esteem and depression.

809   _____. "Depressive Neurosis." In ADULT CLINICAL PSYCHIATRY, edited by Silvano Arieti and Eugene Brody, chapter 4. American Handbook of Psychiatry, 2d ed., vol. 3. New York: Basic Books, 1974.

Presents the clinical picture, classification of affective forces, cause and prognosis, measurement, sociological and demographic aspects, and biological approaches to depression. Includes 229 references.

810   Becker, Joseph. DEPRESSION: THEORY AND RESEARCH. New York: Halsted, 1974. 239 p.

Reviews theory and empirically oriented studies of depression.

811   Blinder, Martin G. "Differential Diagnosis and Treatment of Depressive Disorders." JOURNAL OF THE AMERICAN MEDICAL ASSOCIATION 195, no. 1 (1966): 8-12.

Reports that depression may be recognized as one of three syndromes whose cardinal feature may be: physiological retardation, prolonged unresolved tension, a schizoid personality disorder overlayed with depressive episodes, or an acute organic lesion.

812   _____. "The Pragmatic Classification of Depression." AMERICAN JOURNAL OF PSYCHIATRY 123, no. 3 (1966): 259-69.

813 Braceland, Francis J., and Copparell, Homer U. "Symposium: Psychiatry in General Practice." NEW YORK STATE JOURNAL OF MEDICINE 72, no. 14 (1972): 1825-33.

Reports that depression is probably the diagnosis most frequently made in psychiatric consultations. Presents a history of the concept, and discusses etiology, characteristics of the depressive personality, differentiation from grief, risks of suicide, and prognosis.

814 Coble, Patrick; Foster, Gordon; and Kupfer, David J. "Electroencephalographic Sleep Diagnoses of Primary Depression." ARCHIVES OF GENERAL PSYCHIATRY 33, no. 9 (1976): 1124-27.

815 Fabrega, Horacio. "Problems Implicit in the Cultural and Social Study of Depression." PSYCHOSOMATIC MEDICINE 36, no. 5 (1974): 377-98.

Discusses depression, to illustrate the relationship between psychiatric disease and social symptoms. Forty-six references.

816 Fann, William E.; Karacan, Ismet; Pokorny, Alex D.; and Williams, Robert L., eds. PHENOMENOLOGY AND TREATMENT OF DEPRESSION. New York: Spectrum Publications, 1977. 350 p.

Discusses the etiology, diagnosis, and treatment of clinical depression.

817 Flach, F.F., and Draghi, S.C. THE NATURE AND TREATMENT OF DEPRESSION. New York: John Wiley and Sons, 1975. 422 p.

Contains a wide range of current data and viewpoints on the etiology and operant processes of depression, including psychodynamics and biological theories.

818 Friedman, Raymond J., and Katz, Martin M., eds. THE PSYCHOLOGY OF DEPRESSION: CONTEMPORARY THEORY AND RESEARCH. Washington, D.C.: Winston, 1974. 317 p.

Contains three theoretical papers representing cognitive, behavioral, and psychodynamic models.

819 Gallant, Donald M., and Simpson, George M., ed. DEPRESSION: BEHAVIORAL, BIOCHEMICAL, DIAGNOSTIC AND TREATMENT CONCEPTS. New York: Spectrum Publications, 1976. 351 p.

Stresses the biological and pharmacological aspects of depression, and includes a chapter on childhood depression.

820 Jacobsen, Edith. DEPRESSION: COMPARATIVE STUDIES OF NORMAL, NEUROTIC AND PSYCHOTIC CONDITIONS. New York:

International Universities Press, 1971. 353 p.

Presents clinical descriptions of depression in neurotic, borderline, and ambulatory psychotic clients, as seen through psychoanalytic treatment.

821   Klein, Donald F. "Endogenomorphic Depression." ARCHIVES OF GENERAL PSYCHIATRY 31, no. 4 (1974): 447-54.

Reviews conflicts in delineating the phenomenon of depression, with an emphasis on the central role of the symptomatic pattern of nonprecipitated depression.

822   *Levitt, Eugene E., and Lubin, Bernard, eds. DEPRESSION: CONCEPTS, CONTROVERSIES AND SOME NEW FACTS. New York: Springer, 1975. 171 p.

Reviews the literature on depression, and reports findings and conclusions of a national survey conducted to examine the frequency and distribution of depressive affect and depressive illness in the United States. Twenty-four pages of references.

823   Linsky, Arnold S. "Community Structure and Depressive Disorders." SOCIAL PROBLEMS 17, no. 1 (1969): 120-31.

Notes that the distribution of depressives is better explained by the ratio of "opportunities" to "independently measured aspirations" than it is by the opportunity level alone.

824   Mendels, Joseph. CONCEPTS OF DEPRESSION. New York: John Wiley and Sons, 1970. 124 p.

Covers clinical descriptions, case studies, history, and theory.

825   _____, ed. THE PSYCHOBIOLOGY OF DEPRESSION. New York: Spectrum Publications, 1975. 175 p.

Emphasizes chemical, genetic, and endocrine factors and clinical issues.

826   Moss, Gene R., and Boken, John H. "Depression as a Model for Behavioral Analysis." COMPREHENSIVE PSYCHIATRY 13, no. 6 (1972): 581-90.

Offers a classification based on behavioral analysis. Thirty references.

827   Raskin, Allen; Crook, Thomas H.; and Herman, Kenneth D. "Psychiatric History and Symptom Differences in Black and White Depressed Patients." JOURNAL OF CONSULTING AND CLINICAL PSYCHOLOGY 43, no. 1 (1975): 73-80.

828   Roth, Martin, and Kerr, T.A. "Diagnosis of the Reactive Depressive
       Illnesses." In MODERN TRENDS IN PSYCHOLOGICAL MEDICINE:
       II, edited by J.H. Price, chapter 7. New York: Appleton-Century-
       Crofts, 1970.

       Describes the characteristics of and relationship between neu-
       rotic and endogenous depression. Includes 115 references.

829   Schildkraut, Joseph J. "Neuropsychopharmacology and the Affective
       Disorders: I." NEW ENGLAND JOURNAL OF MEDICINE 281, no.
       4 (1969): 197-201.

       Discusses variation and classification of affective disorders.
       Describes three groups of drugs commonly used in the treat-
       ment of depression: psychomotor stimulants, monamine oxi-
       dase inhibitors, and tricyclic antidepressants.

830   Schuyler, Dean. THE DEPRESSIVE SPECTRUM. New York: Jason
       Aronson, 1974. 174 p.

831   Scott, John Paul, and Senay, Edward C., eds. SEPARATION AND
       DEPRESSION: CLINICAL AND RESEARCH ASPECTS. American Asso-
       ciation for the Advancement of Science, no. 94. Washington, D.C.:
       1973. 256 p.

       Contains twelve papers from behavioral biology, animal be-
       havior studies, clinical psychopharmacology, psychoanalysis,
       and social systems research on the relationship between sep-
       aration and depression.

832   Seligman, Martin E. HELPLESSNESS: IN DEPRESSION, DEVELOP-
       MENT AND DEATH. San Francisco: W.H. Freeman, 1975. 250 p.

       Reviews animal research and other relevant material, to pre-
       sent evidence that anxiety and depression grow out of a feel-
       ing of helplessness and that this feeling must be learned.
       Suggests that when depressed individuals are guided through
       situations in which they learn to exert greater control on
       their environments, their depression dissipates. Thirty pages
       of references.

833   Sewado, Steven K., ed. THE DEPRESSIVE DISORDERS: SPECIAL
       REPORT: 1973. Department of Health, Education and Welfare, no.
       (HSM) 73-9157. Washington, D.C.: Government Printing Office,
       1973. 57 p.

       Presents a synthesis of current research findings on the cause
       and treatment of depressive disorders. Includes topics such
       as transcultural studies, diagnostic studies, epidemiological
       research, psychobiological factors, and various theories.
       One hundred references.

834 Toolan, James M. "Depression and Suicide." In CHILD AND ADO-
LESCENT PSYCHIATRY, SOCIO-CULTURAL AND COMMUNITY PSY-
CHIATRY, 2d ed., edited by Gerald Caplan, chapter 20. American
Handbook of Psychiatry, vol. 2. New York: Basic Books, 1974.

Presents a comprehensive review of literature, and reveals
the controversy as to whether children under twelve years
become depressed. Offers evidence indicating that they do,
but the clinical picture varies considerably from adult depressives. Discusses children and adolescents and depression,
diagnosis, therapy, and suicide. Forty-eight references.

835 Usdin, Gene, ed. DEPRESSION: CLINICAL, BIOLOGICAL AND
PSYCHOLOGICAL PERSPECTIVES. New York: Brunner/Mazel, 1976.
346 p.

Emphasizes the value of multiple systems, and offers an intensive introduction to the psychopharmacology of depression
in the context of psychodynamic and social reality.

836 Weissman, Myrna M., and Paykel, Eugene S. THE DEPRESSED
WOMAN: A STUDY OF SOCIAL RELATIONSHIPS. Chicago: University of Chicago Press, 1974. 296 p.

Describes a study of the behavior of forty depressed women
over twenty months, examining them during acute depression,
recovery, and, in some cases, relapse.

837 Wright, Shelle, and McDonald, Claudia. "Review of Behavioral
Treatment of Depression." PSYCHOLOGICAL REPORTS 34, no. 3,
part 2 (1974): 1335-41.

Reviews behavioral treatments of depression, and categorizes
them according to Wolpe's description of three types of circumstances in which pathologic reactive depression is observed. Twenty-three references.

OBSESSIVE-COMPULSIVE BEHAVIOR

838 Barnett, Joseph. "On Cognitive Disorders in the Obsessional."
CONTEMPORARY PSYCHOANALYSIS 2, no. 2 (1966): 122-34.

839 Beech, H.R., ed. OBSESSIONAL STATES. London: Methuen, 1974.
352 p.

840 *Carr, Anthony F. "Compulsive Neurosis: A Review of the Literature." PSYCHOLOGICAL BULLETIN 81, no. 5 (1974): 311-18.

Examines the literature relating to obsessions and compulsions, from the early identification of the syndrome to contemporary theorizing. Fifty-three references.

841   Lisse, Stanley. "Anxiety: Its Relationship to the Development of Obsessive-Compulsive Disorders." AMERICAN JOURNAL OF PSYCHOTHERAPY 26, no. 3 (1972): 330-37.

Discusses the patterns of anxiety development and amelioration observed over a period of years. Illustrates these with a case history.

842   Makhlouf-Norris, Fawzeya, and Norris, Hugh. "The Obsessive Compulsive Syndrome as a Neurotic Device for the Reduction of Self Uncertainty." BRITISH JOURNAL OF PSYCHIATRY 122, no. 568 (1973): 277-88.

Compares personal construct systems for eleven obsessional neurotic and matched control individuals.

843   Rachman, S. "Obsessional Ruminations." BEHAVIOR RESEARCH AND THERAPY 9, no. 3 (1971): 229-35.

Suggests that obsessional ruminations may be viewed as noxious stimuli to which patients fail to habituate.

844   Rado, Sandor, and Monroe, Russell R. "Obsessive Behavior." In ADULT CLINICAL PSYCHIATRY, edited by Silvano Arieti and Eugene Brody, chapter 9. American Handbook of Psychiatry, 2d ed., vol. 3. New York: Basic Books, 1974.

Includes two sections on obsessive behavior. Part A deals with obsessive-compulsive neuroses, their pathology, chemical picture, and dynamics. Seventeen references. Part B discusses the integration of psychoanalytic, phenomenological, and other approaches. Thirty-one references.

845   Scarbrough, H.E. "The Nature of the Dialogue with the Obsessive Compulsive." PSYCHOTHERAPY: THEORY, RESEARCH AND PRACTICE 3, no. 1 (1966): 33-35.

Suggests that therapists work better with the obsessive-compulsive person when they are sensitive to the patient's idiosyncratic methods of communicating.

846   Solyom, Leslie. "A Case of Obsessive Neurosis Treated by Aversion Relief." CANADIAN PSYCHIATRIC ASSOCIATION JOURNAL 14, no. 6 (1969): 623-26.

Describes the technique of reciprocal inhibition by aversion relief.

847　Templer, Donald I. "The Obsessive-Compulsive Neurosis: Review of Research Findings." COMPREHENSIVE PSYCHIATRY 13, no. 4 (1972): 375-83.

Reviews research from the American and British literature. Forty references.

848　Walls, L.L.; Supinski, C.R.; Cotton, W.K.; and McFadden, J.W. "Compulsive Water Drinking: A Review with Report of an Additional Case." JOURNAL OF FAMILY PRACTICE 5, no. 4 (1977): 531-33.

NEUROSES OF CHILDHOOD

Because the whole area of childhood neurosis is still open to debate, we have combined all of the items which refer to various types of neurotic conditions in children into one general section. Thus, there is no attempt to divide the hysterias or the depressive disorders or any of the other specific types of disorders, as we have done with adult neuroses. Again, rather than try to decide the type of definition or behavior that should be so labeled, we have taken the author's word in the various works presented, and we cite them because we feel that they contribute to the understanding of disorders of childhood without requiring any real statement concerning the label. One exception is that we have set off a group of items on "school phobia" as a specific childhood condition of some importance.

849　Abrahams, M.J., and Mitlock, F.A. "Childhood Experience and Depression." BRITISH JOURNAL OF PSYCHIATRY 115, no. 525 (1969): 883-88.

Reports research on 152 depressed patients matched with controls. Found no marked difference in the number that lost one or both parents in childhood. Notes that unhappy childhoods were common in the depressed patients, particularly those diagnosed as mixed and neurotic depressives.

850　Adams, Paul L. OBSESSIVE CHILDREN: A SOCIOPSYCHIATRIC STUDY. New York: Brunner/Mazel, 1973. 289 p.

Presents forty-nine case histories of obsessive and compulsive behaviors in children. Sixteen pages of references.

851　*Annell, Anna-Lisa, ed. DEPRESSIVE STATE IN CHILDHOOD AND ADOLESCENCE. New York: Halsted, 1972. 541 p.

Papers from the fourth congress of the Union of Pedo-Psychiatrists, held in Stockholm, Sweden, in 1971.

852　Anthony, E. James. "Neuroses of Children." In THE CHILD: HIS

PSYCHOLOGICAL AND CULTURAL DEVELOPMENT: II. THE MA-
JOR PSYCHOLOGICAL DISORDERS AND THEIR TREATMENT, edited
by A.M. Freedman and H.I. Kaplan, chapter 5. New York: Atheneum, 1972.

Cites Freud's findings that an authentic psychoneurotic incident in childhood is almost invariably found in adult neurotic
patients. Suggests that a lack of specificity in defining
childhood neuroses is the cause of their infrequent diagnosis.
Twenty-nine references.

853 Anthony, E. James, and Gilpin, D.C., eds. THREE CLINICAL
PHASES OF CHILDHOOD. New York: Spectrum Publications, 1976.
255 p.

Presents a series of interdisciplinary seminars about three types
of children: oppositional children (those who do not do what
they are supposed to do); inhibited children (slow to warm
up, nonengaging, inhibited, and similar to adult neurotics);
and depressive children.

854 Bowlby, John. ATTACHMENT AND LOSS. Vol. 1: ATTACHMENT.
New York: Basic Books, 1969. 428 p.

Reviews child development research, evolutionary theory,
principles and research of ethology and other studies of animal behavior and control, systems theory, and theoretical
and classic writings of psychoanalysts and psychiatrists.

855 _____. ATTACHMENT AND LOSS. Vol. 2: SEPARATION: ANX-
IETY AND ANGER. New York: Basic Books, 1973. 444 p.

856 Chess, Stella. "Marked Anxiety in Children." AMERICAN JOUR-
NAL OF PSYCHOTHERAPY 27, no. 3 (1973): 390-95.

Discusses the etiology and treatment of severe anxiety in
children.

857 Clarizio, Harvey. "Stability of Deviant Behavior Through Time."
MENTAL HYGIENE 52, no. 2 (1968): 288-93.

Reviews the literature and concludes that in the present state
of knowledge there is at best only mild or moderate evidence
to support the notion that disturbed children turn into disturbed adults.

858 Cytryn, Leon; McKnew, Donald H., Jr.; and Levy, Edeoiu Z. "Proposed Classification of Childhood Depression." AMERICAN JOURNAL
OF PSYCHIATRY 129, no. 21 (1972): 149-55.

Classifies neurotic depressive reactions in childhood in three categories: masked depression; acute depression; and chronic depression. Eleven references.

859 Dale, B.T. "Preventing Childhood Emotional Distrubance." CAN-ADA'S MENTAL HEALTH 17, no. 3-4 (1969): 28.

Proposes a program for early detection of emotional disturb-ance, in which a multidisciplinary advisory board interviews mothers of five-year-old children about their children's adjust-ment and requires teachers to complete a questionnaire on each child six months after the school term begins.

860 Delgado, Rafael A., and Mannino, Fortune V. "Some Observations in Trichotillomania in Children." JOURNAL OF THE AMERICAN ACADEMY OF CHILD PSYCHIATRY 8, no. 2 (1969): 229-46.

Discusses trichotillomania, defined as "the compulsive pulling of a person's own hair from any part of the body over a per-iod of time so that actual loss of hair is obvious." Fifteen references. (See also item no. 873.)

861 Egan, Merritt H., and Robinson, Ora L. "Home Treatment of Severely Disturbed Children and Families." AMERICAN JOURNAL OF OR-THOPSYCHIATRY 36, no. 4 (1966): 730-35.

862 Fahl, Mary A. "Emotionally Distrubed Children. Effects of Cooper-ative Competitive Activity on Peer Interaction." AMERICAN JOUR-NAL OF OCCUPATIONAL THERAPY 24, no. 1 (1970): 31-33.

Empirically demonstrates that cooperative activities are more conducive to peer interaction than are competitive activities.

863 Friedman, Ronald J., and Doyal, Grey T. "Depression in Children: Some Observations for the School Psychologist." PSYCHOLOGY IN THE SCHOOL 11, no. 10 (1974): 19-23.

Presents case material and treatment modalities.

864 Gardner, Lytt I. "Deprivation Dwarfism." SCIENTIFIC AMERICAN 227, no. 1 (1972): 76-82.

Reports that the reaction of some children to an adverse emo-tional environment is a reduction in growth rate. Addresses psychosocial and physiological interactions.

865 Graham, Phillip. "Depression in Pre-Pubertal Children." DEVELOP-MENTAL MEDICINE IN CHILD NEUROLOGY 16, no. 3 (1974): 340-49.

Views depression in childhood as a reaction to environmental stress rather than a disease or illness.

866   Halpern, Werner I.; Hammond, Judith; and Cohen, Rhonda. "A Therapeutic Approach to Speech Phobia: Elective Mutism Re-examined." JOURNAL OF THE AMERICAN ACADEMY OF CHILD PSYCHIATRY 10, no. 1 (1971): 94–107.

Reports on partial speech avoidance in young children, known as elective mutism, in which they will not speak in front of anyone but a select few, for example, parents and siblings. Thirty-two references.

867   Halpern, Werner I., and Kissel, Stanley. HUMAN RESOURCES FOR TROUBLED CHILDREN. New York: John Wiley and Sons, 1976. 263 p.

Discusses a wide range of resources and treatment for child therapy, including environmental change, parent education, family and group counseling, behavior modification, and pharmacotherapy.

868   Laybourne, Paul C., and Churchill, Stephen W. "Symptom Discouragement in Treating Hysterical Reactions of Childhood." INTERNATIONAL JOURNAL OF CHILD PSYCHOTHERAPY 1, no. 3 (1972): 111–23.

Considers that conversion reactions in children, contrary to classic formulations, are often learned defenses against anxiety-producing situations. Twenty-one references.

869   Lester, Eva P. "Symbol and Symptom in Childhood." CANADIAN PSYCHIATRIC ASSOCIATION JOURNAL 18, no. 5 (1973): 421–26.

Outlines the sequence in the development of anxiety, conflict, symbolic behavior, and neurotic symptoms in children. Nineteen references.

870   Lo, W.H. "Aetiological Factors in Childhood Neurosis." BRITISH JOURNAL OF PSYCHIATRY 115, no. 525 (1969): 889–94.

Compares forty-nine neurotic children with controls, to identify a number of significant causes of neurosis.

871   Looff, David H. "Psychophysiologic and Conversion Reactions in Children." JOURNAL OF THE AMERICAN ACADEMY OF CHILD PSYCHIATRY 9, no. 2 (1970): 318–31.

Reports information on 100 children "selected for psychiatric consultation by their hospital attending physicians," who felt that emotional factors were prominent in the children's problems.

872   *Malmquist, Carl P. "Depression in Childhood and Adolescence."
       NEW ENGLAND JOURNAL OF MEDICINE 284 (April 1971): 887-
       93, 933-61.

       Discusses the nature and description of childhood and adoles-
       cent depressions, and reports epidemiological studies. Three
       pages of references.

873   Mannino, Fortune V., and Delgado, Rafael A. "Trichotillomania in
       Children: A Review." AMERICAN JOURNAL OF PSYCHIATRY 120,
       no. 4 (1969): 505-11.

       Suggests that the disease, although not a common occurrence,
       appears more frequently in girls than in boys and cuts across
       all ages and a wide range of nosological categories. Thirty-
       three references (see also item no. 860.)

874   Marita, K. "Rarity of Depression in Childhood." ACTA PAEDO-
       PSYCHIATRICA 40, no. 1 (1973): 37-41.

       Criticizes the use of adult psychiatric criteria for the diag-
       nosis of childhood psychiatric conditions, and notes that
       childhood depression is rare. Discusses the psychosomatic
       nature of depressive mood shifts in children.

875   Poznanski, Elva, and Zrull, Joel P. "Childhood Depression: Clini-
       cal Characteristics of Overly Depressed Children." ARCHIVES OF
       GENERAL PSYCHIATRY 23, no. 1 (1970): 8-15.

876   Rada, Richard T.; Krill, Alex E.; Meyer, George G.; and Armstrong,
       Dorothy. "Visual Conversion Reaction in Children: II. Follow-Up."
       PSYCHOSOMATICS 14, no. 5 (1973): 271-76.

       Presents case information on twenty patients.

877   Ritvo, Samuel. "Current Status of the Concept of Infantile Neurosis:
       Implications for Diagnosis and Technique." PSYCHOANALYTIC STUDY
       OF THE CHILD 29 (1974): 159-81.

       Discusses infantile neurosis as the inner structure development,
       with or without manifest symptoms that form the basis of a
       later neurosis. Twenty-eight references.

878   Rock, Nicholas L. "Conversion Reactions in Childhood: A Clinical
       Study of Childhood Neuroses." JOURNAL OF THE AMERICAN ACAD-
       EMY OF CHILD PSYCHIATRY 10, no. 1 (1971): 65-93.

Suggests that conversion reactions in children are more frequent than the literature would lead us to believe. Twenty-eight references.

879 *Schulterbrandt, Joy G., and Raskin, Allen, eds. DEPRESSION IN CHILDHOOD: DIAGNOSIS, TREATMENT AND CONCEPTUAL MODELS. New York: Raven Press, 1977. 176 p.

Reports an National Institute on Mental Health conference on childhood depression. Contains six edited papers, responses to papers, and overviews of the literature.

NEUROSES OF CHILDHOOD—SCHOOL PHOBIA

880 Berecz, John M. "Phobias of Childhood: Etiology and Treatment." PSYCHOLOGICAL BULLETIN 70, no. 6 (1968): 694–720.

Reviews data from 1927 through 1967. Eight pages of references.

881 Berg, Ian; Nichols, Keith; and Pritchard, Colin. "School Phobia: Its Classification and Relationship to Dependency." JOURNAL OF CHILD PSYCHOLOGY AND PSYCHIATRY AND ALLIED DISCIPLINES 10, no. 2 (1969): 123–41.

Studies twenty-nine school phobic children in their early teens in a psychiatric unit. Reports that the diagnosis of school phobia was made when there was a severe difficulty in attending school, severe emotional upset at the prospect of having to go to school, staying home during school hours with parental knowledge, and the absence of significant antisocial disorder. Twenty references.

882 Gardner, George E., and Sperry, Bessie M. "School Problems--Learning Disabilities and School Phobia." In CHILD AND ADOLESCENT PSYCHIATRY, SOCIO-CULTURAL AND COMMUNITY PSYCHIATRY, 2d ed., edited by Gerald Caplan, chapter 7. American Handbook of Psychiatry, vol. 2. New York: Basic Books, 1974.

Deals with childhood school difficulties in which an organic factor does not appear to be evident. Forty-one references.

883 *Gordon, D.A., and Young, R.D. "School Phobia: A Discussion of Etiology, Treatment and Evaluation." PSYCHOLOGICAL REPORTS 39 (December 1976): 783–804.

Reviews the literature dealing with childhood school phobia. Seventy references.

884 Hersen, Michel. "The Behavioral Treatment of School Phobia."
JOURNAL OF NERVOUS AND MENTAL DISEASE 153, no. 2 (1971):
90-107.

Presents clinical evidence in support of the application of
behavioral principles to the treatment of school phobia.
Thirty-three references.

885 Kelly, Eugene W. "School Phobia: A Review of Theory and Treatment." PSYCHOLOGY IN THE SCHOOLS 10, no. 1 (1973): 33-
42.

Reviews theoretical conceptions of school phobia and their
influence on treatment. Discusses causal explanations, dynamics, symptoms, and other correlates of school phobia.
Forty-five references.

886 Poznanski, Elva Orlow. "Children with Excessive Fears." AMERICAN
JOURNAL OF ORTHOPSYCHIATRY 43, no. 3 (1973): 428-38.

Compares a sample of twenty-eight children (under age twelve)
with excessive fears with a control group from the same outpatient psychiatric population. Nineteen references.

887 Shapiro, Theodore, and Jegede, R. Olukayode. "School Phobia: A
Babel of Tongues." JOURNAL OF AUTISM AND CHILDHOOD SCHIZ-
OPHRENIA 3, no. 2 (1973): 168-86.

Reviews the literature on school avoidance, a new conception
of school phobia, and presents a symptom analysis. Fifty-
nine references.

888 Tyrer, Peter, and Tyrer, Stephen. "School Refusal, Truancy, and
Adult Neurotic Illness." PSYCHOLOGICAL MEDICINE 4, no. 4
(1974): 416-21.

Reports interviews with 240 adult psychiatric patients about
problems of school attendance during childhood. Twenty-two
references.

PSYCHOSOMATIC AND SOMATOPSYCHIC MANIFESTATIONS AND CONDITIONS

889 Ananth, J. Psychopharmacology and Psychosomatic Illness." PSY-
CHOSOMATICS 16, no. 3 (1975): 124-28.

Reviews principles, models, and therapeutic applications of
psychopharmacology in the psychosomatic illnesses. Sixty references.

890   Blacher, Richard S. "On Awakening Paralyzed During Surgery: A Syndrome of Traumatic Neurosis." JOURNAL OF THE AMERICAN MEDICAL ASSOCIATION 234, no. 1 (1975): 67-68.

Reviews cases of post-operative patients displaying symptoms of traumatic neurotic syndromes.

891   Dorfman, Wilfred. "Depression and Psychosomatic Illness." PSYCHO-THERAPY AND PSYCHOSOMATICS 23, no. 1-6 (1974): 87-92.

Suggests that current views of depression recognize that it may have genetic, constitutional, biochemical, neurophysio-logical, sociocultural, and psychodynamic factors. Sixteen references.

892   Eissler, R.S.; Freud, Anna; Kris, M.; and Solnit, Albert J., eds. PHYSICAL ILLNESS AND HANDICAP IN CHILDREN: AN ANTHOL-OGY OF THE PSYCHOANALYTIC STUDY OF THE CHILD. New Haven: Yale University Press, 1977. 321 p.

Contains papers originally published between 1952 and 1963 in THE PSYCHOANALYTIC STUDY OF THE CHILD.

893   Engel, George Z. "Psychological Aspects of Gastrointestinal Dis-orders." In ORGANIC DISORDERS AND PSYCHOSOMATIC MEDI-CINE, edited by Morton F. Reiser, chapter 27. American Handbook of Psychiatry, 2d ed., vol. 4. New York: Basic Books, 1975.

Summarizes the present status of knowledge with respect to interrelationships of psychic and somatic processes as they affect gastrointestinal anxiety. Includes 168 references.

894   Fischer, H. Keith, and Dlin, Barney M. "Psychosomatic Medicine." In PROGRESS IN NEUROLOGY AND PSYCHIATRY: AN ANNUAL REVIEW: XXVII, edited by Ernest A. Spiegel, chapter 20. New York: Grune and Stratton, 1972.

Reviews research and case reports in psychosomatic medicine. Seventy-four references.

895   Fabrega, Horacio. DISEASE AND SOCIAL BEHAVIOR: AN INTER-DISCIPLINARY PERSPECTIVE. Cambridge: M.I.T. Press, 1974. 341 p.

Reviews the recent literature on ethnomedicine, social epi-demiology, and medical biology. Thirty pages of references.

896   Frank, Jerome D. "Psychotherapy of Bodily Disease: An Overview." PSYCHOTHERAPY AND PSYCHOSOMATICS 26, no. 4 (1975): 192-202.

Reviews clinical and experimental studies of the interaction between psychological states and bodily diseases, and considers implications for the role of psychotherapists in diagnosis, prevention, and treatment of these conditions. Thirty-two references.

897   Frazier, Shervert H. "Complex Problems of Pain as Seen in Headache, Painful Phantoms and Other States." In ORGANIC DISORDERS AND PSYCHOSOMATIC MEDICINE, edited by Morton F. Reiser, chapter 34. American Handbook of Psychiatry, 2d ed., vol. 4. New York: Basic Books, 1975.

Discusses transmission and perception of pain, headaches, hypochondriasis, and painful phantoms. Fifty-six references.

898   Fulton, Robert. "Death and the Self." JOURNAL OF RELIGION AND HEALTH 3, no. 4 (1964): 359-68.

Discusses studies on the relationship between grief and psychosomatic responses.

899   Gottschalk, Louis A.; Knapp, P.H.; Reiser, Morton F.; Sapira, J.D.; and Shapiro, A.P., eds. PSYCHOSOMATIC CLASSICS: SELECTED PAPERS FROM PSYCHOSOMATIC MEDICINE, 1939-1958. Basel: S. Karger, 1972. 252 p.

Contains fourteen articles.

900   *Grinker, Roy R. PSYCHOSOMATIC CONCEPTS. New York: Jason Aronson, 1974. 319 p.

Reissue of a classic text in the area of psychosomatic medicine.

901   Knapp, Peter H. "Psychosomatic Aspects of Bronchial Asthma." In ORGANIC DISEASES AND PSYCHOSOMATIC MEDICINE, edited by Morton F. Reiser, chapter 28. American Handbook of Psychiatry, 2d ed., vol. 4. New York: Basic Books, 1975.

Reviews recent work in biological observations, psychophysiological studies, psychosocial studies, and therapy studies. Ninety-three references.

902   Krakowski, Adam J. "Non-Specific Factors in Psychopharmacology." PSYCHOSOMATICS 16, no. 3 (1975): 132-34.

Discusses the psychosomatic model of treatment of mental illness, based on the principles that the causes of mental illness are multiple and that biological and psychosocial approaches to treatment are required.

903 Levi, Lenart. "Stress, Distress, and Psychosocial Stimuli." OCCU-
PATIONAL MENTAL HEALTH 3, no. 3 (1973): 2-10.

Suggests that psychosocial stimuli (stress-evoking factors within an individual's environment) can cause diseases. Sixteen
references.

904 Lipowski, Zbigniew J. "Physical Illness and Psychopathology." IN-
TERNATIONAL JOURNAL OF PSYCHIATRY IN MEDICINE 5, no. 4
(1974): 483-97.

Discusses the relationship between physical illness and psychiatric disorders. Sixty-five references.

905 _____. "Psychiatry of Somatic Disease: Epidemiology, Pathogenesis,
Classification." COMPREHENSIVE PSYCHIATRY 16, no. 2 (1975):
105-24.

Reviews epidemiological data on the association of psychiatric
and physical illness, determinants of psychological responses
to disease and injury, and illness-related psychiatric syndromes. Ninety-three references.

906 _____, ed. ADVANCES IN PSYCHOSOMATIC MEDICINE: PSY-
CHOSOCIAL ASPECTS OF PHYSICAL ILLNESS. Vol. 8. Basel: S.
Karger, 1972. 275 p.

907 *Lipowski, Zbigniew [J.]; Lipsitt, Don R.; and Whybrow, Peter C.,
eds. PSYCHOSOMATIC MEDICINE: CURRENT TRENDS AND CLIN-
ICAL APPROACHES. New York: Oxford University Press, 1977.
625 p.

Reviews psychosomatic medicine in the 1970s, and examines
key theoretical concepts as well as research methods and
clinical applications.

908 Mason, John W. "Clinical Psychophysiology: Psychoendocrine Mechanisms." In ORGANIC DISORDERS AND PSYCHOSOMATIC MEDI-
CINE, edited by Morton F. Reiser, chapter 24. American Handbook
of Psychiatry, 2d ed., vol. 4. New York: Basic Books, 1975.

Describes theoretical implications of psychoendocrinology.
Includes 100 references.

909 Meissner, W.W. "Family Process and Psychosomatic Disease." IN-
TERNATIONAL JOURNAL OF PSYCHIATRY IN MEDICINE 5, no. 4
(1974): 411-30.

Reviews the psychosomatic literature on the relationship between patterns of illness and aspects of family interaction.
Includes 164 references.

910   Minuchin, Salvador; Bater, Lester; Roseman, Bernice L.; Liebman, Ronald; Milman, Leroy; and Todd, Thomas C. "A Conceptual Model of Psychosomatic Illness in Children." ARCHIVES OF GENERAL PSY-CHIATRY 32 (August 1975): 1031-38.

Reports on family therapy strategies based on the results of family treatment with forty-eight cases of diabetes, psychosomatic asthma, and anorexia nervosa. Thirty-seven references.

911   Moos, Rudolf H., ed. COPING WITH PHYSICAL ILLNESS. New York: Plenum Publishing Corp., 1977. 440 p.

912   Musaph, Herman. "The Role of Aggression in Somatic Symptom Formation." INTERNATIONAL JOURNAL OF PSYCHIATRY IN MEDICINE 5, no. 4 (1974): 449-60.

Notes that the role of repressed aggression in the onset of a somatic symptom remains ambiguous. Seventy-four references.

913   Robbins, Paul R. "Personality and Psychosomatic Illness: A Selective Review of Research." GENETIC PSYCHOLOGY MONOGRAPHS 80, no. 1 (1969): 51-90.

Reviews research relating to personality and various psychosomatic disorders for the period 1931-65. Ninety-four references.

914   Roessler, Richard, and Bolton, Brian. PSYCHOSOCIAL ADJUSTMENT TO DISABILITY. Baltimore: University Park Press, 1978. 220 p.

Emphasizes the processes and strategies for enhancing psychosocial adjustment, and attempts a practical rather than a theoretical approach to the problem.

915   Shontz, Franklin C. "Body Image and Its Disorders." INTERNATIONAL JOURNAL OF PSYCHIATRY IN MEDICINE 5, no. 4 (1974): 461-72.

Notes that body image is best described in terms of the functions it serves and the levels at which it is experienced. Twenty-nine references.

916   Wender, E.H.; Palmer, F.D.; Herbst, J.J.; and Wender, P.H. "Behavioral Characteristics of Children with Chronic Nonspecific Diarrhea." AMERICAN JOURNAL OF PSYCHIATRY 133, no. 1 (1976): 20-25.

917   Wittkower, Eric D., and Warnes, Hector. "Transcultural Psychosomatics." PSYCHOTHERAPY AND PSYCHOSOMATICS 23, no. 1-6 (1974): 1-12.

Surveys current knowledge regarding the cultural-etiological parameter of psychosomatic diseases. Thirty-seven references.

918 _____, eds. PSYCHOSOMATIC MEDICINE: ITS CLINICAL APPLI-CATIONS. New York: Harper and Row, 1977. 356 p.

Contains thirty-two chapters by forty-nine contributors on the treatment of psychosomatic disorders.

Chapter 7

PERSONALITY DISORDERS AND TRANSIENT

SITUATIONAL PERSONALITY DISORDERS

We have tried to stay as close as possible to standard nomenclature in classifying the various forms of abnormal behavior. We have done this both to facilitate the search for specific information concerning these conditions and to avoid professional debates with the authors of the works listed concerning the proper definition or classification of the conditions under discussion. When authors deviate from a standard syndrome or group of symptoms, they are usually careful to explain the kind of deviation they are offering and their reasons for doing so. This approach becomes even more important in the area of personality disorders. Here, not only is the standard nomenclature somewhat confusing, using various terms as though they were synonymous, but also many of the labels, though explicit, do not provide useful indications of the nature of the syndrome or the particular symptoms. A large number of these terms usually found in classification lists are covered in the general texts cited in earlier chapters. Therefore, we have brought together here a number of behaviors that are often treated separately, and, we have included them under the broad heading of personality disorders, both chronic and transient, grouped by some of their more common headings. No attempt has been made to group them in terms of etiology or severity of the disturbance.

The sections of this chapter include a general description of personality disorders; child personality disorders (most of these are described more fully in chapter 8); sociopathic and psychopathic disturbances (here the literature usually cites one term or the other, but the syndromes described are almost identical); drug dependence; alcoholism; and borderline disorders. Under the transient situational disorders, we have included sections on stress, grief, and suicide (including child suicide). The books considered most important are starred: numbers 920, 938, 955, 966, 976, 994, 1001, 1014, 1020, 1049, 1057, 1062, 1064, 1088, 1095, and 1112.

GENERAL DISCUSSION

919 Albert, Joel S. "Sociocultural Determinance of Personality Pathology."
In PERSONALITY DISORDERS: DIAGNOSIS AND MANAGEMENT,
edited by J.R. Lion, chapter 15. Baltimore: Williams and Wilkins,
1974.

Discusses sociocultural aspects of the pathogenesis, diagnosis, and treatment of character disorders, based on the thesis that sociocultural factors have significant effects in determining personality pathology. Forty-one references.

920 *Cleckley, Hervey M. MASK OF SANITY: AN ATTEMPT TO CLAR-IFY SOME ISSUES ABOUT THE SO-CALLED PSYCHOPATHIC PERSON-ALITY. St. Louis: C.V. Mosby Co., 1976. 544 p.

Presents clinical observations to develop a working hypothesis on the nature of psychopathology. Includes clinical anec-dotes and case studies attempting to illustrate the personality of the sociopath, whose appearance of normal behavior is a mask.

921 Covi, Lino, and Alessi, Larry. "Pharmacological Treatment of Person-ality Disorders." In PERSONALITY DISORDERS: DIAGNOSIS AND MANAGEMENT, edited by J.R. Lion, chapter 24. Baltimore: Wil-liams and Wilkins, 1974.

Discusses the use of psychotropic medication in the treatment of personality disorders from a pathogenetic viewpoint. Sixty-three references.

922 Davis, F. James, and Stivers, Richard. THE COLLECTIVE DEFINI-TION OF DEVIANCE. New York: Free Press, 1975. 420 p.

923 Docherty, John P., and Ellis, Jean. "A New Concept and Finding in Morbid Jealousy." AMERICAN JOURNAL OF PSYCHIATRY 133, no. 6 (1976): 679-83.

Presents a typology of morbid jealousy consisting, of exces-sive, obsessional-delusional, and ego dysfunctional forms. Thirty-four references.

924 Izard, Carroll E., ed. EMOTIONS IN PERSONALITY AND PSYCHO-PATHOLOGY. New York: Plenum Publishing Corp., 1979. 590 p.

Notes that an understanding of human emotions is of primary importance in studying personality and psychopathology as well as in analyzing social processes and creativity.

925 Kaplan, Howard B. SELF-ATTITUDES AND DEVIANT BEHAVIOR. Pacific Palisades, Calif.: Goodyear, 1975. 185 p.

Outlines the general theory of behavior which forms in the reciprocal relationship between self-attitudes and deviant be-havior. Describes the influence of preexisting self-attitudes in deviant responses and the effect of deviant responses on changes in self-attitudes. Ten pages of references.

926   Kenyon, Jack M. "A Special Type of Theft."
      CAL JOURNAL 72, no. 4 (1976): 227-29.

      Presents a broad discussion of kleptomania.

927   Kernberg, Otto F. "Contrasting Viewpoints Reg
      Psychoanalytic Treatment of Narcissistic Personal
      Communication." JOURNAL OF THE AMERICA.. .ɔ ı ᴄΗΟΑΝΑLΥΠC
      ASSOCIATION 22, no. 2 (1974): 255-67.

928   Leon, Gloria R. CASE HISTORIES OF DEVIANT BEHAVIOR: AN
      INTERACTIONAL PERSPECTIVE. 2d ed. Boston: Allyn and Bacon,
      1977. 372 p.

      Presents twenty case histories offering research and clinical
      findings on a broad range of psychological disorders. Empha-
      sizes the mutual influence of biological and social factors.

929   Lewis, Aubrey. "Psychopathic Personality: A Most Elusive Category."
      PSYCHOLOGICAL MEDICINE 4, no. 2 (1974): 133-40.

      Reviews the history of the diagnostic concept first called
      "moral insanity," which has been troubling psychiatric nosol-
      ogists for 150 years. Fifty references.

930   Messer, Stanley B., and Nathan, Peter E., eds. "Treatment of Psy-
      chological Disorders." CONTEMPORARY ISSUES OF MENTAL HEALTH
      (Monograph Series) 1, no. 3 (1976): 1-71.

      Contains eight articles dealing with psychoanalytic approaches
      to the individual, behavior modification, and other types of
      treatment.

931   Salzman, Leon. "Other Character-Personality Syndromes: Schizoid
      Inadequate, Passive-Aggressive, Paranoid, and Dependent." In ADULT
      CLINICAL PSYCHIATRY, edited by Silvano Arieti and Eugene Brody,
      chapter 10. American Handbook of Psychiatry, 2d ed., vol. 3. New
      York: Basic Books, 1974.

      Presents the various syndromes of character and personality
      disorders, with suggestions for treatment. Nine references.

932   Schuckit, Marc A. "Alcoholism and Sociopathy: Diagnostic Confu-
      sion." QUARTERLY JOURNAL OF STUDIES ON ALCOHOL 34, no.
      1, part A (1973): 157-64.

      Notes that alcohol abuse may be present either as a primary
      illness, as alcoholism, or as a complication of other psychi-
      atric processes, especially depressive illness and sociopathy.
      Thirty-three references.

33   Spruiell, Vann. "Theories of the Treatment of Narcissistic Personalities." JOURNAL OF THE AMERICAN PSYCHOANALYTIC ASSOCIA-
TION 22, no. 2 (1974): 268-78.

> Presents twelve issues by which to compare and contrast the
> clinical approaches of Kohut, Kermberg, and their coworkers
> on narcissistic personalities. Sixteen references.

934   Witenberg, Earl G. "Some Notes on Narcissism." CONTEMPORARY
PSYCHOANALYSIS 10, no. 4 (1974): 465-68.

> Rejects the concept of "normal narcissism" as a contradiction
> in terms.

CHILD PERSONALITY DISORDERS

935   Cerreto, M.C., and Tuma, J.M. "Distribution of DSM-II Diagnoses
in a Child Psychiatric Setting." JOURNAL OF ABNORMAL CHILD
PSYCHOLOGY 5, no. 2 (1977): 147-55.

> Reports a study in which transient situational disorders and
> behavior disorders were assigned to two-thirds of the sample.
> Found transient situational disorders as a concept to be over-
> utilized for adolescents. Reports that boys have behavior dis-
> orders more frequently than do girls.

936   Chess, Stella. "Childhood Psychopathologies: The Search for Differentiation." JOURNAL OF AUTISM AND CHILDHOOD SCHIZOPHRE-
NIA 2, no. 2 (1972): 111-13.

937   Copeland, Adrian D. TEXT BOOK OF ADOLESCENT PSYCHOPATH-
OLOGY AND TREATMENT. Springfield, Ill.: Charles C Thomas,
1974. 141 p.

> For practitioners and students dealing with emotionally dis-
> turbed youth.

938   *Freehill, Maurice F., ed. DISTURBED AND TROUBLED CHILDREN.
New York: Spectrum Publications, 1973. 216 p.

> Describes problems of autism in adolescents, pseudo-retarda-
> tion, and other syndromes. Provides a review of cases.

939   McPherson, Sigrid. "Communication of Intents Among Parents and
Their Disturbed Adolescent Child." JOURNAL OF ABNORMAL PSY-
CHOLOGY 76, no. 1 (1970): 98-105.

> Demonstrates findings to support the view that there are con-
> sistent relationships between patterns of familial behaviors and
> the symptoms of adolescents.

940 Marsden, Gerald; McDermott, John F.; and Miner, Deanna. "Residential Treatment of Children: A Survey of Institutional Characteristics." JOURNAL OF THE AMERICAN ACADEMY OF CHILD PSYCHIATRY 9, no. 2 (1970): 332-46.

Describes a survey of thirty-nine training institutions providing residential care for emotionally disturbed children. An overview of the nature and type of care provided for a wide variety of disorders in children.

941 Small, Iver F.; Small, Joyce G.; Alig, Vincent B.; and Moore, Donald F. "Passive-Aggressive Personality Disorder: A Search for a Syndrome." AMERICAN JOURNAL OF PSYCHIATRY 126, no. 7 (1970): 973-83.

Presents data from a seven- to fifteen-year follow-up study of 100 patients hospitalized with a diagnosis of "passive-aggressive" personality disorders.

942 Vance, Elizabeth T. "Social Disability." AMERICAN PSYCHOLOGIST 28, no. 6 (1973): 498-511.

Considers social disability as a form of deviance which refers to a broad class of social adaptation based on failure in the development of competence. Includes 114 references.

943 Weiner, I.B., and DelGaudio, A.C. "Psychopathology in Adolescents: An Epidemiological Study." ARCHIVES OF GENERAL PSYCHIATRY 33, no. 2 (1976): 187-93.

Uses a cumulative psychiatric case register to examine patterns of psychopathology in 1,334 adolescent patients. Forty-one references.

944 Wise, Louis J. "Alienation of Present Day Adolescents." JOURNAL OF THE AMERICAN ACADEMY OF CHILD PSYCHIATRY 9, no. 2 (1970): 264-77.

Describes adolescent alienation, rebellion, and dissent.

SOCIOPATHIC AND PSYCHOPATHIC (CHARACTER) DISORDERS

945 Abel, Gene G., and Blanchard, Edward B. "The Role of Fantasy in the Treatment of Sexual Deviation." ARCHIVES OF GENERAL PSYCHIATRY 30, no. 4 (1974): 467-75.

Cites the critical role played by sexual fantasy in the treatment of sexual deviation, from both the psychoanalytic and behavioral viewpoints. Fifty-five references.

946   Bak, Robert C. "Distortions of the Concept of Fetishism." In PSY-
       CHOANALYTIC STUDY OF THE CHILD, vol. 29, pp. 191-214. New
       Haven, Conn.: Yale University Press, 1974.

       Reviews the literature on fetishism, and examines the role of
       inanimate objects in the maturation of infant, child, adoles-
       cent, and adult perversions. Thirty-seven references.

947   Bak, Robert C., and Stewart, Walter A. "Fetishism, Transvestitism
       and Voyeurism: A Psychoanalytic Approach." In ADULT CLINICAL
       PSYCHIATRY, edited by Silvano Arieti and Eugene Brody, chapter
       17, American Handbook of Psychiatry, 2d ed., vol. 3. New York:
       Basic Books, 1974.

       Reviews psychoanalytic concepts by which perversions are
       understood. Describes psychoanalytic theory of drive and ego
       development, psychosexual development, and perversions, and
       attempts to deal with whatever anxiety is related to these
       behaviors. Seventeen references.

948   Bancroft, John. DEVIANT SEXUAL BEHAVIOR: MODIFICATION
       AND ASSESSMENT. New York: Oxford University Press, 1974.
       256 p.

       Reviews modification and assessment of deviant sexual behav-
       ior. Describes procedures and theoretical bases of major
       therapies.

949   Bernard, Frederic. "An Inquiry Among a Group of Pedophiles."
       JOURNAL OF SEX RESEARCH 11, no. 3 (1975): 242-55.

       Discusses sociological data obtained from questionnaires from
       seventy-three pedophiles.

950   Bieber, Irving. "Sadism and Masochism: Phenomenology and Psycho-
       dynamics." In ADULT CLINICAL PSYCHIATRY, edited by Silvano
       Arieti and Eugene Brody, chapter 15. American Handbook of Psychiatry.
       2d ed., vol. 3. New York: Basic Books, 1974.

       Discusses theories of sadism and masochism, various symptoms
       and patterns of behavior, and suggestions for treatment.
       Sixteen references.

951   Blanch, Andrea. "The Problem of Feminine Masochism: An Approach
       Through Theory and Literature." CORNELL JOURNAL OF SOCIAL
       RELATIONS 9, no. 1 (1974): 1-15.

       Examines the existence and nature of the link between maso-
       chism and femininity. Twenty references.

952   Crown, Sidney. PSYCHOSEXUAL PROBLEMS: PSYCHOTHERAPY, COUNSELING AND BEHAVIORAL MODIFICATION. London: Academic Press, 1976. 471 p.

953   Draguns, Juris G. "Values Reflected in Psychopathology: The Case of the Protestant Ethic." ETHOS 2, no. 2 (1974): 115-36.

        Discusses the influence of the Protestant Ethic on the nature of manifestations of psychopathology and on social responsibilities for psychopathology. Five pages of references.

954   Farrall, William R. "Selection and Use of Stimulus Material for Aversion Therapy and Desensitization." BEHAVIORAL ENGINEERING 1, no. 1 (1973): 1-7.

955   *Hare, Robert D. PSYCHOPATHY: THEORY AND RESEARCH. New York: John Wiley and Sons, 1970. 138 p.

        Presents a case history and descriptions of the disorder and a diagnostic orientation. Includes a good review of the literature.

956   _____. "Some Empirical Studies of Psychopathology." CANADA'S MENTAL HEALTH 18, no. 1 (1970): 4-9.

        Hypothesizes that a psychopath lacks the "capacity to acquire conditional anticipatory fear responses" with both the gradient of temporal reward and fear arousal being steeper than a normal person's.

957   Herman, David, and Nelson, Marie C. "The Treatment of Psychosocial Masochism." PSYCHOANALYTIC REVIEW 16, no. 3 (1973): 333-72.

        Discusses aspects of psychosocial masochism, outlining conditions in modern society that lead to a sense of personal hopelessness. Sixty-nine references.

958   Humphrey, John A. "A Study of the Etiology of Sociopathic Behavior." DISEASES OF THE NERVOUS SYSTEM 35, no. 9 (1974): 432-33.

        Reports findings that confirm the hypothesis that early institutionalizations (before age sixteen) among sociopaths were significantly higher than for mental patients diagnosed as other than sociopathic. Supports the suggestion that childhood socialization that takes place under conditions of secondary relations between the child and society will be ineffective for the development of a self with adequate role-taking ability. Twenty-two references.

959 Lester, David. UNUSUAL SEXUAL BEHAVIOR: THE STANDARD
DEVIATIONS. Springfield, Ill.: Charles C Thomas, 1975. 242 p.

960 Mathis, James L., and Collins, Mabelle. "Mandatory Group Therapy
for Exhibitionists." AMERICAN JOURNAL OF PSYCHIATRY 126,
no. 8 (1970): 1162-67.

Describes a program of group therapy for men arrested for exhibitionism.

961 Money, John. "Intersexual and Transsexual Behavior and Syndromes."
In ADULT CLINICAL PSYCHIATRY, edited by Silvano Arieti and
Eugene Brody, chapter 16. American Handbook of Psychiatry, 2d
ed., vol. 3. New York: Basic Books, 1974.

Discusses the determination of gender identity differentiation,
core gender identity, and ambiguous gender identity and sex
reassignment. Thirty references.

962 Ostow, Mortimer. SEXUAL DEVIATION: PSYCHOANALYTIC IN-
SIGHTS. New York: Quadrangle/New York Times Books, 1974.
187 p.

963 Panken, Shirley. THE JOY OF SUFFERING: PSYCHOANALYTIC
THEORY AND THERAPY OF MASOCHISM. New York: Jason Aronson, 1973. 242 p.

964 Rappeport, Jonas R. "Antisocial Behavior." In ADULT CLINICAL
PSYCHIATRY, edited by Silvano Arieti and Eugene Brody, chapter 12.
American Handbook of Psychiatry, 2d ed., vol. 3. New York: Basic
Books, 1974.

Discusses the history, diagnosis, causation, and proposed
treatment of antisocial behaviors. Eighty-five references.

965 Reckless, John B. "Enforced Out-Patient Treatment of Advantaged
Pseudosociopathic Neurotically Disturbed Young Women." CANADIAN
PSYCHIATRIC ASSOCIATION JOURNAL 15, no. 4 (1970): 335-45.

Reviews the psychotherapeutic treatment of twenty-five young
women with antisocial behavior problems, including promis-
cuity, failure in school, alcohol and drug abuse, and general
social ineptitude.

966 *Reid, William H. THE PSYCHOPATH: A COMPREHENSIVE STUDY
OF ANTISOCIAL DISORDERS AND BEHAVIORS. New York: Brun-
ner/Mazel, 1978. 352 p.

Offers a comprehensive view of research and treatment of
antisocial disorders and behaviors.

967 Robins, Lee N. DEVIANT CHILDREN GROWN UP: A SOCIOLOG-
ICAL AND PSYCHIATRIC STUDY OF SOCIOPATHIC PERSONALITY.
Baltimore: Williams and Wilkins, 1966. 351 p.

968 Rooth, Grahma. "Exhibitionism, Sexual Violence and Paedophilia."
BRITISH JOURNAL OF PSYCHIATRY 122, no. 571 (1973): 705-10.

969 Sack, Robert L., and Miller, Warren. "Masochism: A Clinical and
Theoretical Overview." PSYCHIATRY 38, no. 3 (1975): 244-57.

Reviews the literature on masochism, from several disciplines
and theoretical frameworks. Fifty-one references.

970 Serber, Michael. "Shame Aversion Therapy." JOURNAL OF BE-
HAVIOR THERAPY AND EXPERIMENTAL PSYCHIATRY 1, no. 3
(1970): 213-15.

Describes shame aversion therapy, a new technique for the
treatment of persons practicing deviant sexual acts.

971 Siomopoulos, V., and Goldsmith, Jewett. "Sadism Revisited." AMER-
ICAN JOURNAL OF PSYCHOTHERAPY 30, no. 4 (1976): 631-40.

Reviews briefly the literature of sadism, and reports and comments on several cases of sadistic individuals. Twenty-one
references.

972 Smith, Robert J. THE PSYCHOPATH IN SOCIETY. New York:
Academic Press, 1978. 176 p.

Takes a broad cultural (Western) overview of the psychopath
as a logical extreme of what the system demands for success.
Discusses the concept from both learning theory and societal-
philosophical approaches.

973 Stoeler, Robert J. "Male Childhood Transsexualism." JOURNAL OF
THE AMERICAN ACADEMY OF CHILD PSYCHIATRY 7, no. 2 (1968):
193-209.

Describes a character disorder, childhood transsexualism, that
can be differentiated from other character disorders clinically,
psychodynamically, and etiologically. Ten references.

974 Tauber, Edward S. "Reflections on Sexual Perversions." CONTEM-
PORARY PSYCHOANALYSIS 11, no. 1 (1975): 1-14.

975 Whitely, Stuart; Briggs, Rennie; and Turner, Merfyn. DEALING WITH
DEVIANCE: THE TREATMENT OF ANTISOCIAL BEHAVIOR. New
York: Schocken, 1973. 248 p.

DRUG DEPENDENCE

976   *Ball, John C., and Chambers, Carl D., eds. THE EPIDEMIOLOGY OF OPIATE ADDICTION IN THE UNITED STATES. Springfield, Ill.: Charles C Thomas, 1970. 337 p.

> Presents major research findings resulting from a six-year study at the Addiction Research Center at Lexington, Kentucky, based on data from 43,215 addicts between 1935 and 1967.

977   Bourne, Peter G., ed. ADDICTION. New York: Academic Press, 1974. 256 p.

> Notes that the increase in heroin addiction in the United States has brought about an enormous amount of new information. Provides insights into the heroin epidemic of the late 1960s.

978   Brill, Leon, and Harms, Ernest, eds. YEAR BOOK OF DRUG ABUSE. New York: Behavioral Press, 1973. 386 p.

> Contains articles on treatment modalities, legislation, and drug problems in specific cities and countries.

979   Callner, Dale A. "Behavioral Treatment Approaches to Drug Abuse: A Critical Review of the Research." PSYCHOLOGICAL BULLETIN 82, no. 2 (1975): 143-64.

> Reviews treatment techniques for drug abuse, derived from contemporary theories of classical and operant learning. Ninety-two references.

980   Coleman, James W. "The Myth of Addiction." JOURNAL OF DRUG ISSUES 6, no. 2 (1976): 135-41.

> Challenges a central feature of the concept of addiction: the belief in the power of narcotic drugs to produce a chemical euphoria or to "hook" the careless user.

981   Galanter, Marc. "The Intoxication State of Consciousness: A Model for Alcohol and Drug Abuse." AMERICAN JOURNAL OF PSYCHIATRY 133, no. 6 (1976): 635-40.

> Describes a model of intoxicant use based on altered states of consciousness. Reviews research on marijuana, to illustrate the utility of the model. Seventy-one references.

982   Gillies, Oliver. "Drug Addiction: Facts and Folklore." SCIENCE JOURNAL 5A, no. 6 (1969): 75-80.

983   Grant, Igor, and Lynn, Mohns. "Chronic Cerebral Effects of Alcohol and Drug Abuse." INTERNATIONAL JOURNAL OF ADDICTION 10, no. 5 (1975): 883-920.

Suggests that a minority of alcohol and drug users develop a severe cerebral dysfunction in the form of Wernicke-Korsakoff syndrome. Reports that cerebral dysfunction (impaired abstracting ability) is also evident in a larger population who do not develop Wernicke-Korsakoff syndrome.

984   Howard, Kay; Rickels, Karl; Mock, John E.; Lipman, Ronald S.; Covi, Lino; and Bauman, Craig U. "Therapeutic Style and Attention Rate from Psychiatric Drug Treatment." JOURNAL OF NERVOUS AND MENTAL DISEASE 150, no. 2 (1970): 102-10.

Suggests that the therapists' approach to treatment might fruitfully be described in terms of a bipolar continuum ranging from activity to passivity.

985   Kurzman, Teresa A. "Communication Skills Seminar: A Non-Drug Approach to Drug Education." CONTEMPORARY DRUG PROBLEMS 3, no. 2 (1974): 187-96.

Describes a seminar approach to improving parent-adolescent communication, with the immediate aim of lowering the adolescent's anxiety level and raising self-esteem, and the long-range goal of reducing drug abuse.

986   McGlothlin, William H. "Drug Use and Abuse." ANNUAL REVIEW OF PSYCHOLOGY 26 (1975): 45-64.

Discusses recent data on trends, patterns of use, and etiologies of heroin and other nonmedical drug use. Includes 109 references.

987   Miller, Peter M. "Behavioral Treatment of Drug Addiction: A Review." INTERNATIONAL JOURNAL OF THE ADDICTIONS 8, no. 3 (1973): 511-19.

Reviews the literature on behavioral modification techniques used in the treatment of drug addiction. Thirty references.

988   Nyswander, Marie. "Drug Addiction." In ADULT CLINICAL PSYCHIATRY, edited by Silvano Arieti and Eugene Brody, chapter 19. American Handbook of Psychiatry, 2d ed., vol. 3. New York: Basic Books, 1974.

Defines addiction, gives some of the historical background, discusses addiction and crime, and suggests treatment models including treatment of withdrawal stages. Fifty-one references.

989   Perry, David D. "The Pharmacology of Addictions and Drug Dependence." PHARM-CHEM NEWSLETTER 5, no. 6 (1976): 1-7.

> Notes that current thinking has identified three factors in the
> development of drug dependence: the pharmacology of the
> drug, the personality of the user, and the sociocultural en-
> vironment of the user.

990   Platt, Jerome J., and Labate, Christina. HEROIN ADDICTION:
THEORY, RESEARCH AND TREATMENT. New York: John Wiley
and Sons, 1976. 417 p.

> Reviews the current state of knowledge about heroin addiction
> and its treatment. Covers the historical-legal background of
> addiction in the United States and various theories dealing
> with heroin abuse and the characteristics of the addict.

991   Segal, Mark. "Drug Education: Logic Versus Rationalization."
DRUG FORUM 4, no. 4 (1975): 273-78.

> Argues that drug education programs designed to prevent use
> are inadequate because of society's ability to rationalize the
> use of the desired substances. Twenty-seven references.

992   Steffenhagen, R.A. "Motivation for Drug and Alcohol Use: A Social
Perspective." In RESEARCH ON METHODS AND PROGRAMS OF
DRUG EDUCATION, edited by M.S. Goodstadt, pp. 85-96. Toronto:
Alcoholism and Drug Addiction Research Foundation of Ontario, 1974.

> Explores the motivation for taking drugs, by means of a re-
> view of research projects conducted over six years at the
> University of Vermont. Seventeen references.

993   Stimson, Gerry V. HEROIN AND BEHAVIOR: DIVERSITY AMONG
ADDICTS ATTENDING LONDON CLINICS. New York: John Wiley
and Sons, 1973. 246 p.

> Provides an extensive description of the background and social
> adjustment of 111 individuals receiving heroin at a London
> clinic. Addresses the controversy concerning the legitimate
> availability of heroin.

994   *Tobias, Lester L., and MacDonald, Marian L. "Withdrawal of Maintenance Drugs with Long-Term Hospitalized Mental Patients: A Critical
Review." PSYCHOLOGICAL BULLETIN 81, no. 2 (1974): 107-25.

> Reports that the advisability of drug withdrawal has become
> an important issue in light of several effects of long-term
> drug maintenance: undesirable side effects, unexplained
> deaths, mounting costs, problems in drug state, and question-
> able utility. Five pages of references.

995   Van Stone, William W. "Peer Groups and Drug Rehabilitation."
       JOURNAL OF MUSIC THERAPY 10, no. 1 (1973): 7-12.

       Describes a peer group structure that appears to have been
       successful in "turning on" its members to an exciting but
       drug-free way of life.

996   Wg, Lorenz K., and Szara, Stephen. "On Understanding and Treat-
       ing Narcotic Dependence: A Neuropsychopharmacological Perspec-
       tive." BRITISH JOURNAL OF ADDICTION 70, no. 3 (1975): 311-
       24.

       Examines the complex etiology of narcotic dependence and
       how social, psychological, and pharmacological factors play
       important roles in the genesis of this disorder.

997   Zinberg, Norman E. "Addictions and Ego Function." PSYCHOAN-
       ALYTIC STUDY OF THE CHILD 30 (1975): 567-88.

       Presents an overview of the clinical picture for the chronic
       polydrug abuser. Fifty-one references.

ALCOHOLISM

998   Allen, I.R. "Note on the Position of the Alcoholic in the Therapeu-
       tic Program." PSYCHOLOGICAL REPORTS 24, no. 3 (1969): 695-
       97.

       Describes the similarities between student volunteers for ther-
       apy and alcoholic volunteers for treatment. Sixteen refer-
       ences.

999   Beckman, Linda J. "Women Alcoholics: A Review of Social and
       Psychological Studies." JOURNAL OF STUDIES ON ALCOHOL 36,
       no. 7 (1975): 797-824.

       Reviews research on social history variables, personality char-
       acteristics, social roles and role confusion, and possible treat-
       ment methods for women alcoholics. Includes 109 references.

1000   Blume, Sheila B. "Psychodrama and Alcoholism." ANNALS OF THE
       NEW YORK ACADEMY OF SCIENCE 233 (April 1974): 123-27.

       Briefly presents the history of formal psychodrama, a descrip-
       tion of its methods, and its use in treating alcoholics.

1001   *Bourne, Peter G., and Fox, Ruth, eds. ALCOHOLISM: PROGRESS
       IN RESEARCH AND TREATMENT. New York: Academic Press, 1973.
       439 p.

Surveys recent research on alcoholism, including biochemical, social, cross-cultural, and treatment aspects.

1002   Bowen, Murray. "Alcoholism as Viewed Through Family Systems Theory and Family Psychotherapy." ANNALS OF THE NEW YORK ACADEMY OF SCIENCE 233 (April 1974): 115-22.

Outlines the principles of family systems theory in which alcoholism is conceptualized as a system of the larger family or social unit.

1003   Burnett, G.B. "Common Alcohol-Related Disorders: Recognition and Management." SOUTHERN MEDICAL JOURNAL 71, no. 5 (1978): 561-65.

Notes that appropriate medical treatment of alcoholics often falls between the clinical specialties of psychiatry, internal medicine, toxicology, and neurology. Reports that the diagnosis of alcohol dependence is often overlooked, and medical complications may be inadequately treated or unrecognized.

1004   Butts, Stanley V., and Shontz, Franklin C. "Invitation of Punishment by Excessive Drinkers in Treatment." JOURNAL OF CONSULTING AND CLINICAL PSYCHOLOGY 34, no. 2 (1970): 216-20.

Employs an experimental analogy of interpersonal relationships presumed to exist in everyday life, to test the idea that alcoholics in treatment invite punishment from others by means of passive and aggressive behavior. Nineteen references.

1005   Chafetz, Morris E., and Demone, Harold W., Jr. "Programs to Control Alcoholism." In CHILD AND ADOLESCENT PSYCHIATRY. SOCIO-CULTURAL AND COMMUNITY PSYCHIATRY, 2d ed., edited by Gerald Caplan, chapter 48. American Handbook of Psychiatry, vol. 2. New York: Basic Books, 1974.

Discusses the extent and distribution of alcoholism and alcohol problems as well as voluntary organizations working with alcoholics, industrial programs, government programs, and prevention. Twenty-six references.

1006   Chafetz, Morris E.; Hertzman, Marc; and Berenson, David. "Alcoholism: A Positive View." In ADULT CLINICAL PSYCHIATRY, edited by Silvano Arieti and Eugene Brody, chapter eighteen. American Handbook of Psychiatry, 2d ed., vol. 3. New York: Basic Books, 1974.

Gives definition and criteria of alcoholism, discusses the etiology and the consequences, and presents some of the natural history and suggestions for therapy. Includes 147 references.

1007 Cohen, Sidney. "Alcoholism Halfway Houses: Relationships to Other Programs and Facilities." SOCIAL WORK 14, no. 2 (1969): 50-60.

Describes and evaluates the characteristics of problem drinkers, treatment services, and the place of the halfway house as a helping service.

1008 _____. "The Many Causes of Alcoholism." DRUG ABUSE AND ALCOHOLISM NEWSLETTER 4, no. 3 (1975): 1-4.

Discusses three causes of alcoholism (biological, psychological, and sociocultural), and outlines contributing factors of each, recognizing that alcoholism is usually a combination of several factors.

1009 Davis, D.L. "Is Alcoholism Really a Disease?" CONTEMPORARY DRUG PROBLEMS 3, no. 2 (1974): 197-212.

Suggests that the concept of alcoholism as a disease may be outdated and may blind physicians to its rational prevention. Twenty references.

1010 DeVito, Robert A.; Flaherty, Lawrence A.; and Mozdzierz, Gerald J. "Toward a Psychodynamic Theory of Alcoholism." DISEASES OF THE NERVOUS SYSTEM 31, no. 1 (1970): 43-49.

Suggests that the early excessive use of alcohol serves as an alternate chemical defense against ego-threatening situations caused by a breakdown in the usual personality defense system.

1011 Ditman, Keith S. "Review and Evaluation of Current Drug Therapies in Alcoholism." INTERNATIONAL JOURNAL OF PSYCHIATRY 3, no. 4 (1967): 248-66.

Reviews the use of psychotropic drugs in the treatment of alcoholism, and discusses the difficulties in assessing treatment because of poor understanding of the condition. Twenty-one references.

1012 Edwards, Patricia; Harvey, Cheryl; and Whitehead, Paul C. "Wives of Alcoholics: A Critical Review and Analysis." QUARTERLY JOURNAL OF STUDIES ON ALCOHOL 34, no. 1, part A. (1973): 112-32.

Reviews the literature on the personality structure and characteristics of wives of alcoholics. Forty references.

1013 Elkins, R.L. "A Note on Aversion Therapy for Alcoholism." BEHAVIOR RESEARCH AND THERAPY 14, no. 2 (1976): 159-60.

Strongly recommends covert sensitization as an alternative to chemical aversion therapy for alcoholism. Nineteen references.

1014 *Estes, Nada J., and Heinemann, M. Edith, eds. ALCOHOLISM: DEVELOPMENT, CONSEQUENCES, AND INTERVENTIONS. St. Louis: C.V. Mosby Co., 1977. 332 p.

Contains papers providing a comprehensive overview of alcoholism and alcoholics. Discusses treatment and prevention of alcoholism.

1015 Fillmore, Kaye M. "Relationships Between Specific Drinking Problems in Early Adulthood and Middle Age: An Exploratory Twenty Year Follow-Up Study." JOURNAL OF STUDIES ON ALCOHOL 36, no. 7 (1975): 882-907.

1016 Forrest, Gary G. THE DIAGNOSIS AND TREATMENT OF ALCOHOLISM. Springfield, Ill.: Charles C Thomas, 1975. 257 p.

Deals with the global process of alcoholic rehabilitation. For undergraduate students or persons with little clinical experience.

1017 Freed, Earl X. "Drug Abuse by Alcoholics: A Review." INTERNATIONAL JOURNAL OF THE ADDICTIONS 8, no. 3 (1973): 451-73.

Discusses methodological problems in studies of alcoholism and drug abuse, and hypothesizes similarities and differences between drug addiction and alcoholism. Seven pages of references.

1018 Gitlow, Stanley E. "The Pharmacological Approach to Alcoholism." JOURNAL OF DRUG ISSUES 2, no. 3 (1972): 32-41.

Stresses the fact the ethyl alcohol is a sedative drug that operates in two opposing ways: it lowers the level of psychomotor activity in a short-term effect lasting two to three hours and reduces tension and anxiety; and in a slower, long-term effect lasting about twelve hours it increases psychomotor activity, renewing tension and permitting further intake.

1019 Jones, Kenneth I., and Smith, David W. "The Fetal Alcohol Syndrome." TERATOLOGY 12, no. 1 (1975): 1-10.

Discusses the fetal alcohol syndrome, which reflects a pattern of altered growth and morphogenesis. Reports case studies including data relative to the maternal history of alcoholism, early neonatal course, and subsequent performance. Nineteen references.

1020 *Kissin, Benjamin, and Begleiter, Henri, eds. THE BIOLOGY OF ALCOHOLISM: TREATMENT AND REHABILITATION OF THE CHRONIC ALCOHOLIC. 5 vols. New York: Plenum Publishing Corp., 1976.

Notes that alcoholism, traditionally neglected as a "soft disorder," is now recognized as a disease. Includes fifteen articles written by leaders in the field on the range of biological and psychological treatments.

1021 Kohn, Paul M. "Motivation for Drug and Alcohol Use." In RESEARCH ON METHODS AND PROGRAMS OF DRUG EDUCATION, edited by M.S. Goodstadt, pp. 53-84. Toronto: Alcoholism and Drug Addiction Research Foundation of Ontario, 1974.

Examines reasons for society's concern about personal motives for drug use and why, from the late 1960s to the present, there has been a drug crisis. Includes 139 references.

1022 Madden, J.S.; Walker, Robin; and Kenyon, W.H., eds. ALCOHOLISM AND DRUG DEPENDENCE: A MULTIDISCIPLINARY APPROACH. New York: Plenum Publishing Corp., 1977. 479 p.

Reports on the International Conference on Alcoholism and Drug Dependence in 1976. Includes thirty-three papers on alcohol, nine on drugs, and two on both.

1023 Malikin, David. SOCIAL DISABILITY: ALCOHOLISM, DRUG ADDICTION, CRIME AND SOCIAL DISADVANTAGE. New York: New York University Press, 1973. 266 p.

1024 Marlatt, G. Alan. "Alcohol Stress and Cognitive Control." In STRESS AND ANXIETY: III, edited by I.G. Sarason and Charles D. Spielberger, chapter 14. Washington, D.C.: Hemisphere, 1976.

Reviews the literature on the relationship between stress and alcohol consumption. Points out that there is no constant support for the tension reduction theory, and suggests that methodological issues may account for some equivocal findings. Three pages of references.

1025 Mello, Nancy K., and Mendelson, Jack H. "Alcoholism: A Biobehavioral Disorder." In ORGANIC DISORDERS AND PSYCHOSOMATIC MEDICINE, edited by Morton F. Reiser, chapter 15. American Handbook of Psychiatry. 2d ed., vol. 4. New York: Basic Books, 1975.

Reviews the current state of knowledge on the actions of alcohol, the disease of alcoholism, and patterns of use and abuse in contemporary American society. Includes 194 references.

1026   Ottenberg, Donald J. "Teenage Alcohol Abuse: Focusing Our Concern." PSYCHIATRIC OPINION 12, no. 3 (1975): 6-11.

Asserts the need to focus on the network of interacting forces involved in addiction, rather than on the particular substance being abused. Forty-one references.

1027   Paredes, Alfonso. "Denial, Deceptive Maneuvers and Consistency in the Behavior of Alcoholics." ANNALS OF THE NEW YORK ACADEMY OF SCIENCE 233 (April 1974): 23-33.

Presents the thesis that the repetitive, compulsive, and chronic behavior that is alcoholism can only be maintained if it is supported by an array of physiological and psychological mechanisms and social conditions, all of which require considerable organization and work output. Forty-three references.

1028   Paredes, Alfonso; Hood, William R.; and Seymour, Harry. "Sobriety as a Symptom of Alcohol Intoxication: A Clinical Commentary on Intoxication and Drunkenness." BRITISH JOURNAL OF ADDICTION 70, no. 3 (1975): 233-43.

Discusses intoxication and drunkenness as related but not identical phenomena. Notes that certain biological, psychomotor, and psychological effects define intoxication. Thirty-nine references.

1029   Pattison, E. Mensell; Sobell, Mark B.; and Sobell, L.C., eds. EMERGING CONCEPTS OF ALCOHOL DEPENDENCE. New York: Springer, 1977. 369 p.

Presents evidence and a fresh outlook on alcoholic dependence and treatment implications.

1030   Schramm, Carl J., and DeFilligi, Robert J. "Characteristics of Successful Alcoholism Treatment Programs for American Workers." BRITISH JOURNAL OF ADDICTION 70, no. 3 (1975): 271-75.

1031   Seixas, Frank A. "New Priorities in Diagnosing and Treating Alcoholism." ALCOHOL HEALTH AND RESEARCH WORLD Experimental issue (1973): 69 p.

Discusses the official statement, issued in 1970 by the American College of Physicians, that alcoholism is a disease.

1032   Swinyard, Chester A.; Chaube, Slakuntale; and Sutton, David B. "Neurological and Behavioral Aspects of Transcendental Meditation Relevant to Alcoholism: A Review." ANNALS OF THE NEW YORK ACADEMY OF SCIENCE 233 (April 1974): 162-73.

Summarizes the literature concerning neurophysiological aspects of the state of consciousness. Reviews studies on the use of transcendental meditation in alcoholism and drug addiction. Thirty-seven references.

1033 Tarter, Ralph E., and Sugarman, A. Arthur, eds. ALCOHOLISM: INTERDISCIPLINARY APPROACH TO AN ENDURING PROBLEM. Reading, Mass.: Addison-Wesley, 1976. 857 p.

Presents twenty-two papers by writers from several disciplines, discussing current knowledge about the causes, processes, and treatment of alcoholism, which is seen not simply as a disease but as an array of disorders of similar topography with complex manifestations.

1034 Tyndel, Milo. "Psychiatric Study of the Chronic Drunkenness Offender." CANADIAN PSYCHIATRIC ASSOCIATION JOURNAL 14, no. 3 (1969): 275-85.

Studies 237 chronic drunkenness offenders, with an average age of forty-five years, who had been drinking excessively for twenty years. Notes that interviews and medical and police reports revealed psychopathological, psychiatric, and social disorders in all subjects.

1035 Wallgren, Henrik, and Barry, Herbert III. ACTIONS OF ALCOHOL I: BIOCHEMICAL, PHYSIOLOGICAL AND PSYCHOLOGICAL ASPECTS. New York: Elsevier, 1970. 400 p.

1036 _____. ACTIONS OF ALCOHOL II: CHRONIC AND CLINICAL ASPECTS. New York: Elsevier, 1970. 468 p.

Presents an integrated summary of scientific knowledge about all aspects of alcohol effects on living organs and organisms. Reviews experimental, clinical, and epidemiological literature.

1037 Westermeyer, Joseph. A PRIMER ON CHEMICAL DEPENDENCY: A CLINICAL GUIDE TO ALCOHOL AND DRUG PROBLEMS. Baltimore: Williams and Wilkins, 1976. 231 p.

Presents a brief clinical introduction to alcohol and drug dependence for "the busy practitioner with limited knowledge or experience in the field."

1038 Wilson, George C. "The Management of the Alcoholic." MEDICAL JOURNAL OF AUSTRALIA 22, no. 20 (1968): 875-84.

Discusses principles in the management of alcoholics, including the needs for a concept of alcoholism, for abstinence as a therapeutic goal, and for cooperation between agencies. Twenty-five references.

1039 Young, Alex W. "Cutaneous Stigma of Alcoholism." ALCOHOL HEALTH AND RESEARCH WORLD Experimental issue (1974): 24-28.

Discusses various categories of cutaneous stigmata of alcoholism. Fifty-one references.

1040 Zimering, Stanley, and Calhoun, James F. "Is There an Alcoholic Personality?" JOURNAL OF DRUG EDUCATION 6, no. 2 (1976): 97-103.

Discusses the existence of an alcoholic personality type, given the high rate of alcoholism in the United States. Seventeen references.

BORDERLINE STATES

1041 Fast, Irene. "Multiple Identities in Borderline Personality Organization." BRITISH JOURNAL OF MEDICAL PSYCHOLOGY 47, no. 4 (1974): 291-300.

Discusses the multiplicity of identities as a particular characteristic of borderline personality organization. Twenty-one references.

1042 Gunderson, John G., and Singer, Margaret F. "Defining Borderline Patients: An Overview." AMERICAN JOURNAL OF PSYCHIATRY 132, no. 1 (1975): 1-10.

Reviews the literature, noting that accounts of borderline patients vary, depending upon who is describing them and in what context, how the samples are selected, and what data are collected. Eighty-seven references.

1043 Hartocollis, Peter, ed. BORDERLINE PERSONALITY DISORDERS. New York: International Universities Press, 1977. 535 p.

Reviews the issues associated with the borderline patient. Report of a conference at the Menninger Foundation in 1976.

1044 Kernberg, Otto F. BORDERLINE CONDITIONS AND PATHOLOGI-CAL NARCISSISM. New York: Jason Aronson, 1975. 361 p.

k, John E., ed. BORDERLINE STATES IN PSYCHIATRY. New Grune and Stratton, 1975. 224 p.

usses historical perspectives, usefulness of the concept in otherapy, and therapeutic intervention.

1046 Masterson, James J. "Intensive Psychotherapy of the Adolescent with a Borderline Syndrome." In CHILD AND ADOLESCENT PSYCHIATRY, SOCIO-CULTURAL AND COMMUNITY PSYCHIATRY, 2d ed., edited by Gerald Caplan, chapter 16. American Handbook of Psychiatry, vol. 2. New York: Basic Books, 1974.

Briefly outlines borderline syndrome theory and applies it to the diagnosis, psychodynamics, and treatment of the borderline adolescent. Sixty-nine references.

1047 _____. PSYCHOTHERAPY OF THE BORDERLINE ADULT. New York: Brunner/Mazel, 1976. 377 p.

1048 _____. TREATMENT OF THE BORDERLINE ADOLESCENT. New York: Wiley-Interscience, 1972. 289 p.

1049 *_____, ed. NEW PERSPECTIVES ON PSYCHOTHERAPY OF THE BORDERLINE ADULT. New York: Brunner/Mazel, 1977. 181 p.

Presents papers by four clinicians in the area of borderline states, and includes their interaction and discussion as part of a conference on this topic.

1050 Pfeiffer, Eric. "Borderline States." DISEASES OF THE NERVOUS SYSTEM 35, no. 5 (1974): 212-19.

Considers the historical development of the concept of borderline states, the phenomenology of this state, and treatment methods. Twenty-three references.

1051 Wolberg, Arlene Robbins. THE BORDERLINE PATIENT. New York: Intercontinental Medical Book Corp., 1973. 288 p.

Provides a description of the psychodynamics and psychopathology of borderline patients. Traces the development of modern concepts of the syndrome, and stresses differential diagnosis and treatment methods, illustrated by case material and documented with a comprehensive bibliography.

PERSONALITY AND TRANSIENT SITUATIONAL DISORDERS

Stress

The following sections are related primarily to transient situational personality disorders and cover elements which in some instances might be considered etiological (stress or grief), or primarily reaction formations (suicide). The use of the word "transient" implies that they are not fixed characterological disturbances; however, the reaction may produce behaviors just as deviant as in the more "fixed" personality disorders.

1052   Coleman, James C. "Life Stress and Maladaptive Behavior." AMER-
        ICAN JOURNAL OF OCCUPATIONAL THERAPY 27, no. 4 (1973):
        169-80.

        Discusses the nature of stress and factors that determine its
        severity. Includes 119 references.

1053   DeFazio, Victor J. "The Vietnam Era Veteran: Psychological Prob-
        lems." JOURNAL OF CONTEMPORARY PSYCHOTHERAPY 7, no. 1
        (1975): 9-15.

        Studies a large number of Vietnam veterans who are seen as
        experiencing considerable readjustment difficulties and symp-
        tom development. Compares them with other groups exposed
        to psychic trauma. Twenty-four references.

1054   Dressler, David M.; Donovan, James M.; and Geller, Ruth A. "Life
        Stress and Emotional Crisis: The Idiosyncratic Interpretation of Life
        Events." COMPREHENSIVE PSYCHIATRY 17, no. 4 (1976): 549-
        58.

        Reports a study of forty patients in which the subjects' pre-
        stress lives were characterized by conflicting interpersonal
        relationships with a high degree of communicative impair-
        ment, few friends, and a lack of success in handling earlier
        stresses. Fifteen references.

1055   Horowitz, Mardi J. STRESS RESPONSE SYNDROMES. New York:
        Jason Aronson, 1976. 366 p.

1056   Horowitz, Mardi J., and Solomon, George F. "A Prediction of De-
        layed Stress Response Syndromes in Vietnam Veterans." JOURNAL
        OF SOCIAL ISSUES 31, no. 4 (1975): 67-80.

        Posits that over the next year civilian mental health profes-
        sionals will encounter stress response syndromes in Vietnam
        veterans, misread etiological factors, and be unable to treat
        such persons effectively. Twenty-five references.

1057   *Janis, Irving L. PSYCHOLOGICAL STRESS: PSYCHOANALYTIC
        AND BEHAVIORAL STUDIES OF SURGICAL PATIENTS. New York:
        Academic Press, 1974. 439 p.

        Describes an empirical and theoretical investigation of emo-
        tional reactions and thought processes in times of external
        threat and danger.

1058   Levi, Lennart, ed. SOCIETY, STRESS AND DISEASE II: CHILD-
        HOOD AND ADOLESCENCE. London: Oxford University Press,
        1975. 551 p.

Contains papers from the six sessions of the 1971 international interdisciplinary symposium dealing with various aspects of childhood and adolescent adaptation to psychosocial stresses and other intervening variables.

1059　Mechanic, David. "Stress, Illness and Illness Behavior." JOURNAL OF HUMAN STRESS 2, no. 2 (1976): 2-6.

Examines adaptation as a transactive process involving skills and capacities of individuals and their supporting groups as well as the types of challenges they face.

1060　Moore, Terence. "Stress in Normal Childhood." HUMAN RELATIONS 22, no. 3 (1969): 235-50.

Reviews studies on sources of stress in childhood and factors influencing the child's response to stress. Sixty-five references.

1061　Pilowsky, I. "Psychiatric Aspects of Stress." ERGONOMICS 16, no. 5 (1973): 691-98.

Suggests that the observation that diseases tend to occur in clusters, usually following a series of life changes, has led to attempts to quantify the stress potential of life events and to relate these to the incidence and severity of disability.

1062　*Sarason, Irwin G., and Spielberger, Charles D., eds. STRESS AND ANXIETY: II. Washington, D.C.: Hemisphere, 1975. 397 p.

Discusses the physiological, personality, and social dimensions of human distress and the need to adapt to persistent, unforeseen, and unwanted conditions of life. See also item 1064.

1063　Selye, Hans. "Implications of Stress Concept." NEW YORK STATE JOURNAL OF MEDICINE 75, no. 12 (1975): 2139-45.

Discusses a theory suggesting that work is necessary to reduce negative effects of stress. Defines stress as the nonspecific response of the body to any demand, positive or negative. Notes that the stress or stress-producing factor leads to a condition of nonadjustment, which must be corrected to reestablish normality. Views stress as an inevitable concomitant of life.

1064　*Spielberger, Charles D., and Sarason, Irwin G., eds. STRESS AND ANXIETY: I. Washington, D.C.: Hemisphere, 1975. 397 p.

Reports developments in research and theory on anxiety and stress, from the proceedings of the International Advanced Institute on Stress and Anxiety in Modern Life, held in June, 1973. See Also item 1062.

1065   Titchener, James L., and Ross, Donald W. "Acute or Chronic Stress
        as Determinants of Behavior, Character and Neurosis." In ADULT
        CLINICAL PSYCHIATRY, edited by Silvano Arieti and Eugene Brody,
        chapter 3. American Handbook of Psychiatry, 2d ed., vol. 3. New
        York: Basic Books, 1974.

        Presents a general theory of psychic stress, varieties of stress,
        and clinical processes of acute and chronic stress. Seventy-
        one references.

1066   Ursin, Holger; Baade, Fivind; and Levine, Seymour, eds. PSYCHO-
        BIOLOGY OF STRESS: A STUDY OF COPING MEN. New York:
        Academic Press, 1978. 256 p.

        Describes an interdisciplinary study of psychobiological re-
        sponses in a life-stress situation.

1067   Wild, Bradford S., and Hanes, Carolyn. "A Dynamic Conceptual
        Framework of Generalized Adaptation to Stressful Stimuli." PSYCHO-
        LOGICAL REPORTS 38, no. 1 (1976): 319-34.

        Reviews the popular definitions and theoretical arguments of
        the stress perspective, with the purpose of integrating this
        material into a general paradigm. Twenty-nine references.

Grief

1068   Anthony, E. James, and Koupernik, Cyrille, eds. THE CHILD IN
        HIS FAMILY II: THE IMPACT OF DISEASE AND DEATH. New York:
        John Wiley and Sons, 1973. 509 p.

        Deals comprehensively with the variety of reactions of chil-
        dren and their parents to the impact of disease, dying, and
        death.

1069   Ball, Justine F. "Widow's Grief: The Impact of Age and Mode of
        Death." OMEGA: JOURNAL OF DEATH AND DYING 7, no. 4
        (1976): 307-33.

        Reports a test of these two variables to determine whether
        they could predict the intensity of the grief reaction. Fifty
        references.

1070   Becker, Ernest. THE DENIAL OF DEATH. New York: Free Press,
        1973. 314 p.

        Analyzes the philosophies and theories of Freud, Jung,
        Kierkegaard, Rank, and others on the subject of death.

1071   Clayton, Paula J. "The Clinical Morbidity of the First Year of Be-
        reavement: A Review." COMPREHENSIVE PSYCHIATRY 14, no. 2
        (1973): 151-57.

Reviews papers dealing with the morbidity of widowhood. Twenty-four references.

1072   Epstein, Gerald; Weitz, Laurence; Roback, Howard; and McKee, Embry. "Research on Bereavement: A Selection and Critical Review." COMPREHENSIVE PSYCHIATRY 16, no. 6 (1975): 537-46.

Reviews studies of parental loss and conjugal loss and predictors of unfavorable bereavement outcomes.

1073   Gut, Emmy. "Some Aspects of Adult Mourning." OMEGA: JOURNAL OF DEATH AND DYING 5, no. 4 (1974): 323-42.

Discusses the subjective experience of mourning. Thirty-eight references.

1074   Mushatt, Cecil. "Mind-Body Environment: Toward Understanding the Impact of Loss on Psyche and Soma." PSYCHOANALYTIC QUARTERLY 44, no. 1 (1975): 81-106.

Notes that the special vulnerability of individuals to loss or separation may precipitate emotional as well as somatic disorders. Two pages of references.

1075   Parkes, Colin Murray. BEREAVEMENT: STUDIES OF GRIEF IN ADULT LIFE. New York: International Universities Press, 1973. 233 p.

1076   Pattison, E. Mansell. "The Fatal Myth of Death in the Family." AMERICAN JOURNAL OF PSYCHIATRY 133, no. 6 (1976): 674-78.

Hypothesizes that the observed pathogenic effects of the death of a parent on a child are the result of the family's culture-bound inability to integrate death as a natural part of the process of living.

1077   Salzberger, Ruth C. "Death: Belief, Activities, and Reactions of the Bereaved: Some Psychological and Anthropological Observations." HUMAN CONTEXT 7, no. 1 (1975): 103-16.

Examines the question: "Why is it that loss, especially loss through death, may have effects on the loser so devastating that he may be thrown into illness, even into fatal illness?" Twenty-nine references.

1078   Schoenberg, Bernard; Carr, Arthur C.; Kutscher, Austin H.; Peretz, David; and Goldberg, Ivan K. ANTICIPATORY GRIEF. New York: Columbia University Press, 1974. 381 p.

Contains forty-one articles from a conference on anticipatory grief.

1079   Volkan, Vamik D. "More on Re-Grief Therapy." JOURNAL OF
        THANATOLOGY 3, no. 2 (1975): 77-91.

>   Describes re-grief therapy, a short-term psychotherapy for es-
>   tablished pathological mourners. Provides case studies.

1080   Wahl, Charles W. "The Differential Diagnosis of Normal and Neu-
        rotic Grief Following Bereavement." PSYCHOSOMATICS 11, no. 2
        (1970): 104-6.

>   Studied patients whose precomplaint was grief following be-
>   reavement, to identify characteristics of neurotic grief reac-
>   tions.

Suicide

Recognizing that suicide is, in effect, a result rather than an ongoing disorder, the discussions concerning this question in both children and adults
have been brought together in one section. Thus, various aspects of research
and philosophical investigations relating to the etiology of suicide, its prevention, and the possible treatment of suicidal personalities can be easily
located. No effort has been made to establish a particular theoretical position.

1081   Blaker, Karen P. "Systems Theory and Self-Destructive Behavior: A
        New Theoretical Base." PERSPECTIVES IN PSYCHIATRIC CARE 10,
        no. 4 (1972): 168-72.

>   Questions the use of the medical model in dealing with sui-
>   cide. Describes systems theory, and proposes it as an alter-
>   native to the medical approach.

1082   Choron, Jacques. SUICIDE. New York: Charles Scribner's Sons,
        1972. 182 p.

>   Discusses facts and figures about suicide, national and inter-
>   national rates, and various methods as influenced by sex and
>   by country.

1083   Farberow, Norman L. BIBLIOGRAPHY ON SUICIDE AND SUICIDE
        PREVENTION: 1897-1957; 1958-1967. Public Health Service Publi-
        cation, no. 1970, 1-203. Washington, D.C.: Government Printing
        Office, 1969.

1084   _____, ed. SUICIDE IN DIFFERENT CULTURES. Baltimore: Univer-
        sity Park Press, 1975. 286 p.

1085   Finch, Stuart M., and Poznanski, Elva O. ADOLESCENT SUICIDE.

Springfield, Ill.: Charles C Thomas, 1971. 66 p.

1086   Fisher, Sheila. SUICIDE AND CRISIS INTERVENTION. New York: Springer, 1973. 279 p.

Surveys methods and techniques for operating a suicide or crisis prevention service.

1087   Gnepp, Eric H. "A Causal Theory of Suicide." PSYCHOLOGY 13, no. 1 (1976): 45-53.

Examines suicide as a biological and psychological phenomenon. Regards culture as a correlative but not causal factor.

1088   *Grollman, Earl A. SUICIDE: PREVENTION, INTERVENTION AND POSTVENTION. Boston: Beacon Press, 1971. 145 p.

Surveys the literature on suicide, and offers suggested readings.

1089   Haim, Andre. ADOLESCENT SUICIDE. New York: International Universities Press, 1974. 310 p.

Analyzes probable causes, incidence, characteristics, and theories of adolescent suicide.

1090   Hopkins, Mary T. "Patterns of Self-Destruction Among Orthopedically Disabled." REHABILITATION RESEARCH AND PRACTICE REVIEW 3, no. 1 (1971): 5-16.

Reviews research on suicide among persons with spinal cord injuries and amputations. Fifty-six references.

1091   Humphrey, John A.; French, Lawrence; Niswander, G. Donald; and Casey, Thomas M. "The Process of Suicide: The Sequence of Disruptive Events in the Lives of Suicide Victims." DISEASES OF THE NERVOUS SYSTEM 35, no. 6 (1974): 275-77.

Reviews case histories of 160 suicides, in an attempt to determine whether there were consistent patterns of problematic events in their lives which may have resulted in their self-destruction.

1092   Jacobs, Jerry. ADOLESCENT SUICIDE. New York: John Wiley and Sons, 1971. 147 p.

Suggests that only through a phenomenological understanding of the statements of suicidal persons can we understand the true meaning of their behavior.

1093   Kiev, Ari. THE SUICIDAL PATIENT: RECOGNITION AND MAN-
        AGEMENT. Chicago: Nelson Hall, 1976. 157 p.

        Discusses factors known to be present in attempted and suc-
        cessful suicides, including social-psychological, historical,
        and phenomenological characteristics.

1094   Lester, David. WHY PEOPLE KILL THEMSELVES: A SUMMARY OF
        RESEARCH FINDINGS ON SUICIDAL BEHAVIOR. Springfield, Ill.:
        Charles C Thomas, 1972. 353 p.

1095   *Lester, Gene, and Lester, David. SUICIDE: THE GAMBLE WITH
        DEATH. Englewood Cliffs, N.J.: Prentice-Hall, 1971. 176 p.

        Presents data from psychological and sociological research on
        reasons for suicide. Considers the influences of heredity,
        environment, childhood experiences, drugs, and mental ill-
        ness. Offers demographic data from suicide attempts and
        completions.

1096   Mattsson, Ake; Seese, Lynne R.; and Hawkins, James W. "Suicidal
        Behavior as a Child Psychiatric Emergency." ARCHIVES OF GENERAL
        PSYCHIATRY 20 (January 1969): 100–109.

        Reports the results of a retrospective and follow-up study of
        seventy-five children and adolescents with suicidal behavior.

1097   Mikawa, James K. "An Alternative to Current Analyses of Suicide
        Behavior." PSYCHOLOGICAL REPORT 32, no. 1 (1973): 323–30.

        Recommends that suicidal acts be assessed within a broader
        framework of coping styles and stress situations occurring over
        a period of time. Forty-seven references.

1098   Mintz, Ronald S. "Some Practical Procedures in the Management of
        Suicidal Persons." AMERICAN JOURNAL OF ORTHOPSYCHIATRY
        36, no. 5 (1966): 896–903.

        Discusses procedures found to be useful in the psychotherapy
        and management of suicidal persons. Forty-six references.

1099   Niswander, G. Donald; Casey, Thomas M.; and Humphrey, John A.
        A PANORAMA OF SUICIDE. Springfield, Ill.: Charles C Thomas,
        1973. 149 p.

        Presents case studies and interview data of families and friends
        of deceased persons, to describe their life-styles, significant
        life events, and deaths.

1100   Parker, A. Morgan. SUICIDE AMONG YOUNG ADULTS. New

York: Exposition Press, 1974. 164 p.

Combines personal experiences with findings of authorities on attempted and completed suicide cases. Ten pages of references.

1101 Perlin, Seymour, ed. A HANDBOOK FOR THE STUDY OF SUICIDE. New York: Oxford University Press, 1975. 236 p.

Presents critical notions, hypotheses, theories, and research on suicide.

1102 Ranshaw, Domeena C. "Suicide and Depression in Children." JOURNAL OF SCHOOL HEALTH 44, no. 9 (1974): 487–89.

Discusses the difficulty of diagnosing depression in childhood and infancy.

1103 Retterstol, Nils. LONG TERM PROGNOSIS AFTER ATTEMPTED SUICIDE: A PERSONAL FOLLOW UP EXAMINATION. Springfield, Ill.: Charles C Thomas, 1971. 110 p.

Describes a research study begun in 1958, with follow-up data in 1966, 1967, and 1968.

1104 Rosen, David H. "The Serious Suicide Attempt: Five Year Follow Up Study of 886 Patients." JOURNAL OF THE AMERICAN MEDICAL ASSOCIATION 235, no. 19 (1976): 2105–9.

Confirms the hypothesis that persons who had seriously attempted suicide (21 percent) would have a higher suicide rate on long-term follow-up.

1105 Schneer, Henry I.; Perlstein, Abraham; and Brozovsky, Morris. "Hospitalized Suicidal Adolescents." JOURNAL OF THE AMERICAN ACADEMY OF CHILD PSYCHIATRY 14, no. 2 (1975): 268–80.

Describes two generations of adolescents, thirteen years apart, hospitalized for suicidal behavior, noting similarities and differences from non-suicidal adolescents admitted to the same wards. Twenty-two references.

1106 Schneidman, Edwin S. "Community Programs in Suicidology." In CHILD AND ADOLESCENT PSYCHIATRY. SOCIO-CULTURAL AND COMMUNITY PSYCHIATRY, edited by Gerald Caplan, chapter 49. American Handbook of Psychiatry, 2d. ed., vol. 2. New York: Basic Books, 1974.

Discusses prevention, intervention, and postvention. Seventeen references.

1107   Schneidman, Edwin S.; Farberow, Norman L.; and Litman, Robert E.
THE PSYCHOLOGY OF SUICIDE. New York: Jason Aronson, 1970.
719 p.

Contains forty-four articles written during the period 1955-66,
covering a wide range of topics relating to the psychology of
suicide.

1108   Sendbriehler, J.M. "Attempted Suicide: A Description of the Pre
and Post Suicidal States." CANADIAN PSYCHIATRIC ASSOCIATION
JOURNAL 18, no. 2 (1973): 113-16.

Compares pre- and postsuicidal states in terms of clinical,
biochemical, and physiological changes. Fifteen references.

1109   Shaffer, David. "Suicide in Childhood and Early Adolescence."
JOURNAL OF CHILD PSYCHOLOGY AND PSYCHIATRY 15 (October
1974): 275-91.

Surveys all childhood suicides in England and Wales over a
seven-year period. Reports all cases as between ages twelve
and fourteen, with twice as many boys as girls. Three pages
of references.

1110   Spalt, Lee. "Death Thoughts in Hysteria, Antisocial Personality and
Anxiety Neurosis." PSYCHIATRIC QUARTERLY 48, no. 3 (1974):
441-44.

1111   Waldenstrom, Jon; Larsson, Tage; and Ljungstedt, Nils, eds. SUICIDE
AND ATTEMPTED SUICIDE. Stockholm: Nordiska Bokhandelns Forlag,
1972. 320 p.

Contains papers presented at the Sixth International Symposium
held in Stockholm, Sweden, in 1971. Provides a broad overview of suicidal behaviors.

1112   *Weiss, James M.A. "Suicide." In ADULT CLINICAL PSYCHIATRY,
edited by Silvano Arieti and Eugene Brody, chapter 33. American
Handbook of Psychiatry, 2d ed., vol. 3. New York: Basic Books,
1974.

Gives definitions, etiological approaches, epidemiological
patterns, and suggestions for treatment. Includes 136 references.

1113   Wetzel, Richard D., and McClure, James N. "Suicide in the Men-
strual Cycle: A Review." COMPREHENSIVE PSYCHIATRY 13, no.
4 (1972): 369-74.

Reviews the literature since 1900. Twenty-eight references.

1114   Winokur, George, and Tsuang, Ming. "The Iowa 500: Suicide in Mania, Depression and Schizophrenia." AMERICAN JOURNAL OF PSYCHIATRY 132, no. 6 (1975): 650–51.

   See item no. 723 for annotation.

Chapter 8

BEHAVIOR DISORDERS WITH EMPHASIS ON BEHAVIOR DISORDERS OF CHILDHOOD AND ADOLESCENCE

This chapter covers a variety of abnormal behaviors that do not fit into any of the previous classifications. They include such responses as hyperkinetic reactions, withdrawing reactions, overanxious reactions, runaway reactions, and unsocialized aggressive reactions. However, these descriptive headings apply to behaviors that may fall under more generic psychosociological concepts. That is, these behaviors may be symptoms of broader classifications of behaviors. Thus, we have divided this chapter into sections under the headings of these broader behaviors and discuss general questions surrounding behavior disorders, their potential etiology, and treatment; child abuse; self-destructive behavior; feeding disorders; enuresis; hyperactivity; and sleep disorders. Most of this research applies to children and adolescents. The reason for this is not entirely clear but is evidently related to classification systems which imply that when adults have these problems they are classified under psychoses, neuroses, or personality disorders. Key references in this section are marked with an asterisk and include numbers 1115, 1141, 1143, 1158, 1164, 1195, 1203, 1204, 1219, 1236, and 1238.

GENERAL BEHAVIOR DISORDERS OF CHILDHOOD AND ADOLESCENCE

1115   *Anthony, E. James. "The Behavior Disorders of Childhood." In CARMICHAEL'S MANUAL OF CHILD PSYCHOLOGY, edited by Paul H. Mussen, vol. 2, pp. 667-764. New York: John Wiley and Sons, 1970.

Offers a comprehensive description and critique of current diagnostic and classification models, from a clinical, investigative, and actuarial framework. Includes a review of theories and research relating to the etiology, incidence, prevalence, treatment, and prevention of behavior disorders.

1116   Bemporad, Jules R.; Pfeifer, Carl M.; Cortner, Robert H.; and Bloom, Wallace. "Characteristics of Encopretic Patients and Their Families." JOURNAL OF THE AMERICAN ACADEMY OF CHILD PSYCHIATRY 10, no. 2 (1971): 272-92.

Describes seventeen patients with symptoms of encopresis seen at a child psychiatry clinic. Discusses family organization, cause of symptoms, and treatment patterns. Five references.

1117   Chess, Stella; Thomas, Alexander; and Birch, Herbert G. "Behavior Problems Revisited: Findings of an Anterospective Study." JOURNAL OF THE AMERICAN ACADEMY OF CHILD PSYCHIATRY 6, no. 2 (1967): 321-31.

Investigates the genesis and evolution of behavior problems, and tests the validity of theories concerning the origin and nature of behavior problems in childhood. Fourteen references.

1118   Clarizio, Harvey F., and McCoy, George F. BEHAVIOR DISORDERS IN SCHOOL AGED CHILDREN. Scranton, Pa.: Chandler, 1970. 519 p.

Presents a psycho-educational discussion with a general empirical orientation.

1119   Everett, Craig A. "Family Assessment and Intervention for Early Adolescent Problems." JOURNAL OF MARRIAGE AND FAMILY COUNSELING 2, no. 2 (1976): 155-65.

Discusses a model aimed at clinical assessment and therapeutic intervention with early adolescents and their parents. Twenty-five references.

1120   Gardner, Richard A. PSYCHOTHERAPEUTIC APPROACHES TO THE RESISTANT CHILD. New York: Jason Aronson, 1975. 384 p.

Discusses therapeutic techniques designed to involve resistant or withdrawn children in the therapeutic process.

1121   Glavin, John P., and Quay, Herbert C. "Behavior Disorders." REVIEW OF EDUCATIONAL RESEARCH 39, no. 1 (1969): 83-102.

Surveys research on aspects of behavior disorders: prevalence, characteristics, therapeutic educational provisions, teacher behavior and training, and the role of the teacher.

1122   Groves, Marion H. "The Systematic Application of the Goal Gradient Principle in the Treatment of Behavior Disorders." INTERNATIONAL HEALTH RESEARCH NEWSLETTER 16, no. 3 (1974): 7-9.

Describes the rationale and application of this method of behavioral therapy, which is based partly on systematic desensitization principles and partly on providing alternative responses to previously troublesome behaviors.

1123   Jenkins, Richard L. BEHAVIOR DISORDERS IN CHILDHOOD AND
ADOLESCENCE. Springfield, Ill.: Charles C Thomas, 1973. 140 p.

1124   McAuley, Roger, and McAuley, Patricia. CHILD BEHAVIOR PROB-
LEMS: AN EMPIRICAL APPROACH TO MANAGEMENT. New York:
Free Press, 1978. 240 p. Bibliog. Glossary.

Contains standard text material.

1125   Milton, Ohmer, and Wahler, Robert G., eds. BEHAVIOR DISORDERS:
PERSPECTIVES AND TRENDS. 3d ed. Philadelphia: J.B. Lippincott,
1973. 326 p.

Contains readings to supplement textbooks in abnormal psychology. Criticizes the medical model, and presents an alternative psychosocial model. Stresses the importance of environmental determinants.

1126   Monroe, Russell R. "Episodic Behavioral Disorders--An Unclassified
Syndrome." In ADULT CLINICAL PSYCHIATRY, edited by Silvano
Arieti and Eugene Brody, chapter 11. American Handbook of
Psychiatry. 2d ed., vol. 3. New York: Basic Books, 1974.

Discusses episodic dyscontrol, episodic reactions and behavior
associated with chronic psychopathology, neurophysiologic
mechanisms, and treatment. Twenty-four references.

1127   Novak, Arthur L., and van der Vien, Ferdinand. "Perceived Parental Relationships as a Factor in the Emotional Adjustment of Adolescence." PROCEEDINGS OF THE 77TH ANNUAL CONVENTION OF
THE AMERICAN PSYCHOLOGICAL ASSOCIATION 4, part 2 (1969):
563-64.

1128   Symonds, Martin. "The Management of the Troubled Child at Home."
AMERICAN JOURNAL OF PSYCHOANALYSIS 29, no. 1 (1969):
18-23.

1129   Thomas, Alexander, and Chess, Stella. "Development in Middle
Childhood." SEMINARS IN PSYCHIATRY 4, no. 4 (1972): 331-41.

Describes the New York longitudinal study in which the behavioral development of 136 children was followed from the
first month of infancy. Provides data on a number of features of development during the six to twelve year age period. Thirty references.

1130   _____. "Evolution of Behavior Disorders into Adolescence." AMER-
ICAN JOURNAL OF PSYCHIATRY 133, no. 5 (1976): 539-42.

Contains more information from the New York longitudinal study. Seventeen references. (See also item 1129.)

1131   Tobias, Jerry J. "Deviation in Affluent Suburbs." In CHILDHOOD DEVIATION, edited by A.R. Roberts, chapter 8. Springfield, Ill.: Charles C Thomas, 1974.

Discusses factors within the home, school, and community environments that appear to be associated with delinquency and antisocial behaviors of affluent adolescents.

CHILD ABUSE AND FAMILY VIOLENCE

1132   Alvy, Kerby T. "Preventing Child Abuse." AMERICAN PSYCHOL-OGIST 30, no. 9 (1975): 921-28.

Discusses preventive implications of different approaches to child abuse, emphasizing the need to raise public conscious-ness. Two pages of references.

1133   Ebeling, Nancy B., and Hill, Deborah A., eds. CHILD ABUSE: INTERVENTION AND TREATMENT. Acton, Mass.: Publishing Sciences Group, 1975. 182 p.

1134   Elmer, Elizabeth, and Gregg, Grace S. "Developmental Characteris-tics of Abused Children." PEDIATRICS 40, no. 4, part 1 (1967): 596-602.

Describes the developmental characteristics of abused children when admitted to a children's hospital and when evaluated some years later. Twelve references.

1135   Fontana, Vincent J. THE MALTREATED CHILD: THE MALTREATMENT SYNDROME IN CHILDREN. 2d ed. Springfield, Ill.: Charles C Thomas, 1971. 96 p.

Discusses current concepts of child abuse as well as its diag-nosis and treatment.

1136   _____. SOMEWHERE A CHILD IS CRYING: THE BATTERED CHILD. New York: Macmillan, 1973. 264 p.

1137   Franklin, Alfred W., ed. THE CHALLENGE OF CHILD ABUSE. New York: Grune and Stratton, 1977. 298 p.

Relates child abuse to general study of aggression and the moral background of the way the individual values self con-trol.

1138 Gelles, Richard J. "Demythologizing Child Abuse." FAMILY CO-
ORDINATOR 25, no. 2 (1976): 135-41.

Discusses myths about child abuse, including definition, esti-
mate of incidence, and statements of cause. Nineteen references.

1139 Gil, David G. "Unraveling Child Abuse." AMERICAN JOURNAL
OF ORTHOPSYCHIATRY 45, no. 3 (1975): 346-50.

Attempts to clarify the dynamics of child abuse, and suggests
approaches to primary prevention. Six references.

1140 _____. VIOLENCE AGAINST CHILDREN: PHYSICAL CHILD ABUSE
IN THE UNITED STATES. Cambridge: Harvard University Press, 1970.
204 p.

Reports on a national HEW survey of public opinion and
knowledge about child abuse.

1141 *Helfer, Ray E., and Kempe, C. Henry, eds. THE BATTERED CHILD.
Chicago: University of Chicago Press, 1974. 262 p.

Contains studies of parents of abused infants and small children and suggestions on treatment approaches and public responsibility. See also item 1143.

1142 Kaplun, David, and Reich, Robert. "The Murdered Child and His
Killers." AMERICAN JOURNAL OF PSYCHIATRY 133, no. 7 (1976):
804-13.

Studies 112 cases of child homicide. Identifies contributing
social and psychiatric factors, and attempts to determine the
fate of the surviving siblings as well as the degree of involvement of the city social agencies with the families.

1143 *Kempe, C. Henry, ed. THE BATTERED CHILD. Chicago: University
of Chicago Press, 1968. 268 p.

Describes theoretical and diagnostic aspects of child abuse,
along with empirical studies of specific cases. Presents multidisciplinary aspects of the problem. An earlier edition of
Helfer and Kempe's work (see item 1141).

1144 Kempe, C. Henry, and Helfer, Ray E., eds. HELPING THE BATTERED
CHILD AND HIS FAMILY. Philadelphia: J.B. Lippincott, 1972.
313 p.

Discusses practical matters involving the establishment of
treatment programs for children who are battered and for
parents who do the battering.

1145 Lystad, Mary Hanemann. "Violence at Home: A Review of the Literature." AMERICAN JOURNAL OF ORTHOPSYCHIATRY 45, no. 3 (1975): 328-45.

Analyzes studies on family violence, and describes the phenomenon from psychological, social, and cultural perspectives. Concludes that a comprehensive theory of violence at home must take into account factors at all these levels. Seven pages of references.

1146 Mitchell, Ross G. "The Incidence and Nature of Child Abuse." DEVELOPMENTAL MEDICINE IN CHILD NEUROLOGY 17, no. 5 (1975): 641-44.

Discusses abusive mothers.

1147 Scott, P.D. "Battered Wives." BRITISH JOURNAL OF PSYCHIATRY 125 (November 1974): 433-41.

Defines the battered wife as a woman who has suffered serious or repeated injury from the man with whom she lives.

1148 Smith, Selwyn, ed. THE MALTREATMENT OF CHILDREN: A COMPREHENSIVE GUIDE TO THE BATTERED BABY SYNDROME. Baltimore: University Park Press, 1978. 350 p.

Covers medical, psychiatric, sociological, and legal aspects of child abuse. Examines the nature of the problem and its causes and effects, and offers suggestions for remediation.

SELF-DESTRUCTIVE BEHAVIOR

1149 Bach-y Rita, George. "Habitual Violence and Self-Mutilation." AMERICAN JOURNAL OF PSYCHIATRY 131, no. 9 (1974): 1018-20.

Reports that 57 percent of a group of twenty-two habitually violent male patients in a prison facility have scars resulting from self-inflicted wounds. Nineteen references.

1150 Frankel, Fred, and Simmons, James Q. III. "Self-Injurious Behavior in Schizophrenic and Retarded Children." AMERICAN JOURNAL OF MENTAL DEFICIENCY 80, no. 5 (1976): 512-22.

Suggests that self-injurious behavior is a problem with children who are primarily nonverbal and low functioning. Sixty references.

1151 Geiger, Jane K.; Sindberg, Ronald M.; and Barnes, Charles M.

"Head Hitting in Severely Retarded Children." AMERICAN JOURNAL OF NURSING 74, no. 10 (1974): 1822-25.

1152 Goldberg, George. "The Psychological, Physiological and Hypnotic Approach to Bruxism in the Treatment of Periodontal Disease." JOURNAL OF THE AMERICAN SOCIETY OF PSYCHOSOMATIC DENTISTRY AND MEDICINE 20, no. 3 (1973): 75-91.

Presents a comprehensive review of the effects of tension in dental problems.

1153 Goldfield, Michael D., and Glick, Ira D. "Self Mutilation of the Genitalia." MEDICAL ASPECTS OF HUMAN SEXUALITY 7, no. 4 (1973): 219-36.

1154 Lester, David. "Self Mutilating Behavior." PSYCHOLOGICAL BULLETIN 78, no. 2 (1972): 119-28.

Discusses the varieties of self-mutilating behavior, and reviews studies on their prevalence, with special focus on head banging, trichotilomania, wrist cutting, and self castration.

1155 Lovaas, O. Ivar, and Simmons, James Q. III. "Manipulation of Self-Destruction in Three Retarded Children." JOURNAL OF APPLIED BEHAVIOR ANALYSIS 2, no. 3 (1969): 143-57.

1156 Pao, Ping N. "The Syndrome of Delicate Self-Cutting." BRITISH JOURNAL OF MEDICAL PSYCHOLOGY 42, no. 3 (1969): 193-206.

Discusses the experience of self-cutting from both the patient's and the therapist's view. Forty-one references.

1157 Podvall, Edward M. "Self-Mutilation within a Hospital Setting: A Study of Identity and Social Compliance." BRITISH JOURNAL OF MEDICAL PSYCHOLOGY 42, no. 3 (1969): 213-21.

1158 *Roberts, Albert R., ed. SELF-DESTRUCTIVE BEHAVIOR. Springfield, Ill.: Charles C Thomas, 1975. 215 p.

Contains articles concerning patterns of direct and indirect self-destruction and the social, medical, psychological, and psychiatric correlates of such behavior.

1159 Williams, Cyril. "Self Injury in Children." DEVELOPMENTAL MEDICINE AND CHILD NEUROLOGY 16, no. 1 (1974): 88-90.

Reviews the literature on self-injurious behavior. Suggests that, in the absence of good classification of the nature and cause of such behavior, most treatment has to be pragmatic.

FEEDING DISORDERS: ANOREXIA NERVOSA AND OBESITY

1160   Amdur, Millard J.; Tucker, Gary J.; Detre, Thomas; and Markhus, Kathryn. "Anorexia Nervosa: An Interactional Study." JOURNAL OF NERVOUS AND MENTAL DISEASE 148, no. 5 (1969): 559–66.

        Observes fluctuations of behavioral symptoms and weight in relationship to treatment and stress periods.

1161   Blinder, Barton J.; Freeman, Daniel M.; and Stunkard, Albert J. "Behavior Therapy of Anorexia Nervosa: Effectiveness of Activity as a Reinforcer of Weight Gain." AMERICAN JOURNAL OF PSYCHIATRY 126, no. 8 (1970): 1093–98.

        Reports application of operant reinforcement to patients by making access to physical activity contingent upon weight gain; treatment resulted in rapid weight restoration. Twenty-eight references.

1162   Bruch, Hilde. "Anorexia and Its Differential Diagnosis." JOURNAL OF MENTAL AND NERVOUS DISEASE 141, no. 5 (1966): 555–66.

1163   . "Anorexia Nervosa." In ORGANIC DISORDERS AND PSYCHOSOMATIC MEDICINE, edited by Morton F. Reiser, chapter 32. American Handbook of Psychiatry, 2d ed., vol. 4. New York: Basic Books, 1975.

        Gives the history of the concept and discusses primary anorexia nervosa, atypical anorexia nervosa, and treatment concepts. Forty-nine references.

1164   *   . EATING DISORDERS: OBESITY AND ANOREXIA NERVOSA. New York: Basic Books, 1973. 396 p.

        Reviews biological, psychological, metabolic, and physiological studies on these eating disorders.

1165   . "Eating Disturbances in Adolescents." In CHILD AND ADOLESCENT PSYCHIATRY. SOCIO-CULTURAL AND COMMUNITY PSYCHIATRY, edited by Gerald Caplan, chapter 18. American Handbook of Psychiatry, 2d ed., vol. 2. New York: Basic Books, 1974.

        Discusses definitions of growth in adolescents and various biological, social, and psychiatric aspects. Describes therapeutic implications, and gives case illustrations. Twenty-five references.

1166   . "Psychotherapy in Primary Anorexia Nervosa." JOURNAL OF NERVOUS AND MENTAL DISEASE 150, no. 1 (1970): 51–67.

1167 Cappon, Daniel. EATING, LOVING AND DYING: A PSYCHOL-
OGY OF APPETITE. Toronto: University of Toronto Press, 1973.
118 p.

Discusses the psychological causes and treatment for persons
who are either very much overweight or very much under-
weight.

1168 Chinn, Terrance A. "Compulsive Water Drinking: A Review of the
Literature and an Additional Case." JOURNAL OF NERVOUS AND
MENTAL DISEASE 158, no. 1 (1974): 78-86.

Reviews medical literature to identify cases of compulsive
water drinking. Assigns each case to the appropriate psychiatric diagnostic category. Sixteen references.

1169 Crisp, A.H. "Premorbid Factors in Adult Disorders of Weight with
Particular Reference to Primary Anorexia Nervosa (Weight Phobia): A
Literature Review." JOURNAL OF PSYCHOSOMATIC RESEARCH 14,
no. 1 (1970): 1-22.

Reviews the literature on anorexia nervosa in terms of premorbid features, determinants of obesity, determinants of birth
weight, menarche, and the validity of reports based on memory. Includes 137 references.

1170 _____. "A Treatment Regime for Anorexia Nervosa." BRITISH
JOURNAL OF PSYCHIATRY 112, no. 486 (1966): 505-12.

1171 Gailand, Hugh; Sumner, David; and Fourman, Paul. "The Kleine-
Levin Syndrome." NEUROLOGY 15, no. 12 (1965): 1161-67.

Describes the Kleine-Levin syndrome as a "clinical entity
characterized by recurring episodes of excessive eating, intermittent withdrawal sometimes amounting to excessive sleep,
and behavior disorders of which uninhibited sexuality is the
most specific."

1172 Geller, Jeffrey L. "Treatment of Anorexia Nervosa by the Integration
of Behavior Therapy and Psychotherapy." PSYCHOTHERAPY AND
PSYCHOSOMATICS 26, no. 3 (1975): 167-77.

Notes that anorexia nervosa has been approached by a variety
of therapeutic regimens addressed to either the underlying
psychological problems or the eating disorder itself. Suggests
integrating behavior therapy and psychotherapy in a treatment
plan to address both problems simultaneously. Sixty-eight
references.

1173 Gluckman, Myron L., and Hirsch, Jules. "The Response of Obese

Patients to Weight Reduction." PSYCHOSOMATIC MEDICINE 31, no. 1 (1969): 1-7

1174 Halmi, Katherine A. "Anorexia Nervosa: Demographic and Clinical Features in 94 Cases." PSYCHOSOMATIC MEDICINE 36, no. 1 (1974): 18-26.

1175 _____. "Anorexia Nervosa: Recent Investigations." ANNUAL RE-VIEW OF MEDICINE 29 (1978): 137-48.

Discusses blood and chemical studies in anorexia nervosa and reviews endocrine investigations. Notes that no single hypothesis of etiology has been supported.

1176 Halmi, Katherine A.; Powers, Pauline; and Cunningham, Sheila. "Treatment of Anorexia Nervosa with Behavior Modification: Effectiveness of Formula Feeding and Isolation." ARCHIVES OF GENERAL PSYCHIATRY 32, no. 1 (1975): 93-96.

Notes that data from a short-term follow-up assessment indicate that all subjects are maintaining or continuing to gain toward their normal weight range on individualized positive reinforcement programs. Thirty references.

1177 Kiell, Norman, ed. THE PSYCHOLOGY OF OBESITY: DYNAMICS IN TREATMENT. Springfield, Ill.: Charles C Thomas, 1973. 458 p.

Contains papers representing a multidisciplinary approach to the study of obesity. Forty-two pages of references.

1178 Kline, Milton V.; Coleman, Lester L.; and Wick, Erika E., eds. OBESITY: ETIOLOGY, TREATMENT AND MANAGEMENT. Springfield, Ill.: Charles C Thomas, 1976. 480 p. Illus.

Classifies obesity within a psychodynamic and clinical orientation. Discusses types of obesity encountered in the daily practice of psychotherapy. Ninety pages of references.

1179 Lucos, Alexander R.; Duncan, Jane W.; and Piens, Violet. "The Treatment of Anorexia Nervosa." AMERICAN JOURNAL OF PSYCHIATRY 133, no. 9 (1976): 1034-38.

1180 Masserman, Jules H. "Syndromes Resulting from Overlax Control: II Man-Family." In EXPERIMENTAL BEHAVIOR: A BASIS FOR THE STUDY OF MENTAL DISTURBANCE, edited by J.H. Cullen. New York: John Wiley and Sons, 1974.

1181 Nagaraja, Jaya. "Anorexia and Cyclic Vomiting in Children: A

Psychogenic Study." CHILD PSYCHIATRY QUARTERLY 7, no. 4 (1974): 1-5.

Examines etiological factors that contribute to psychosomatic diseases manifested through anorexia and cyclic vomiting in children.

1182 Rau, John H., and Green, Richard S. "Compulsive Eating: A Neuropsychologic Approach to Certain Eating Disorders." COMPREHENSIVE PSYCHIATRY 16, no. 3 (1975): 223-31.

Defines compulsive eating as irregular, unpredictable episodes of ego-dystonic excessive eating during which large quantities of food are consumed. Fifty references.

1183 Robin, Judith. "Causes and Consequences of Time Perception Differences in Overweight and Normal People." JOURNAL OF PERSONALITY AND SOCIAL PSYCHOLOGY 31, no. 5 (1975): 898-904.

1184 Rowland, Christopher V., Jr., ed. ANOREXIA AND OBESITY: INTERNATIONAL PSYCHIATRY CLINICS. Vol. 7, no. 1. Boston: Little, Brown, 1970. 360 p.

1185 Steele, Carolyn I. "Obese Adolescent Girls: Some Diagnostic and Treatment Considerations." ADOLESCENTS 9, no. 33 (1974): 81-96.

Suggests that adolescence is a period of mourning for one's dependence on parents and that obesity in adolescent girls may be caused by their anxiety about attaining an independent existence. Thirty references.

1186 Stinbert, Vaughn E., and Coffey, Kitty R. "Obese Children and Adolescents: A Review." ERIC CLEARINGHOUSE ON EARLY CHILDHOOD: RESEARCH RELATING TO CHILDREN 30 (March 1972): 1-30.

Discusses confusion in the definition of overweight and obesity, and describes various calibration methods for determining obesity. Reviews research on physical and psychosocial factors involved in the causes, consequences, and cures of obesity. Thirteen pages of references.

1187 Stunkard, Albert J. "Obesity." In ORGANIC DISORDERS AND PSYCHOSOMATIC MEDICINE, edited by Morton F. Reiser, chapter 31. American Handbook of Psychiatry, 2d ed., vol. 4. New York: Basic Books, 1975.

Discusses the epidemiology, genetics, etiology, and treatment of obesity in childhood. Sixty-four references.

1188   Tolstrup, Kai. "The Treatment of Anorexia Nervosa in Childhood and Adolescence." JOURNAL OF CHILD PSYCHOLOGY AND PSYCHIATRY AND ALLIED DISCIPLINES 16, no. 1 (1975): 75-78.

1189   Warren, W. "A Study of Anorexia Nervosa in Young Girls." JOURNAL OF CHILD PSYCHOLOGY AND PSYCHIATRY 9 (October 1968): 27-40.

1190   Winick, Myron, ed. CHILDHOOD OBESITY. New York: John Wiley and Sons, 1975. 189 p.

    Contains thirteen papers on the causes and effects of obesity during the developmental years.

1191   Young, J.K. "A Possible Neuroendocrine Basis of Two Clinical Syndromes: Anorexia Nervosa and the Kleine-Levin Syndrome." PHYSIOLOGICAL PSYCHOLOGY 3, no. 4 (1975): 322-30.

    Reviews the two clinical syndromes, and proposes a neuroendocrine basis for both. Three pages of references.

SPECIAL SYMPTOMS

Enuresis

1192   Bindelglos, Paul M. "The Enuretic Child." JOURNAL OF FAMILY PRACTICE 2, no. 5 (1975): 375-80.

    Notes that enuresis is a symptom believed to result from a variety of etiological factors including genitourinary disease, neurological disturbances, delayed development, allergic reactions, deep sleep, and psychological factors. Thirty-nine references.

1193   Dimitriov, E.; Konfas, K.; and Logothetis, J. "Relationship Between Parental Attitudes Towards the Emotionally Distrubed Child and Nocturnal Enuresis." BEHAVIORAL NEUROPSYCHIATRY 8, nos. 1-12 (1976-77): 76-77.

1194   Fermaglich, Joseph L. "Electroencephalographic Study of Enuretics." AMERICAN JOURNAL OF DISEASES OF CHILDREN 118, no. 3 (1969): 473-78.

    Reports that of thirty-nine four- to eighteen-year-old enuretics, thirteen had distinctly abnormal EEGs, and four others showed some sign of abnormality.

1195 *Freeman, Ellen D. "The Treatment of Enuresis: An Overview." INTERNATIONAL JOURNAL OF PSYCHIATRY IN MEDICINE 6, no. 3 (1975): 403-12.

Reviews the history of the treatment of enuresis as described in world medical literature. Fifty-four references.

1196 Novick, Jack. "Symptomatic Treatment of Acquired and Persistent Enuresis." JOURNAL OF ABNORMAL PSYCHOLOGY 71, no. 5 (1966): 363-68.

1197 Ritvo, Edward R.; Ornitz, Edward M.; Gottlieb, Fred; Poussaint, Alvin S.; Maron, Barry J.; Ditman, Keith S.; and Blinn, Kenneth A. "Arousal and Non-Arousal Enuretic Events." AMERICAN JOURNAL OF PSYCHIATRY 126, no. 1 (1969): 77-84.

Presents a somatopsychic model for the etiology of enuresis. Fifteen references.

1198 Umphress, Agnes; Murphy, Solbritt; Nickols, Jackson; and Hammar, Sherrell. "Adolescent Enuresis: A Sociological Study of Family Interaction." ARCHIVES OF GENERAL PSYCHIATRY 22, no. 3 (1970): 237-74.

Studies family relationships in homes of enuretic and nonenuretic clinic patients and normal nonenuretic adolescents from neighboring schools. Fifteen references.

1199 Vernia, J.K.; Shah, D.K.; and Bhatia, S.C. "Enuresis in Children: A Psychological Study." CHILD PSYCHIATRY QUARTERLY 5, no. 2 (1972): 28-34.

Studies 26 cases of enuresis among 200 emotionally disturbed children. Twenty-one references.

Hyperactivity

1200 Anderson, Robert P., and Halcomb, Charles G., eds. LEARNING DISABILITY/MINIMAL BRAIN DYSFUNCTION SYNDROME: RESEARCH PERSPECTIVES AND APPLICATIONS. Springfield, Ill.: Charles C Thomas, 1976. 283 p.

Contains proceedings of a conference held in Texas in 1973.

1201 Arnold, L. Eugene. "Minimal Brain Dysfunction: A Hydraulic Parfait Model." DISEASES OF THE NERVOUS SYSTEM 37, no. 7 (1976): 171-73.

Demonstrates the overlap of minimal brain dysfunction, behavior disorders, and learning disorders.

1202   Barcie, Avner, and Rabkin, Leslie Y. "A Precursor of Delinquency: The Hyperkinetic Disorder of Childhood." PSYCHIATRIC QUARTERLY 48, no. 3 (1974): 387-99.

Examines behavior and personality variables identified as common to theories and etiology of delinquency and to the life histories of hyperkinetic children. Thirty-seven references.

1203   *Bradley, Charles. "The Behavior of Children Receiving Benzedrine." AMERICAN JOURNAL OF PSYCHIATRY 94 (November 1937): 577-85.

Classic article which initiated the movement to use stimulant medication for children with behavior disorders; the first to publicize the paradoxical effect of stimulant medication.

1204   *Cantwell, Dennis P., ed. THE HYPERACTIVE CHILD: DIAGNOSIS, MANAGEMENT, CURRENT RESEARCH. New York: Spectrum Publications, 1975. 209 p.

Describes the clinical picture, epidemiology, and classification of the hyperactive child syndrome.

1205   Clements, Sam D. TASK FORCE ONE: MINIMAL BRAIN DYSFUNCTION IN CHILDREN. National Institute of Neurological Diseases and Blindness Monograph No. 3. Washington, D.C.: U.S. Department of Health, Education and Welfare, 1966. 18 p.

Includes definitions, nomenclature, symptomatologies, diagnosis, and evaluation criteria. Includes 124 references.

1206   Cole, Sherwood O. "Hyperkinetic Children: The Use of Stimulant Drugs Evaluated." AMERICAN JOURNAL OF ORTHOPSYCHIATRY 45, no. 1 (1975): 28-37.

Reviews the use of stimulant drugs in the treatment of hyperkinetic children. Thirty-five references.

1207   Fish, Barbara. "The 'One Child One Drug' Myth of Stimulants in Hyperkinesis." ARCHIVES OF GENERAL PSYCHIATRY 25, no. 3 (1971): 193-203.

Points out that hyperkinesis is not a unitary disorder and that different types of behaviors require different treatment. Describes many types of hyperactive children, and suggests the use of stimulants for only some of them. Discusses the popular myth that stimulants are the most useful drugs for all hyperactive children.

1208   Freedman, Daniel X.; Brazelton, T. Berry; Comer, James; Cruickshank,

William; Crump, Edward P.; Fish, Barbara; Garrison, George H.; Hewett, F.; Hollister, Leo E.; Kornetsky, Conan; Ladd, Edward T.; Levine, Robert J.; Morisey, Patricia; Shulman, Irving; and Smith, Martin. "Report of the Conferences on the Use of Stimulant Drugs in the Treatment of Behaviorally Disturbed Young School Children." JOURNAL OF LEARNING DISABILITIES 4, no. 9 (1971): 59-66.

Presents guidelines for using stimulant medication with hyperkinetic children. Supports the assumption that one needs therapy in conjunction with a drug regimen to produce effective treatment results.

1209   Gardner, Richard A. MBD: THE FAMILY BOOK ABOUT MINIMAL BRAIN DYSFUNCTION. New York: Jason Aronson, 1973. 185 p.

For families of hyperactive or MBD children.

1210   Gross, Mortimer B., and Wilson, William C. MINIMAL BRAIN DYS-FUNCTION. New York: Brunner/ Mazel, 1974. 206 p.

1211   Howell, Mary C.; Reve, George W.; Scholl, Mary L.; and Rutledge, Anne. "Hyperactivity in Children: Types, Diagnosis, Drug Therapy, Approaches to Management." CLINICAL PEDIATRICS 11, no. 1 (1972): 30-39.

1212   Langhorne, John E.; Loney, Jam; Paternite, Carl E.; and Bechtoldt, Harold P. "Childhood Hyperkinesis: A Return to the Source." JOURNAL OF ABNORMAL PSYCHOLOGY 85, no. 2 (1976): 201-9.

Discusses the most widely agreed upon primary or core symptoms of hyperkinesis. Fifty references.

1213   Laufer, M.W. "In Osler's Day It Was Syphilis." In EXPLORATIONS IN CHILD PSYCHIATRY, edited by E. James Anthony, pp. 105-24. New York: Plenum Publishing Corp., 1975.

Offers a historical approach to the recognition of hyperkinesis and the evolution of the clinical syndrome, with possible etiological explanations. Thirty-nine references.

1214   Oetingor, Leon. "Learning Disorders, Hyperkinesis, and the Use of Drugs in Children." REHABILITATION LITERATURE 32, no. 6 (1971): 162-67, 170.

Reviews the literature on the relationship between the use of drugs in children and learning disorders and other behavioral variants, particularly hyperactivity.

1215   O'Malley, John E., and Eisenberg, Leon. "The Hyperkinetic Syndrome." In MINIMAL CEREBRAL DYSFUNCTION IN CHILDREN, edited by S. Walzer and P.H. Wolff, pp. 95-103. New York: Grune and Stratton, 1973.

Discusses hyperkinesis as a chronic and serious abnormality. Describes behavior characteristics, epidemiology, and etiology.

1216 Paternite, Carl E.; Loney, Jan; Langhorne, John E., Jr. "Relationships Between Symptomatology and SES-Related Factors in Hyperkinetic/MBD Boys." AMERICAN JOURNAL OF ORTHOPSYCHIATRY 46, no. 2 (1976): 291-301.

1217 Renshaw, Domeena. THE HYPERACTIVE CHILD. Chicago: Nelson Hall, 1974. 197 p.

Presents an elementary description of hyperactivity and major treatment modalities. For parents.

1218 Rie, Herbert E. "Hyperactivity in Children." AMERICAN JOURNAL OF DISEASES IN CHILDREN 129, no. 7 (1975): 783-89.

Suggests that various childhood problems that are often subsumed under the heading of hyperactivity occur in combinations, apparently for several reasons. Notes that the designation does not define a homogeneous group of children or consistently point to a common cause. Forty references.

1219 *Ross, Dorothea M., and Ross, Sheila A. HYPERACTIVITY: RESEARCH, THEORY, AND ACTION. New York: John Wiley and Sons, 1976. 385 p.

Provides details of research findings, and offers a blueprint for coping with hyperactive children. Includes etiology, drug intervention, psychotherapy and education, prevention, team management, and potential control of the problem. Includes an extensive bibliography.

1220 Safer, Daniel J., and Allen, Richard P. HYPERACTIVE CHILDREN: DIAGNOSIS AND MANAGEMENT. Baltimore: University Park Press, 1976. 239 p.

Discusses and synthesizes information about hyperactivity and practical details of daily clinical management. Assesses interdisciplinary input in developing management plans.

1221 Satterfield, James M.; Cantwell, Dennis P.; and Satterfield, Breena T. "Pathophysiology of the Hyperactive Child Syndrome." ARCHIVES OF GENERAL PSYCHIATRY 31, no. 12 (1974): 839-44,

Suggests that some hyperactive children may be characterized as having a low central nervous system arousal level. Three pages of references.

1222 Schain, R.J. "Minimal Brain Dysfunction." CURRENT PROBLEMS IN PEDIATRICS 5, no. 10 (1975): 3-30.

Contains a brief but fairly comprehensive review of the literature on the major areas of MBD.

1223 Schrag, Peter, and Divoky, Diane. THE MYTH OF THE HYPERACTIVE CHILD. New York: Pantheon, 1975. 285 p.

Considers the term "hyperactive" as a "vogue" term, and takes the position that children are overmedicated. Reports epidemiological studies to support this view.

1224 Weiss, Gabrielle; Minde, Klaus; Werry, John S.; Douglas, Virginia; and Nemeth, Elizabeth. "Studies on the Hyperactive Child: Five Year Follow Up." ARCHIVES OF GENERAL PSYCHIATRY 24 (May 1971): 409-14.

1225 Wender, Paul H. THE HYPERACTIVE CHILD: A HANDBOOK FOR PARENTS. New York: Crown, 1973. 120 p.

1226 _____. MINIMAL BRAIN DYSFUNCTION IN CHILDREN. New York: Wiley-Interscience, 1971. 242 p.

Describes a broad concept of MBD that includes not only hyperactive behavior and specific learning disabilities but also neurotic, psychopathic, and schizophrenic subvariants.

1227 Werry, John S. "Studies on the Hyperactive Child: An Empirical Analysis of the Minimal Brain Dysfunction Syndrome." ARCHIVES OF GENERAL PSYCHIATRY 19 (July 1968): 9-16.

Reports on a variety of neurological, EEG, medical history, cognitive, and psychiatric measures, taken on 103 hyperactive children of normal intelligence, subjected to factor analysis. Seventeen references.

Disorders of Sleep

1228 Anders, Thomas F., and Weinstein, Pearl. "Sleep and Its Disorders in Infants and Children: A Review." JOURNAL OF PEDIATRICS 50, no. 2 (1972): 311-24.

Discusses polygraphic studies of sleep to assess the central nervous system functioning in newborn infants and to diagnose sleep disorders in children. Eighty-four references.

1229 Bonkalo, Alexander. "Impulsive Acts of Confusional States During Incomplete Arousal from Sleep: Criminological and Forensic Implications." PSYCHIATRIC QUARTERLY 48, no. 3 (1974): 400-409.

Suggests that "sleep drunkenness" is a syndrome in its own right and that this condition is probably more common than is generally believed. Twenty-three references.

1230 Kales, Anthony, and Kales, Joyce D. "Sleep Disorders: Recent Findings in the Diagnosis and Treatment of Disturbed Sleep." NEW ENGLAND JOURNAL OF MEDICINE 290, no. 9 (1974): 487-99.

Describes laboratory studies, psychological evaluations, and management of sleep disorders, somnambulism, night terrors and nightmares, enuresis, narcolepsy, hypersomnia, and hypnotic-drug dependence. Ninety-five references.

1231 _____. "Somnambulism: Psychophysiological Correlates II: Psychiatric Interviews, Psychological Testing and Discussion." ARCHIVES OF GENERAL PSYCHIATRY 14, no. 6 (1966): 595-604.

1232 Kales, Anthony; Paulson, Morris, J.; Jacobson, Alan; and Kales, Joyce D. "Somnambulism: Psychophysiological Correlates I: All-Night EEG Studies." ARCHIVES OF GENERAL PSYCHIATRY 14, no. 6 (1966): 586-94.

1233 Moldofsky, Harvey; Scarisbrick, Phillip; England, Robert; and Smythe, Hugh. "Musculoskeletal Symptoms and Non-REM Sleep Disturbance in Patients with 'Fibrositis Syndrome' and Healthy Subjects." PSYCHOSOMATIC MEDICINE 37, no. 4 (1975): 341-51.

1234 Nagaraja, Jaya. "Somnambulism in Children: Clinical Communication." CHILD PSYCHIATRY QUARTERLY 7, no. 1 (1974): 18-19.

1235 Regestein, Quentin R. "A Clinical Framework for Insomnia." MASSACHUSETTS JOURNAL OF MENTAL HEALTH 4, no. 1 (1975): 4-15.

Suggests that insomnia is a mask for many psychopathological conditions and that these should not be ignored. Nineteen references.

1236 *Usdin, Gene, ed. SLEEP RESEARCH IN CLINICAL PRACTICE. New York: Brunner/Mazel, 1973. 94 p.

1237 Williams, Richard Q., and Karacon, Ismet. "Clinical Disorders of Sleep." In SLEEP RESEARCH IN CLINICAL PRACTICE, edited by Gene Usdin, chapter 2. New York: Brunner/Mazel, 1973.

Defines and presents clinical data on sleep disorders. Includes 220 references.

1238 *_____. "Sleep Disorders and Disordered Sleep." In ORGANIC DIS-
ORDERS AND PSYCHOSOMATIC MEDICINE, edited by Morton F.
Reiser, chapter 35. American Handbook of Psychiatry, 2d ed., vol.
4. New York: Basic Books, 1975.

Discusses primary sleep disorders, secondary sleep disorders,
parasomnia, and sleep-modified disorders. Includes 446 references.

Appendix

JOURNALS AND SERIALS

The following is a selected list of technical journals and serials on all aspects of abnormal behavior. This listing is limited to national and some international periodicals. All international journals listed provide English translations of their articles. Most of the items not only contain articles of interest in the field of abnormal psychology, but also include book reviews, notes, information on additional sources and reference materials.

ACTA NEUROLOGICA. Universita di Napoli, Facolta di Medicina e Chirurgia, Clinica Malattie Nervose e Mentali, Nuova Policlinico, Cappella dei Cangiani, 80100 Naples, Italy. 1946-- . Bimonthly.

ACTA NEUROLOGICA SCANDINAVICA. Munksgaard, Noerre Soegade 35, DK-1370 Copenhagen K, Denmark. 1961-- . Monthly.

ACTA PAEDOPSYCHIATRICA. Schwabe und Co., Steinenforstr. 13, 4010 Basel, Switzerland. 1934-- . 6/year.

ACTA PSYCHIATRICA SCANDINAVICA. Munksgaard, Noerre Soegade 35, DK-1370 Copenhagen K, Denmark. 1926-- . 10/year.

ADVANCES IN BEHAVIOR RESEARCH AND THERAPY. Pergamon Press, Maxwell House, Fairview Park, Elmsford, N.Y. 10523. 1976-- . Quarterly.

AMERICAN ACADEMY OF CHILD PSYCHIATRY JOURNAL. Yale University Press, Journals Department, 92 A Yale Station, New Haven, Conn. 06520. 1962-- . Quarterly.

AMERICAN ACADEMY OF PSYCHIATRY AND NEUROLOGY JOURNAL. American Academy of Psychiatry and Neurology, 17 Kingston Road, Scarsdale, N.Y. 10583. 1976-- . Quarterly.

AMERICAN ACADEMY OF PSYCHOANALYSIS JOURNAL. Wiley-Interscience, 605 Third Avenue, New York, N.Y. 10016. 1973-- . Quarterly.

Journals and Serials

AMERICAN JOURNAL OF MENTAL DEFICIENCY. American Association on Mental Deficiency, 5201 Connecticut Avenue, N.W., Washington, D.C. 20015. 1876-- . Bimonthly.

AMERICAN JOURNAL OF ORTHOPSYCHIATRY. American Orthopsychiatric Association, 1775 Broadway, New York, N.Y. 10019. 1930-- . Quarterly.

AMERICAN JOURNAL OF PSYCHIATRY. American Psychiatric Association, 1700 Eighteenth Street, N.W., Washington, D.C. 20009. 1844-- . Monthly.

AMERICAN JOURNAL OF PSYCHOANALYSIS. APS Publications, 150 Fifth Avenue, New York, N.Y. 10011. 1941-- . Quarterly.

AMERICAN JOURNAL OF PSYCHOTHERAPY. Association for the Advancement of Psychotherapy, 114 East Seventy-eighth Street, New York, N.Y. 10021. 1946-- . Quarterly.

AMERICAN PSYCHOANALYTIC ASSOCIATION JOURNAL. International Universities Press, 315 Fifth Avenue, New York, N.Y. 10016. 1953-- . Quarterly.

AMERICAN PSYCHOLOGIST. American Psychological Association, 1200 Seventeenth Street, N.W., Washington, D.C. 20036. 1946-- . Monthly.

ARCHIVES OF GENERAL PSYCHIATRY. American Medical Association, 535 North Dearborn Street, Chicago, Ill. 60610. 1959-- . Monthly.

ARCHIVES OF NEUROLOGY. American Medical Association, 535 North Dearborn Street, Chicago, Ill. 60610. 1959-- . Monthly.

AUSTRALIAN AND NEW ZEALAND JOURNAL OF PSYCHIATRY. Australian and New Zealand College of Psychiatrists, 107 Rathdown Street, Carlton, Victoria, Australia. 1967-- . Quarterly.

AUSTRALIAN JOURNAL OF MENTAL RETARDATION. Group for the Scientific Study of Mental Deficiency, Box 114, Kew, Victoria 3101 Australia. 1970-- . Quarterly.

AUSTRALIAN JOURNAL OF PSYCHOLOGY. Australian Psychological Society, National Science Centre, 191 Royal Parade, Parksville, Victoria 3052 Australia. 1949-- . 3/year.

BEHAVIORAL NEUROPSYCHIATRY. Behavioral Neuropsychiatry Medical Publishers, 61 East 86th Street, New York, N.Y. 10028. 1969-- . Bimonthly.

BEHAVIOR MODIFICATION. Sage Publications, 275 South Beverly Drive, Beverly Hills, Calif. 90212. 1977-- . Quarterly.

BEHAVIOR RESEARCH AND THERAPY. Pergamon Press, Maxwell House, Fairview Park, Elmsford, N.Y. 10523. 1963-- . Bimonthly.

BEHAVIOR THERAPY. Academic Press, 111 Fifth Avenue, New York, N.Y. 10003. 1970-- . 5/year.

BIOLOGICAL PSYCHIATRY. Plenum Publishing Corp., 227 West Seventeenth Street, New York, N.Y. 10011. 1969-- . Bimonthly.

BRITISH JOURNAL OF MENTAL SUBNORMALITY. British Society for the Study of Mental Subnormality, Monyhull Hospital, Birmingham, England. 1955-- . Semiannual.

BRITISH JOURNAL OF PSYCHIATRY. Headley Bros. Ltd., Ashford, Kent. TN24 8H H, England. 1853-- . Monthly.

BRITISH JOURNAL OF PSYCHOLOGY. Cambridge University Press, 200 Euston Road, London NW1 2DB, England. 1904-- . Quarterly.

BRITISH JOURNAL OF SOCIAL AND CLINICAL PSYCHOLOGY. Cambridge University Press, 200 Euston Road, London NW1 2DB, England. 1962-- . Quarterly.

CANADA'S MENTAL HEALTH/HYGIENE MENTALE AU CANADA. Department of National Health and Welfare, Health Programs Branch, Ottawa, Ontario K1A 1B4, Canada. 1953-- . Quarterly.

CANADIAN PSYCHIATRIC ASSOCIATION JOURNAL. Canadian Psychiatric Association, 225 Lisgar Street, Suite 103, Ottawa, Ontario K2P OC6, Canada. 1956-- . 8/year.

CHILD PSYCHIATRY AND HUMAN DEVELOPMENT. Human Sciences Press, 72 Fifth Avenue, New York, N.Y. 10011. 1970-- . Quarterly.

CHILD PSYCHIATRY QUARTERLY. Community Mental Health Center, Indira Health Home, 8-2-547/2 Road No. 7, Banjara Hills, Hyderabad 500034, Andra Pradesh, India. 1967-- .

CLINICAL PSYCHOLOGIST. American Psychological Association, Division 12, c/o Temple University, Philadelphia, Pa. 19122. 1946-- . Quarterly.

COMMUNITY MENTAL HEALTH REVIEW. Haworth Press, 149 Fifth Avenue, New York, N.Y. 10010. 1975-- . Bimonthly.

COMPREHENSIVE PSYCHIATRY. Grune and Stratton, 111 Fifth Avenue, New York, N.Y. 10003. 1960-- . Bimonthly.

CONTEMPORARY PSYCHOLOGY. American Psychological Association, 1200 Seventeenth Street, N.W., Washington, D.C. 20036. 1956-- . Monthly.

DISEASES OF THE NERVOUS SYSTEM. Physicians Postgraduate Press, Box 38293, Memphis, Tenn. 38138. 1940-- . Monthly.

EPILEPSIA. Raven Press, 1140 Avenue of the Americas, New York, N.Y. 10036. 1959-- . Quarterly.

FAMILY THERAPY. Libra Publishers, 391 Willets Road, Rosslyn, N.Y. 11577. 1972-- . 3/year.

GROUP PSYCHOTHERAPY, PSYCHODRAMA AND SOCIOMETRY. Beacon House, 259 Wolcott Avenue, Box 311, Beacon, N.Y. 12508. 1947-- . Quarterly.

HOSPITAL AND COMMUNITY PSYCHIATRY. American Psychiatric Association, 1700 Eighteenth Street, N.W., Washington, D.C. 20009. 1950-- . Monthly.

INTERNATIONAL JOURNAL OF FAMILY COUNSELING. Transaction Periodicals Consortium, Rutgers University, New Brunswick, N.J. 08903. 1973-- . Semiannual.

INTERNATIONAL JOURNAL OF PSYCHIATRY IN MEDICINE. Baywood Publishing Co., 120 Marine Street, Farmingdale, N.Y. 11735. 1970-- . Quarterly.

INTERNATIONAL JOURNAL OF PSYCHOTHERAPY. International Universities Press, 315 Fifth Avenue, New York, N.Y. 10023. 1951-- . Quarterly.

INTERNATIONAL JOURNAL OF SOCIAL PSYCHIATRY. Avenue Publishing Co., 18 Park Avenue, London NW11 755, England. 1955-- . Quarterly.

INTERNATIONAL PHARMACOPSYCHIATRY. S. Karger AG, Arnold Boecklinstr, 25, CH-4011 Basel, Switzerland. 1968-- . Quarterly.

INTERNATIONAL REVIEW OF PSYCHOANALYSIS. Bailliere Tindall, 35 Red Lion Square, London WC1R 4SG, England. 1974-- . Quarterly.

JOURNAL OF ABNORMAL CHILD PSYCHOLOGY. Plenum Publishing Corp., 227 West 17th Street, New York, N.Y. 10011. 1973-- . Quarterly.

JOURNAL OF ABNORMAL PSYCHOLOGY. American Psychological Association, 1200 Seventeenth Street, N.W., Washington, D.C. 20036. 1965-- . Bimonthly.

JOURNAL OF ALTERED STATES OF CONSCIOUSNESS. Baywood Publishing Co., 120 Marine Street, Farmingdale, N.Y. 11735. 1973-- . Quarterly.

JOURNAL OF APPLIED BEHAVIOR ANALYSIS. Society for the Experimental Analysis of Behavior, c/o University of Kansas, Human Development, Lawrence, Kans. 66045. 1968-- . Quarterly.

JOURNAL OF AUTISM AND CHILDHOOD SCHIZOPHRENIA. Plenum Publishing Corp., 227 West Seventeenth Street, New York, N.Y. 10011. 1971-- . Quarterly.

JOURNAL OF BEHAVIOR THERAPY AND EXPERIMENTAL PSYCHIATRY. Pergamon Press, Maxwell House, Fairview Park, Elmsford, N.Y. 10523. 1970-- . Quarterly.

JOURNAL OF CHILD PSYCHOLOGY AND PSYCHIATRY. Pergamon Press, Maxwell House, Fairview Park, Elmsford, N.Y. 10523. 1960-- . Quarterly.

JOURNAL OF CLINICAL CHILD PSYCHOLOGY. American Psychological Association, Division 12, Section I, c/o Child Study Center, 1100 North East Thirteenth Street, Oklahoma City, Okla. 73117. 1972-- . 3/year.

JOURNAL OF CLINICAL PSYCHOLOGY. Clinical Psychology Publishing Co., 4 Conant Square, Brandon, Vt. 05733. 1945-- . Quarterly.

JOURNAL OF COMMUNITY PSYCHOLOGY. Clinical Psychology Publishing Co., 4 Conant Square, Brandon, Vt. 05733. 1973-- . Quarterly.

JOURNAL OF CONSULTING AND CLINICAL PSYCHOLOGY. American Psychological Association, 1200 Seventeenth Street, N.W., Washington, D.C. 20036. 1937-- . Bimonthly.

JOURNAL OF CONTEMPORARY PSYCHOTHERAPY. Long Island Institute for Mental Health, 97-29 Sixth-fourth Road, Forest Hills, N.Y. 11374. 1968-- . Semiannual.

JOURNAL OF COUNSELING PSYCHOLOGY. American Psychological Association, 1200 Seventeenth Street, N.W., Washington, D.C. 20036. 1954-- . Monthly.

JOURNAL OF FAMILY COUNSELING. New York Family Counselors Institute, Rutgers University, New Brunswick, N.J. 08903. 1973-- . Semiannual.

JOURNAL OF HUMAN STRESS. Opinion Publications, 82 Cochituate Road, Framingham, Mass. 01701. 1975-- . Quarterly.

JOURNAL OF MENTAL DEFICIENCY RESEARCH. National Society for Mentally Handicapped Children, Pembridge Hall, 17 Pembridge Square, London WZ 4EP, England. 1957-- . Quarterly.

JOURNAL OF NERVOUS AND MENTAL DISEASE. Williams and Wilkins Co., 428 East Preston Street, Baltimore, Md. 21202. 1874-- . Monthly.

JOURNAL OF PERSONALITY AND SOCIAL PSYCHOLOGY. American Psychological Association, 1200 Seventeenth Street, N.W., Washington, D.C. 20036. 1965-- . Monthly.

JOURNAL OF PHENOMENOLOGICAL PSYCHOLOGY. Humanities Press, Atlantic Highlands, N.J. 07716. 1970-- . Semiannual.

JOURNAL OF PSYCHIATRIC RESEARCH. Pergamon Press, Maxwell House, Fairview Park, Elmsford, N.Y. 10523. 1961-- . Quarterly.

JOURNAL OF PSYCHOSOMATIC RESEARCH. Pergamon Press, Maxwell House, Fairview Park, Elmsford, N.Y. 10523. 1956-- . Bimonthly.

JOURNAL OF THE EXPERIMENTAL ANALYSIS OF BEHAVIOR. Society for the Experimental Analysis of Behavior, Indiana University, Bloomington, Ind. 1958-- . 6/year.

MENNINGER CLINIC BULLETIN. Menninger Foundation, Box 829, Topeka, Kans. 66601. 1936-- . Bimonthly.

MENTAL HEALTH AND SOCIETY. S. Karger AG, Arnold Boecklinstr, 25, CH-4011 Basel, Switzerland. 1974-- . Bimonthly.

MENTAL RETARDATION. American Association on Mental Deficiency, 5201 Connecticut Avenue, N.W., Washington, D.C. 20015. 1963-- . Bimonthly.

NATIONAL ASSOCIATION OF PRIVATE PSYCHIATRIC HOSPITALS JOUR-NAL. National Association of Private Psychiatric Hospitals, 1701 K Street, N.W., Suite 1205, Washington, D.C. 20006. 1969-- . Quarterly.

NEUROPSYCHOLOGIA. Pergamon Press, Maxwell House, Fairview Park, Elmsford, N.Y. 10523. 1963-- . Bimonthly.

NEW ZEALAND PSYCHOLOGIST. New Zealand Psychological Society, Victoria University of Wellington, Department of Psychology, Private Bag, Wellington, New Zealand. 1972-- . Semiannual.

PRACTICAL PSYCHOLOGY FOR PHYSICIANS. Harcourt Brace Jovanovich, 757 Third Avenue, New York, N.Y. 10017. 1974-- . Monthly.

PROFESSIONAL PSYCHOLOGY. American Psychological Association, 1200 Seventeenth Street, N.W., Washington, D.C. 20036. 1969-- . Quarterly.

PROGRESS IN PSYCHIATRIC RESEARCH. Pergamon Press, Maxwell House, Fairview Park, Elmsford, N.Y. 10523. 1975-- . Quarterly.

PSYCHIATRY. William Alanson White Psychiatric Foundation, 1610 New Hampshire Avenue, N.W., Washington, D.C. 20009. 1938-- . Quarterly.

PSYCHOANALYTIC QUARTERLY. 57 West Fifty-seventh Street, New York, N.Y. 10019. 1932-- .

PSYCHOANALYTIC REVIEW. National Psychological Association for Psycho-analysis, 150 West Thirteenth Street, New York, N.Y. 10011. 1913-- . Quarterly.

PSYCHOLOGICAL BULLETIN. American Psychological Association, 1200 Seventeenth Street, N.W., Washington, D.C. 20036. 1904-- . Bimonthly.

PSYCHOLOGICAL MEDICINE. Cambridge University Press, 200 Euston Road, London NW1 2DB England. 1970. Quarterly.

PSYCHOLOGICAL REVIEW. American Psychological Association, 1200 Seventeenth Street, N.W., Washington, D.C. 20036. 1894-- . Bimonthly.

PSYCHONEUROENDOCRINOLOGY. Pergamon Press, Maxwell House, Fairview Park, Elmsford, N.Y. 10523. 1976-- . Quarterly.

PSYCHOSOMATIC MEDICINE. Elsevier North Holland, New York, 52 Vanderbilt Avenue, New York, N.Y. 10017. 1938-- . Bimonthly.

PSYCHOSOMATICS. Academy of Psychosomatic Medicine, 992 Springfield Avenue, Irvington, N.J. 07111. 1960-- . Quarterly.

PSYCHOTHERAPY. University of Chicago, Department of Psychology, 5848 University Avenue, Chicago, Ill. 60637. 1963-- . Quarterly.

SCHIZOPHRENIA BULLETIN. National Institute of Mental Health, 5600 Fishers Lane, Rockville, Md. 20852. 1969-- . Quarterly.

SOCIAL BEHAVIOR AND PERSONALITY. Editorial Services Ltd., Box 6443, Wellington, New Zealand. 1973-- . Semiannual.

SUICIDE AND LIFE THREATENING BEHAVIOR. Human Sciences Press, 72 Fifth Avenue, New York, N.Y. 10011. 1971-- . Quarterly.

VOICES. American Academy of Psychotherapists, 1040 Woodcock Road, Orlando, Fla. 32803. 1965-- . Quarterly.

AUTHOR INDEX

In addition to authors, this index includes all editors, compilers, translators, and other contributors to works cited in the text. References are to entry numbers and alphabetization is letter by letter.

Author Index

Author Index

Author Index

Author Index

Author Index

Author Index

Milton, Ohmer 1125
Milumsky, Aubrey 349
Minde, Klaus 1224
Miner, Deanna 940
Miner, Gary D. 755
Mintz, Ronald S. 1098
Minuchin, Salvador 239, 910
Mitala, Ronald F. 365
Mitchell, Alexander R. 620
Mitchell, Ross G. 1146
Mitlock, F.A. 849
Mittler, Peter 290, 299, 300
Mock, John E. 984
Moen, Marilyn 353
Moldofsky, Harvey 1233
Money, John 961
Monroe, Russell R. 844, 1126
Moore, Byron C. 338
Moore, Donald F. 941
Moore, Terence 1060
Moos, Rudolf H. 911
Mordock, John B. 424
Morehead, Ann E. 387
Morehead, Donald M. 387
Moreno, Jacob L. 69
Morgan, Sam B. 399
Morisey, Patricia 1208
Morris, J. 1231
Morris, Richard 105
Morrison, Gilbert C. 240
Morrison, James R. 642–43, 646,
721
Moser, Atanna M. 601
Moser, Hagow W. 332
Mosher, Loren R. 604
Moss, Gene R. 826
Moustakes, Clark 228
Mozdrierz, Gerald J. 1010
Mugckari, Lovas H. 581
Muhlfelder, Warren J. 366
Mulla, Dawood 720
Murdock, Charles W. 411
Murphy, Solbritt 1198
Murray, Robert F. 339
Musaph, Herman 912
Musella, L. 467
Mushatt, Cecil 1074
Mussen, Paul H. 24, 534, 1115

N

Nagaraja, Jaya 1181, 1234
Nagler, Simon H. 753
Nathan, Peter E. 106, 930
Naylor, G.J. 428
Neale, John M. 107
Neil, John F. 720
Nell, Renee 621
Nelson, Marie C. 957
Nemeth, Elizabeth 1224
Nemiah, John C. 756
Newbauer, Peter B. 137
Nicholi, Armand M., Jr. 108
Nichols, Keith A. 776, 881
Nichtern, Sol 301
Nickols, Jackson 1198
Nicol, Charles F. 798
Nirje, Benjit 412
Nisbett, R.E. 641
Niswander, G. Donald 1091, 1099
Noland, Robert L. 400
Norris, Hugh 842
Norton, James A. 417
Novak, Arthur L. 1127
Novick, Jack 1196
Noyes, Russell 735
Nyswander, Marie 988

O

Obrador, Sixto 456
O'Brien, Charles P. 622
O'Donnell, Patrick A. 388
Oetingor, Leon 1214
Offer, Daniel 109
O'Gorman, J.G. 768
Oliver, Margaret 367
Oliviau, Donald 765
Olshansky, Simon 412
O'Malley, John E. 1215
Ornitz, Edward M. 676–77, 679,
1197
Ostow, Mortimer 962
Ottenberg, Donald J. 1026

P

Packara, R.C. 500

234

TITLE INDEX

This index includes titles of books which are cited in this text. The titles are listed in their shortened form. Journals and titles of articles within journals are not listed. References are to entry numbers and alphabetization is letter by letter.

Title Index

Title Index

Title Index

SUBJECT INDEX

References are to entry numbers. Underlined numbers refer to major topics or subtopics within the book. Alphabetization is letter by letter.

Subject Index

Genetic disorders 57, 168, 327,
334, 339, 449, 691, 701,
707, 743
and psychoses 557-72
German measles. See Rubella, congenital
Gerontology
and mental retardation 289-90
Gestalt therapy 201. See also
Psychotherapy
Gilles de la Tourette's disease 481,
486, 504, 512
Grief 1068-80
anticipatory 1078
in children 1068
neurotic 1080
Group therapy
childhood psychoses 363, 535
desensitization 776
and schizophrenia 622, 629
See also Psychotherapy

H

Habilitation 385
Habitual violence 1149
Hallucinosis 500
Handicapped persons 45
attitude towards 315
children 402-3
identification 330
See also Developmental disabilities;
Mental retardation
Head Hitting 1151. See also Self-
injurious behaviors
Head traumas 471-73, 477. See also
Brain damage
Hebephrenia 638, 646
Helplessness 178, 832. See also
Anxiety; Depression
Hereditary Disorders. See Genetic
disorders
Historical perspective
alcohol use 88
clinical psychology 84
institutions 81-82, 89-90, 310,
313, 320
mental illness 78-90
mental retardation 307-19
narcotics 88

psychiatry 78, 80, 85
psychology 83
Homocystinuria 354
Homosexuality 639
Hospitalization
involuntary 259-60
for schizophrenia 60
See also Institutions
Human services 412
Huntington's chorea 449, 510
Hyperactivity 451, 1199-1227
classification 1211
diagnosis 1211
etiology 1213
management 1211
research 1219, 1224
treatment 1203, 1206-8, 1211,
1214, 1219
Hypersomnia. See Sleep Disorders
Hypnosis 198-99
and multiple personalities 791
Hypochondriasis 784, 787, 897.
See also Psychosomatic
illness
Hysteria 487, 509, 779-805, 868
diagnosis 783
epidemic 802
psychophysiology 793
psychotherapy 782, 799-801
Hysterical conversion reaction 779,
789, 804
Hysterical personality 779-81, 788,
790

I

Infanticide 480
Infantile autism
Inhibited children 854
Insomnia 1235, 1237-38. See also
Sleep disorders
Institutions 81, 82, 89-90, 355
alternatives 208
for children 223, 233
history 90
for mentally retarded 266-68,
277, 302, 310, 313-14,
320, 373, 407
Intelligence 52, 357
Intoxication 1028. See also Alcoholism, Drug dependence

Subject Index

Subject Index

and alcohol 484–85, 500
brain traumas 466–77
cerebral conditions 466–77
childbirth 480, 492, 495
classification systems 438
drug intoxication 482, 494
endocrine disorders 483, 490,
     501–2
etiology 489
intracranial infections 458–65
metabolic disorders 492, 511
physical conditions 480–512
poison intoxication 497
post-gastrectomy hypoglycemia 489
renal failure 499
rheumatoid arthritis 488
See also Epilepsy; Gilles de la
     Tourette's disease; Hunting-
     ton's chorea
Orthomolecular psychiatry 528
Overlax control syndromes 1180

P

Paedophilia 948, 968
Paranoia 634, 635, 639, 644, 645,
     931
Paranoid schizophrenia 506, 640,
     646, 714
Paresis, general 461
Parkinson's disease 446
Passive-aggressive personality 931,
     941
Patient rights 245–59, 403–12
Perceptual disturbances 436
Personality disorders 49, 165, 557,
     731, 749, 757, 919–1113
     alcoholism 998–1040
     borderline states 1041–51
     child 935–44
     drug dependence 976–97
     grief 1068–80
     psychopathic 945–75
     sociocultural factors 919
     sociopathic 945–75
     stress 1052–67
     suicide 1068–80
     theories 165, 661
Pervasive anxiety 733
Phenylketonuria 354

Phobias 91, 765–78
     avoidance 771
     behavior therapy 773
     childhood 768, 880–88
     classification 772, 775
     epidemiology 765
     maintenance 768
Physical illness 892, 904, 911.
     See also Psychosomatic ill-
     ness
Physiological habituation 778
Play therapy 218, 224, 228, 232,
     660
Polyneuropathy 500
Porphyria 449
Post-gastrectomy hypoglycemia 489
Postpartum reactions 480, 492, 494,
     495, 507
Post-traumatic disability 472
Primal therapy 522
Prophylactic physiotherapy 346
Pseudodementia 726
Pseudosociopathic neuroses 965
Psychiatry 9, 16, 78, 85, 89,
     91–92, 108
     adolescent 20
     diagnosis 33
     reference books 17, 23, 26, 29,
     37
     reforms 260
     theory 22, 108
Psychoanalysis 1, 12–13, 26, 63,
     124, 170, 196, 201, 206,
     252, 758, 892
     dictionary 32
     See also Psychotherapy
Psychodrama 69
Psychogenic illness 556
Psychoneuroendocrinology 483, 490,
     501–2, 511, 908
Psychoneurotic disturbances. See
     Neuroses
Psychopathology 95, 106–7, 110,
     116, 121, 127, 143, 150,
     157, 165, 178, 426, 431–
     32, 452, 904, 920, 929,
     953, 955–56, 966, 972
     adolescent 132, 142, 145, 147,
     937, 943
     child 1, 31, 122–23, 125–30,